"Finally, a book for those on the 'outside' trying to get 'in' from someone who, until very recently, was also on the 'outside.' That Fran manages also to be honest and funny without dissuading those who've been bitten by the film bug from trying to pursue their passions is a testament to her OWN passion for the business; a terrific, must-read book!"

— Liz Owen, Producer/President, Girlie Girl Productions

"Fran's brutally honest roadmap of Hollywood realities might spook as many people away from the 'biz' as she helps break into it; but she's doing those folks running away just as big a favor."

— Larry Hill, Screenwriter, *The Bar*

"Fresh and funny! With her tongue firmly implanted in cheek, Fran still gets to the very real heart of the biz, and as anyone in Hollywood knows, finding a heart anywhere is a tough task."

— Jerry Penacoli, Entertainment Correspondent, *Extra*

"*Crashing Hollywood* is an amazingly insightful book that reveals what it really takes to make it in the entertainment industry... had I known this information sooner, I might have never taken my clothes off."

— Sean O'Brien, Turn & Cough Productions

"As close to the way things really work in Hollywood as you'll get. Fran has managed both to en'   ntful and laugh-out-loud look at LaLaL

— Ana Clavell, Vice F
   Taurus Entertainm

D1114244

"*Crashing Hollywood* is the right metaphor for this timely how-to book. Unless you put on a football helmet and run headlong into the fray, repeatedly, you will not get your big break."

— **Kevin Beggs, President of Production, Lions Gate Television**

"Those seeking the truth, the way, and the spotlight should read Fran's book... but then they might realize that this town is not for them."

— **Leslie Sloan, Winston Davis & Associates**

"This book will bring the dreamers down to earth and show them how to really make it in Hollywood."

— **Johnette Duff, Screenwriter, *The Devil Went Down***

"Not only does Fran offer advice on how to handle yourself in a pitch meeting, she also tells you how to dress and how much to tip the valet! This is the most comprehensive book on breaking into Hollywood that I've seen."

— **Lesley Bracker, *WritersChannel.net***

"In *Crashing Hollywood*, Harris offers the wannabe a metal-toed boot to start kicking down the doors and a Kevlar shield of knowledge to pro- tect the ego. There's not a corner of that godforsaken city to which she won't go to reveal a real-life story. Whether you're on the outside wanting to get in or too fearful of the daily beatings to try, you'll find a sick pleasure in reading the humorous and gut-wrenching stories exposed in her lively and charming prose."

— **Brian Hamm, Novelist, *Roller Coasters & Brass Poles***

"*Crashing Hollywood* is a humorous, energetic, honest, and insightful book! Loved it!"

— **Julia Michels, Vice President, Creative Affairs**
   20th Century Fox Music

MICHAEL WIESE PRODUCTIONS
www.mwp.com

We are delighted that you have found, and are enjoying, our books.

Since 1981, we've been all about providing filmmakers with the very best information on the craft of filmmaking: from screenwriting to funding, from directing to camera, acting, editing, distribution, and new media.

It is our goal to inspire and empower a generation (or two) of film and video-makers like yourself. But we want to go beyond providing you with just the basics. We want to shake you, and inspire you to reach for your dreams and go beyond what's been done before. Most films that come out each year waste our time and enslave our imaginations. We want to give you the confidence to create from your authentic center, to bring something from your own experience that will truly inspire others and bring humanity to its full potential — avoiding those urges to manufacture derivative work in order to be accepted.

Movies, television, the Internet, and new media all have incredible power to transform. As you prepare your next project, know that it is in your hands to choose to create something magnificent and enduring for generations to come.

This is not an impossible goal because you've got a little help. Our authors are some of the most creative mentors in the business, willing to share their hard-earned insights with you. Their books will point you in the right direction but, ultimately, it's up to you to seek that authentic something on which to spend your precious time.

We applaud your efforts and are here to support you. Let us hear from you.

Sincerely,

Michael Wiese
Filmmaker, Publisher

CRASHING HOLLYWOOD

HOW TO KEEP YOUR
INTEGRITY UP,
YOUR CLOTHES ON
& STILL MAKE IT
IN HOLLYWOOD

FRAN HARRIS

Published by Michael Wiese Productions
11288 Ventura Blvd., Suite 621
Studio City, CA 91604
tel. (818) 379-8799
fax (818) 986-3408
mw@mwp.com
www.mwp.com

Cover Design: Objects of Design
Book Layout: Gina Mansfield
Editor: Arthur G. Insana

Printed by McNaughton & Gunn, Inc., Saline, Michigan
Manufactured in the United States of America

© 2003 Fran Harris

Library of Congress Cataloging-in-Publication Data

Harris, Fran, 1965-
   Crashing Hollywood: how to keep your integrity up, your clothes on & still make it in Hollywood / by Fran Harris; foreword by Sheila Gallien.
        p. cm.
    ISBN 0-941188-82-5
    1. Motion pictures--Vocational guidance--United States. I. Title.
    PN1995.9.P75H38 2003
    791.43'028'023--dc21

                                        2003009302

ACKNOWLEDGEMENTS

First, I thank God for love that surrounds and enfolds me every day of my life. I'm grateful to my parents, John and Bessie, for giving me life. To my Extreme Team, Rebecca, Debra, Alonzo, Larry and Chris, who remind me that love's got everything to do with it. Micah and Jon, thanks for the dance lessons.

To Ken Lee and Michael Wiese of Michael Wiese Productions for their speedy and enthusiastic response to my idea and for giving this book a loving home and more importantly, an expedient publication date.

To my literary agent… oh, that's right, I don't have a lit agent, I sold this book on my own. Well, to my alter ego who often serves as agent, publicist, consultant, and anything else I need, thank you.

To Pat Dengler for always opening her home to me while I was doing the L.A. interviews for this book.

To Lisa Hockley, of Angel City Fitness in Marina Del Rey for giving me a place to work out while I made moves in Los Angeles.

To Nan Diacovo, for all of the hook ups.

To all of the people I interviewed for this book, thank you for the sushi, the candid conversations, and encouragement.

And to the millions of wannabes, struggling, working, and kick ass folks in the biz. Remember, the degree to which you are successful (and happy with yourself) in the biz is in direct proportion to how passionate and intentional you are about life, how much you love what you're doing, and how true you stay to that love.

TABLE OF CONTENTS

×

FOREWORD

The image emblazoned on my mind of Fran Harris is from our first meeting at the 2000 Austin Film Festival. I had recently left my job as assistant to screenwriter William Broyles and started my own script consulting business. It was just after my first speaking engagement, and I was flushed from the great turnout and the new experience of people stopping me in the halls to ask me questions. As I made my way through the crowd, I suddenly saw a tall, fabulous woman striding toward me, arm outstretched. The next thing I knew, she was warmly shaking my hand, smiling and saying "Bill Broyles says he trusts you with his work, and I just have to talk to you about mine." She enveloped me in her warmth and enthusiasm, and soon we were talking excitedly about her screenplays and my consulting business.

Fran has a gift for generating excitement. It's contagious. You can feel her enthusiasm, and her passion the moment you meet her. But without the techniques she has worked so hard to develop, our conversation might have drifted to the movies we saw the night before, or we might have been interrupted before she made her point. Instead, before a minute had transpired, she had signed up for a consult, talked me into doing it over Thanksgiving, and lifted several of my cards to pass along to her friends. She had used my time efficiently, earned my trust, and promised me a favor. What a first impression!

What Fran has done in her life and in this book is simple: she has cracked the code of conduct for Hollywood — secrets she willingly shares with you in this entertaining and provocative take on breaking into the business.

As the assistant to an A-list screenwriter, I was privileged to be in meetings at all stages of the development process (on *Cast Away*, *Entrapment*, *Unfaithful,* and more). From early story meetings to eleventh-hour, high-pressure shooting situations, I watched movie stars, directors, executives, producers, writers, and I can tell you that while Hollywood is famous for bad behavior, bad behavior is the deviation, not the norm. The vast majority of truly successful people in all walks of the business are gracious and effective. If they do behave badly, it's when they're among friends and a 50-million-dollar movie they've worked on for five years has just fallen apart. At that point, anyone is entitled to a breakdown.

It's a cliché, but Hollywood is a people business, and people are complex. It's a business of great subtlety in communication. In her book, Fran Harris sneaks a peak behind that curtain of subtlety. She knows that to survive the searing voltage of Hollywood, you must constantly balance between extremes. Be direct but not abrupt; focused but not single-minded; respectful but confident; entertaining but not cloying; passionate but not overpowering.

At the bottom of it all, you must have good, clear ideas, and you must make it pleasant (and safe) to be around you. Hollywood buyers are always looking for ideas. They just don't want bad ideas, and they especially don't want ideas spewed at them by crazy people.

It may seem an unnecessary admonition, but craziness is not coveted in Hollywood. People make the assumption that because it is a creative business, it is an eccentric business. You would be amazed at how many aspiring writers, actors, and directors don't follow even the simplest rules of etiquette when approaching Hollywood. They fancy themselves as "refreshingly frank" or "refreshingly quirky," but how they really appear is arrogant or disorganized. Over the years, I have seen weepers, yellers, and people who get defensive before they have anything to defend. And if, somehow, they were able to slither through the door with this behavior, it quickly kills their careers. One of the first lessons I learned as an assistant at CAA was that given the choice between a crazy, brilliant, difficult writer and a competent, professional one, the common response is "Life is too short," and the job goes to the professional. Eccentricity might be tolerated when accompanied by great brilliance, but don't count on it. And most of us, let's face it, are not oppressed by such luminosity.

So how does one approach Hollywood? This is the subject so well articulated in *Crashing Hollywood*. At the heart of the code of conduct are two qualities that Fran has worked hard to perfect, and which I noticed the first time I met her: focus and tact. But don't be deceived by these simple concepts. Inherent in focus is the brutally hard work it takes to hone a craft, to research a buyer, to define a desire. Inherent in tact is respect, the ability to listen, to read a situation, exercise good timing, and generate positive feelings and energy.

Hollywood is a churning, nail-biting world where failures are as big as dreams, where there is no such thing as job security, and where your sense of self is tested at every turn. Of course, that's also what makes it so exciting. So, if showbiz is in your blood, and Hollywood is in your view, listen to Fran, and you just might get there.

Sheila Gallien, script consultant, screenwriter, author of *So Your Momma Likes It But Is It Ready For The Big time?: 10 Common Mistakes Screenwriters Make and What They Can Do To Avoid Them (www.sheilagallien.com)*

INTRODUCTION

I know what you're thinking. I can hear what you're thinking. You're thinking who is Fran Harris and why is she writing this book and not me? You've read the cover endorsements, seen all of the glowing reviews but you're still saying to yourself, "Why did I buy this book?" Am I right? That's what you were thinking, isn't it? Yes, it was. Don't lie. You're wondering what qualifies me to write a book about breaking into Hollywood when you don't even know who the hell I am. Aren't these books supposed to be written by people who are outrageously rich and famous? Aren't those the only folks knighted to tell the rest of us poor, struggling, oft-starving writers, actors, directors, producers, filmmakers, and so on, how it's done?

Well, who wants to read another book by a fabulous millionaire when you can read a book by someone whose bank account more closely resembles yours? Who wants to read yet another story by an author who engages daily in multimillion-dollar negotiations and attends $25,000-a-plate benefit dinners on the weekend? Wouldn't you rather hear from a person who's probably had a recent close encounter with a container of Ramen Noodles? Someone like you? I thought so. See, I did know what you were thinking!

What's been written about breaking into the business is good, some of it, damn good. What's missing about breaking into the business is the raw, unadulterated truth about what it's like to start at square one and end up one day in the Kodak Theater in March for the Academy Awards. That's where I come in.

Like you, I've seen the end of my movie. I see the lights, the glitz, the glamour, the royalties, and grosses. I've already written my Oscar- (or Grammy-, take your pick) winning speech. I've already told family members that I can't fly them all to Los Angeles for the big night. I've even prayed that certain people who dissed me along the way are still alive so that I can rub just a little of my obscene fame in their faces. I'm just kidding. I'd actually like to rub a LOT of my obscene fame in their faces! (You know who you are, don't make me stop this car.)

Like you, I've blown auditions and nailed pitches to the wall. I've written things so lyrical they scared me and I've penned a few things that I'm certain have scared the living daylights out of other folks. In my short time on this journey I have encountered a few road blocks, but I have succeeded far more than I've fallen short. In fact, there's really no such thing as failure, only lessons. Remember that. And all in all, I've learned a valuable lesson: making it in Hollywood comes down to one thing and only one thing. How much do you want it? I wrote this book to get you to answer that one question. It sounds simple. And everyone who's reading this right now thinks he or she wants it bad. Really bad. But they don't. They want it a little bad. And a little bad won't cut it in this town.

Hollywood is an ongoing, never-ending roller coaster ride. It's filled with dips and dives. Twists and turns. And like every great roller coaster ride, it's chock full of things that might occasionally make you want to vomit. But all in all, if you can hold on to the feeling you have at the end when you're unbuckling the seatbelt and heading to the cotton candy stand, you'll discover that it's a ride well worth taking. And one that will never disappoint. So, suit up, fellow warriors. It's game time.

WHY I WROTE THIS BOOK

Hey, it sounded like a good idea at the time. I had four months with nothing to do and normally when I have nothing to do, which is never, I write. No, but seriously, it was January 1, 1999 and on this day I have this nasty habit of writing down at least two goals that I always manage to forget about by Valentine's Day. But this year was going to be different, I promised. This time I was really going to take The Artist Formerly Known As Prince's advice and party like it's 1999. Mainly because it was. So, I grabbed my writing spiral and wrote the following. In 1999, I will learn how to write a screenplay. I will work out five days a week. That's it. All I had planned for 1999 was writing a movie and pulling myself away from my sofa and those addicting reruns of *Cheers* on Nick at Nite.

Actually, my showbiz career started more than 20 years ago when my sister, Debra, would summon me to the living room to do my recitations of *A Charlie Brown Christmas* for her junior high school friends. Since that day, I've sold toothpaste for a Fortune 500 company, owned a sports marketing company, and worked at Starbucks. But in the end, it's the biz that I've always come home to because nothing makes me happier than being creative. Well, maybe a tall, no foam latte.

Being in this business is akin to having a flu bug. It's easy to catch and hard as hell to shake. It's like I've been struck by lightening and now I can't stop until I've at least put some of this outrageously expensive writing software and 60 lb paper I got on sale at Wal-Mart, to good use. But the main reason I wrote this book is that I kept running into situations in the biz that I wasn't prepared to handle and there were no books that really spoke to me in wannabe language.

Now, don't get me wrong, as I said earlier, there are some great books out there about Hollywood, even a few on how to play the game or navigate through the system but very few of them made me laugh. And let's face it, when you're climbing the stairway to Tinseltown, comic relief is a welcomed addition to your life. When you're spending $100 a week copying videotapes or screenplays, you need something or someone to relieve the tension. This book will help in that department because ya gotta admit, some of the things we wannabes do and say, are pretty funny. So, when you see yourself in these pages, remember that, one day, we'll all look back on some of the things we did and hope no one else remembers.

WHO'S THIS BOOK FOR?

This book was written for anyone trying to break into the entertainment business – actors, producers, directors, writers, recording artists, musicians, you name it. If showbiz is in your present or future, this book's for you. And even if Hollywood's not your ultimate destination, I challenge you to use the principles and tools in these pages to help you succeed in your chosen career field. They will work. Why? Because I said so. Hey, my mother used to use that line and it worked on me!

HOW TO USE THIS BOOK

This book's broken down like a standard screenplay, into three primary sections: Act I, Act II, and Act III. The first section's really about learning the game. The second section's about playing the game and the last section's about mastering the game. I've used mostly short, choppy sections, mainly because it's a widely known fact that once you get to Hollywood your attention span will shrink to the size of a paper clip, so you might as well get in some practice.

Next, this is a new jack "how to" book, which means that it has no real structure. How could I possibly form discernible, cohesive chapters if I'm a starving wannabe? I can't, that's my point. I have lots of points, as you will see as you get to know me better. Another one is that you can't tame rants and ravings. You can't put them in a three-act structure, give them an arc and make them follow the rules. Rants are nothing if they aren't all over the place, so that's what you can expect from this book and me. The A to Zs of making it in Hollywood, but not in that order. Got it?

Now, in addition to lots of useful information and occasional rants, you'll also see a wide array of interviews from people I hand selected because I knew they'd bring a unique perspective to the book. You'll hear from people in very high-profile positions all the way to those who are just starting out. They all have some amazing insights and I'm really glad that I found them or in some cases, that they stumbled into my life through friends and acquaintances whom I bribed.

And last but not least, some very high paid friends have told me that the secret to getting the most out of this book is simple. Check your ego at the door and be open to the many lessons and challenges that will come your way within the next few hundred pages. Here's to many green lights and blue skies. Crash On!

ACT I

———

LEARNING THE GAME:
THINGS YOU NEED
TO KNOW OR DO
BEFORE YOU
HEAD TO HOLLYWOOD

"I don't want to be rich, I just
want to write good movies."

— *Liar, 2002*

FRAN'S GOLDEN RULE #1:
DON'T TAKE IT
(ANYTHING) PERSONALLY

Before I say anything else, let me say one of the most important things anybody "in" the business will tell you.

Hollywood is full of procedures, paper trails, and protocol. You will be asked to sign releases, non-disclosure agreements, contracts, and other legal documents more often than you think. Get used to it. It ain't personal. If you're the kind of person to get bent out of shape because someone asks you to sign a confidentiality agreement, don't pursue Hollywood, you'll be eaten up the first time out.

In addition to the mounds of paperwork that are likely to flow your way — even before you have a deal — you'll also be given strong medicine, as it relates to your talent or work. Feedback will not arrive at your doorstep wrapped in swaddling clothing. Coverage on the script you worked on for three years will not be accompanied by an American Greeting e-card. Input on your latest recording demo is not likely to be delivered to you with a bouquet of flowers saying, "Great job. Gee, you have a really wonderful voice but we can't sign you. Sorry. XoXo."

Nope, feedback will come to you generally in one form: a scud missile. Straight atcha and to the point. No doubt, early on, it will knock you for a loop. Trust me. It may even hurt your feelings. I certainly had my hair blown back a couple of times. But know this: If you cannot handle the bitter, sometimes painful, truth about your work, you might want to think twice about pursuing the entertainment business. If you cannot accept direct communication that's not nestled in a bunch of empty compliments which mean nothing at the end of the day without a deal, please become a tour guide at Disney World, because that's about as close to the business as you'll get.

SO, YA WANNA BE IN THE BIZ?
I don't know you, but I do. I know one thing about you: you want to

sing, write, star in, direct, produce, or make movies. I lied. I know two things about you. You want to *get rich* singing, writing, starring in, directing, producing, or making movies. Yes, you do. (No I don't). Yes, you do. It's okay. Anyone who says that money can't buy happiness shops at Target (and so do I).

What's my point? Where's my arc? Relax for a sec and peep this. I'm gonna let you in on a little secret. Most of the stuff you've read in those "How to Become an Award Winning Actor, Screenwriter, Filmmaker, Director, or Producer" books on your shelf is a rip off. Yes, it is. (No, it's not). Yes, it is. Trust me on this.

Those alluring alliterations, those pages of carefully collected clichés have done nothing but a disservice to you… and me too, for that matter. Why? How? Because we actually believed that if we read what's in those books, we'd become rich and famous, or at least we'd be able to move out of our parent's basement by next Labor Day, right? Wrong. We've been robbed, ladies, gentlemen, and transgenders. And I'm here to set the record straight.

Now, most of the millions of people (and yes, there will be millions) who buy this book will never be rich or famous. No, they *won't*. Why? I'll tell you why. Because most of you suck at whatever it is you do, period. Yes, you *do*. And so did I, that's why I'm an authority on the subject. Everyone who's good at anything sucked at it once upon a time, so get over yourself.

Forget everything you read in *The Hollywood Reporter* last month about first time writer, Brenda Sue Richards from Beeville, Texas, signing a 12-figure deal with Paramount — it doesn't work that way. No, it *doesn't*. Don't believe what you heard at your Saturday morning filmmaker's lab about the virgin producer collaborating with Spielberg on his next project — it ain't gonna happen. And the actor who supposedly went from a non-speaking role to a lead in Woody Allen's film about reviving the eight-track tape deck? Never happened. No, it didn't.

Now, let's be clear. New writers and producers don't suck because they have no talent. Neophyte directors and actors don't suck because they can't get a scene right. Fledgling filmmakers don't suck because they can't find financing. All of these people suck because they have no ethic. Not ethics — although I'll go there later in the book — ethic. Work ethic.

That's what it takes to become wildly successful in this business. And let's face it, what's the point of becoming successful if you can't be *wildly* successful. It's a complete waste of time and effort.

Most wannabes suck because they want to find the perfect idea, nail the perfect role, land the perfect agent or manager, attach the perfect talent to their projects, and marry the perfect studios. Well, it just doesn't work that way... no, it doesn't.

But guess what? This is your lucky day. I'm getting paid a handsome figure to tell you the truth, the absolute truth, about the biz. And that's exactly what I aim to do. Who am I, you say, that I should write this book? Well, glad you asked. I'm a starving writer, producer, actor, director, and filmmaker who's on the fast track to stardom, first-look deals, and million-dollar paydays. But I'm also already a successful screenwriter, producer, director, and filmmaker. I'm sorta bipolar. Wait a minute. How can you be starving *and* successful? Easy. You redefine the word success. But I'm getting ahead of myself; we'll get to that later. For now, just roll with me.

I know what you're thinking. You're thinking, "this woman's a loon." A straight up nut! And guess what? You're right. I'm a nutcase and that's why *you're* reading my book. Nutty, huh?

Anyway, what were we talking about? Oh, yeah, your miserable, failing career that's never going to go anywhere because you have no work ethic. Listen, before I start to get really brutally honest, I should tell you a couple of things.

First, I'm not here to tell you how great you are — that's your mom's or your underpaid assistant's job. And I'm also not here to make you feel worse (as if you could) about your budding or fading Hollywood career. I'm here to lighten the load with a little humor. I'm here to sprinkle a few rays of sunshine and a few bad jokes onto an otherwise dreadfully unproductive day. But that's not all.

I'm also here to ease the burden of that most recent rejection letter you got from Hollywood or Studio City, California. I'm here to tell you what the agent who politely said, "Your project's not quite right for us," really meant. That's my job. That's why I'm here. And I take my job very seriously. So, let's dispense with all of the pleasantries, roll up our sleeves, pop an Exlax, if you need to, and get down to biz. After all, that's the only way you're ever gonna get anywhere in Hollywood anyway. Yes, it is.

> **"How do you get a waiter's attention in an L.A. restaurant? You say, 'Actor?'"**
>
> — *L.A. & Austin-based casting director*

IN THE BEGINNING

God created two kinds of people. Screenwriters, producers, actors, singers, directors, and filmmakers, and those who want to be screenwriters, producers, actors, singers, directors, and filmmakers. Oh, I lied again. There's a third kind of people. People who don't believe in God, therefore, people who can't believe that God made those two kinds of people or those who want to be those two kinds of people.

Sure, there are people roaming the earth who pretend to be lawyers, priests, doctors, engineers, prostitutes, and journalists. They attend college, get advanced degrees, work on jobs they hate and even get paid for them, but what they secretly crave is making movies or being in movies. Think about it. Every breathing adult has left a movie theater and declared, "I could write something better than that!" And you know what? They're probably right. But the key is, they *don't*. They don't write something better than that, they simply talk about it. See, being a critic is easy. Making good movies that millions of people will pay 10 bucks to see, is tough. So, I congratulate you. You're not a wimp and that's good, because by the time you're finished with this book, you'll wish you'd never met me.

INC. YOURSELF!

Before we take the tag off the new pair of jeans, let me say the most important thing I will say in this book. If you are serious about breaking into or becoming more established in the entertainment world, you must embrace the "business" in show business. You are not just an artist, you are a businessperson. You are selling products: you and your art. So, if you haven't already set up your business, now's the time to do it. Depending on your area of specialty, you may either operate as a sole proprietor or you may want to incorporate your business.

For those of you who are scratching your heads, wondering why I'm talking to you about business, let me ask you a quick question. Do you expect to make money at what you're doing? Do you expect people to pay to see you or to have your product? Then you're a business. The IRS will see you as a business, so you should probably see yourself as one, too. If you're going to fight me on this, I suggest you sharpen your anger management skills. You're gonna need them in prison.

Okay, back to the free world. Now, at minimum, you need to go to your county courthouse or the County Clerk's office (requirements vary by state) and file for a DBA (Doing Business As) status. You will need what's called an "assumed name certificate," which should cost less than $20. This is your official business name. It could be something as simple as Your Name, Inc., or you could make up something that signifies what you do: Bad Mutha Records.

Become official as early as you can because this will encourage you to think like a businessperson from now on. You don't know how big of a favor I'm doing you right now. I wish someone had told me this on the first day of Showbiz School. It would have saved me a lot of hassles down the line. You see, when you "Inc." yourself, you're more than just a "show," you're a player in this great game. We'll talk more about how to be in the business later, but I wanted to shift your mindset about how to truly succeed in the entertainment world by putting the Most Valuable Principle in your face, as early as possible.

MAXIMIZE YOUR ISP

We all have 'em. Those things that make us who we are. I call them Individual Selling Points (ISPs). Those things that brand us. Things that make you who you are. Don't fight them, they're a part of your package. Make them work for you. Maybe one of your ISPs is a silky smooth, Ella Fitzgerald-type voice. Maybe, you're one of the most lyrical rappers the music industry's never heard. Maybe you're about to light up Broadway with your acting skills. Just know that whatever you can do to distinguish yourself from the thousands of people in your business, the better chance you'll have at success. One of the biggest problems with today's industry is sameness. There aren't enough originals out there. Everybody is pretty much a clone of someone else. But every now and then the Mozarts and Lenny Kravitzs of the world show up and make the rest of us take notice. It doesn't happen often, but it does happen. Will you be the next masterpiece to give us pause?

WHO'S JOHNNY WALKER?

They say all good things must come to an end and I say "phooey." Actually I say something else but what I say can't be printed in these pages. So, we'll go with "phooey." I think a more accurate axiom is that all good things end for a time, but if you're good at what you do and you're diligent, they return. Take celebrity for instance. Right now, you probably fall somewhere below the celebrity meter, at least in Hollywood. Nationally, nobody knows who you are. If you were to go to Hollywood right now, walk into someone's office, introduce yourself by saying, "Johnny Walker, here to see John Singleton," here's what would happen. The assistant would buzz John on the intercom and say, "Johnny Walker's here to see you."

To which John would say, "Who's Johnny Walker?"

You. You're Johnny Walker and nobody knows who you are. This is the first stage of becoming a celebrity. People don't know you yet. They say, who's Johnny Walker, what's he done? That's when you get to work on building your brand, building your craft so that people will know who you are. Once you build your celebrity wherever you decide to do it, you then move from the "Who's Johnny Walker?" stage to the "Get me Johnny Walker" stage.

At this point you're hotter than a plate of Kung Pao Chicken and everybody in town wants a piece of you, any little piece. (think Ice Cube, post the movie *Barber Shop*). You're starring in movies, Pepsi, and Gap commercials. You've got a bobble head, an action figure, and a small role in *Austin Powers 7*. You get it, you are one hot mama or papi. Your agent's (yes, you now have an agent) telling you how great you are and how great he is for turning you into a star. Hell, you almost believe your own hype. Then it happens. The heat switches over. You move from the "Get me Johnny Walker" stage to the "Get me a Johnny Walker clone" stage. Yep, you were so hot that everybody started copying everything you said and did. But now, they don't want you, they want someone who looks or sounds like you. You're trying to tell them that you're still there, but that's the problem, there was too much you. The market's oversaturated with you. It's you, ad nauseum. Finally you move into the final stage. You move from the "Get me a Johnny Walker look alike" stage to "Who's Johnny Walker?" Again. It's a cycle. Get ready for it and get used to it.

EVERYBODY IS A STAR

Whenever I'm feeling like gumshoe, I put on Sly & The Family Stone's song, *Everybody Is A Star* and I feel better. It's true. You're already a star even if it's only in your own mind. You have to adopt this mentality because the Hollywood waters are often chilly and filled with piranha, sharks, and other slimy things. If you don't think you can swim with the other fish, you should probably drop out of school right now. Get it, school? Fish? Okay, that's my one bad joke for the entire book. Seriously, if you're going to get off to a good start, you have to develop confidence of steel. I'm not talking about being a know-it-all or even a braggadocio. I'm talking about knowing that you have the goods, along with the stamina and work ethic, to see your goal through to completion. Do you have the right stuff? Good, because it's going to take every ounce of skill, seen and unseen, to become successful in showbiz. Ready? Here we go.

TIME OUT WITH AN SOB

SEAN O'BRIEN
PRODUCER | TURN & COUGH PRODUCTIONS

I bumped into Sean at Pete's Coffee in Santa Monica after I'd finished an interview with Lesley Bracker, founder of the WritersChannel.net, whom you'll meet later on in the book. Sean offers some interesting commentary about independent filmmaking that was crucial to this book.

FH: How does a video producer end up in film?
SOB: Ironically enough, I fell into producing, I never wanted to be a producer. I didn't set my sights on being a producer. What happened is that a really well-known writer, who's written for *Roseanne* and *Golden Girls*, did a film called *A Very Brady Sequel*. He'd given me a script and asked me if I'd help him find a director and I read this script and I loved it. And I optioned it for $10.

FH: $10? How do you persuade a writer to let you option his script for 10 bucks?
SOB: I think it's one of those things that everybody in the biz knows happens. If you have the passion and the drive to get behind a project, the money really isn't a factor. I mean, I'm not saying it's not a factor, but it's not the bottom line. It is all about the money, but that will come later on. And if you find the right match, someone who's passionate enough to stand behind your project to get it made and who's willing to option for a low amount, then it's worth pursuing.

FH: When you were younger did you know that you wanted to be in the entertainment business?
SOB: I did. I thought I was going to be the next Michael Jackson.

FH: You could be, you're white.
SOB: That's true.

FH: How has that changed, in light of Jacko's recent forays?
SOB: I realized I couldn't really dance and I couldn't really sing, but I liked to entertain people, so I thought I'd get into the film business.

FH: So, when the Jackson 5 told you that they had no plans to become the Jackson 6, what was your next move?

SOB: It's really funny. I'd been set up with this really well-known writer named Gigi Gaston. She was looking for an assistant, and I thought she was looking for a production manager or location manager, or something in the management area. And it was one of those classic "the wires were crossed" scenarios. She asked me about my background and then realized I had all of this production experience. All along, she thought she was interviewing me for a personal assistant position, so she couldn't understand why I would want to go and pick up her cleaning and walk her dogs. Not that I'm opposed to that because if it's gonna get my movie made, I'll walk your dog. Anyway, the long story short was that she was getting ready to direct a Sophie B. Hawkins video, she liked my style and my experience, and we hit it off really well. And, she presented me with the opportunity of producing the music video.

FH: Hmmm...

SOB: And I snatched it up. I mean, even though I'd never produced before, I thought, "sure I'll do it."

FH: Was it any good?

SOB: It was really good. Actually Calvin Klein used it to launch one of its new jean lines. It was a very difficult project. I called it the neverending video because it just went on and on and on and on. But I learned so much from her and she gave me my first break.

FH: Now you're an Indie filmmaker. What's that been like?

SOB: It's been an interesting experience. I was connected with a really well-known record company and a powerful agency that went bad. I was a little bit shocked, but also excited by it. With the project that I optioned I found myself in a situation where I was swimming with some really heavy hitters, really powerful people and long story short, they tried to take the project away from me because some bigger people got involved and expressed interest and they basically said point blank, "what do we need you for?" They were unaware that I owned the property.

FH: Ummmm...

SOB: I told them that I had an option on it. They were kind of silent on the phone. At that point, I realized that you really gotta cover your butt in the business. And I really learned a valuable lesson: get everything in writing. Protect yourself. I mean, I've worked really hard on this; I've spent my own money. I've made all the calls, I've sent all the scripts and I'm really passionate about this script. And it was really scary for me that someone was basically saying "we don't need you, we don't want you and we're gonna take it away from you." But because I had that paperwork, I was able to have protection.

FH: So, you actually had an attorney draw up an agreement... or you had the necessary documentation?
SOB: I did.

FH: In what form?
SOB: It wasn't even that elaborate. Short paragraph, but it was binding enough that they couldn't sweep it out from underneath me. Looking back, I would have wanted to be a little bit more specific in the option agreement. However it was enough to protect me.

FH: Were you surprised that these big and powerful people would respond the way they did? Literally trying to back door you.
SOB: I wouldn't say I was surprised. I was a little disappointed. I came into this business thinking that if you work really hard and you...

FH: ... play well with others.
SOB: Yeah, and you're persistent and ambitious and stick with it that you'll get a payoff. And that is true, in most cases. But this is a very cutthroat industry and it was a reality check for me. But I am glad I was able to have that protection. Had I not, we wouldn't even be having this conversation.

FH: Wow. Was the writer aware of any of this?
SOB: Yeah, he's aware.

FH: What was his response?
SOB: Well, unfortunately this complicated the situation because there was a split in the camps. He thought it would have been better to stay with this large production company. He's letting his option stand and waiting to see what I can do, but still I think there's a part of him that would have preferred to have stayed with this production company and I understand. They are very well known and powerful and have a lot of clout, which means a lot in this town. But there's also the Indie

filmmaker, like myself, who is very passionate and can also get the job done. Even with very big people trying to, like you said, back door you.

FH: How long is your option?
SOB: Two years.

FH: You got all the money to make the film?
SOB: No, I'm in the process of doing that right now. What I need to do is either piece it together through nontraditional sources or partner up with a finance company or production company that has connections with finance.

FH: What's the level of your experience in this? It sounds over-whelming.
SOB: It is new for me but I have some really great mentors and role models walking me through it. And I'm just taking the necessary steps, just basically covering all of my bases. I'm utilizing all of my resources that I've obtained in my production experience. And I'm sending out query letters to people I don't know.

FH: Having been established in music, in commercials, but heading into the uncertain waters of film, do you feel like a rookie again?
SOB: I do.

FH: You're a total rookie, dude!
SOB: I am. [*Laughs*]. I feel like a rookie, you know it's similar, but on a larger scale. I learned a lot from doing that music video with Gigi. That really was a great foundation for me to move into Indie filmmaking, which has changed a lot in the last five years. The first thing that dis-tribution companies are asking these days is "What names I have attached?" Whereas five years ago, nobody really asked that question. And so that's just the reality. It's pretty much following suit of the Hollywood heavy hitters. Like I said earlier, the bottom line is people want to make money.

FH: So how *are* you making money while you're finding financing for your film? Ya gotta eat!
SOB: I still do location management for commercials. And that's been helpful for me because it allows me to pay my rent and pursue my ultimate goals.

FH: Where do you see yourself in terms of your filmmaking career? Are you pretty true to Indie?
SOB: I am true to Indie. I see myself as a big part of the next generation of filmmakers and staying true to the Indie film world, really telling compelling stories that are thought provoking and interesting.

FH: I always ask people this question and I phrase it this way because I really don't feel like there are mistakes. There are lessons, but no mistakes. What are some of the big ones for you? Best/worst thing you ever did?
SOB: With this particular project? The best/worst thing I did was that I attached a director to the project. In retrospect, I would not do that again. I would option on my own and I wouldn't attach anybody in the beginning.

FH: Why not?
SOB: The more attachments you have, the more problems come with that. You have other people to consider and it just turns into this whole ordeal and you have to talk with multiple people to get anything signed off on to get the simplest task completed. Let's say I wanted to send something off to a production company and I needed to call them, I'd have to call three people....

FH: Just to make a phone call?
SOB: Just to make a phone call. Exactly. And let them know and keep everybody on the same page. It's time consuming.

FH: Did you attach this person because you'd been in business with him or because you were friends?
SOB: Well, I attached this person because this person was so passionate about the script, the project. And I felt very strongly that he was the right person for this job. And I still think that this person is the right person for this job. He's ultimately the right person, but in an effort to obtain financing from production companies and investors and even agencies, it makes things a lot more difficult, because a lot of them may like the script but they want to attach their own directors and a lot of actors want to work with certain directors. And, if you're an unknown director...

FH: The actor's gonna say, who's this guy?
SOB: Exactly. What's he done? I don't know him. I've never even heard of that person.

FH: Best advice for a fledgling filmmaker? Say that three times fast!
SOB: Fledgling filmmaker. Fledgling filmmaker. Fledgling filmmaker. Get everything in writing. Cover your ass and I can't stress that enough. You really need to protect yourself and it doesn't have to be some document...

FH: Filled with hereins, whereofs, theretooths....
SOB: Right, a 16-page document. It could be something as simple as a paragraph, just something that ties you in and protects you — you really have to protect yourself. There are thousands, hundreds of thousands of people who want to be in this business and it's cutthroat. I can't stress that enough.

FH: C'mon, what happened to all of the verbal agreements and deals written on napkins and all of that madness?
SOB: I think that disappeared some time in the '20s. I think it still exists, but you have to have a history in those circumstances. If you don't have a preexisting relationship with that person then that verbal agreement or that napkin is not going to protect you. And people can "yes" you to death in this town but if you don't have it in writing, you have nothing.

SEAN GOES ONE-ON-ONE WITH FRAN

FH: Why/how did you decide to get into the entertainment business?
SOB: I decided to get into the entertainment business because I really enjoyed telling stories that were thought provoking and affected peoples' views on life... that and the malpractice insurance for being an MD in this country was out of control.

FH: What was the one perception you had about being in the business that you found out was inaccurate?
SOB: My one perception (or misconception) about the business was that everyone was into making great quality films, while expressing all of their artistic endeavors... I overlooked the "biz" part.

FH: What do you wish someone had told you prior to your diving in?
SOB: I wish someone had told me that the bottom line was "How much money are we going to make?"

FH: Who are/were some of the people you admire (d) in the biz and why?
SOB: Some of the people I admire most in the biz would be: The Coen brothers, Halle Berry, Pedro Almodovar, Michael Moore, and Oprah Winfrey. Firstly, I admire anyone who can make it in the business, who has faced an unfair disadvantage (e.g., African-Americans, Latinos, and homosexuals). Secondly, I admire anyone who has anything important to say.

FH: What's been the most difficult aspect of being in the biz?
SOB: The most difficult aspect of being in the business is the vast amount of doors that are closed (or get closed in your face), but it only takes one door to open it all up. There also don't seem to be many successful role models out there who want to assist others in achieving their goals and dreams.

FH: What do you think you'd be doing if you weren't in the biz?
SOB: If I weren't in the biz I would be a political activist. Either that or I would work at my local Wal-Mart.

FH: Ever slept with someone to get a job? How'd you feel the next morning?
SOB: I have never slept with someone for a job, but I certainly would-n't judge anyone who has (look how well it worked for Madonna)... hey, it's tough out there.

FH: Share one hard knocks lesson you learned.
SOB: I learned to get everything in writing! People will "yes" you to death in this biz if they want something you have. Just make sure you protect yourself.

FH: Share one pattern or mistake you see newbies make.
SOB: I see "newbies" making the mistake of taking things at face value. Let's face it, it's a business and people lie. All of us have had to do things "gratis" (which means free). Just make sure you're not being taken advantage of... even indentured servants got a plot of land after seven years.

FH: If you had the chance to start your career over, what, if anything, would you do differently?
SOB: If I were to start my career over I would just pick up a camera and start filming. My biggest problem in the beginning was a severe lack of confidence, but have you seen some of these people who are making film today? If they can do it, I can do it better!

FH: How do you handle rejection?
SOB: I handle rejection by placing a Voodoo curse on that very nega-tive and tasteless individual. I also try to keep things as objective as possible... it's not personal, but who really wants to be told they're work is crap?

FH: Best advice given to you.
SOB: The best advice I received was by this writer/director, John Stockwell. I was up in Canada auditioning for a role in this HBO film... I sucked! John took me aside and gently suggested that maybe I tried becoming a writer or a producer. I was so upset, but he (unknowingly to us both at the time) planted a seed.

FH: Your best advice for wannabes?
SOB: My advice for wannabes would be 1) Don't take "no" for an answer (trust me, you'll get a lot of them). 2) Learn Voodoo.

YOU KNOW YOU PO' WHEN....

It's okay. Nobody thinks you're rich, so stop pretending to be independently wealthy. You're a struggling (fill in the blank). Sometimes you're gonna be po'. If you're good at what you do, though, you won't be financially challenged for long. In the meantime, embrace your po'ness and see if you see yourself in any of these bullets.

You know you po' when...
- You keep calling the credit card company to change your billing cycle to coincide with your gig paydays

- You reported identity fraud to your credit card company when you went over your limit

- You get your boy or girl to help you get a fake ID so you could give blood more than once a week

- You go to the grocery store and sample the food in the hot deli until you're full

- You find yourself flipping through your credit cards to see if you have any credits

- You go to the post office to see if they'll give you refunds for old stamps

- You hang around after you and your friends go drinking to retrieve the empty beer bottles

- You keep checking on your ailing grandfather's health to find out when you might be inheriting the estate

- You buy an outfit, leave the tag on and return it the next day (maybe you're just ghetto fab)

- You have more than five packages of Ramen Noodles in your house

- You find yourself eating combinations of foods that you have never eaten together because they're the only things in your cupboards (peanut butter beans, dude?)

- You invite yourself to your friends' homes for dinner every night, even when they tell you that they don't want you there

- You wash your laundry in the kitchen sink with Dawn dish-washing detergent

MAYBE THE HOKEY POKEY IS WHAT IT'S ALL ABOUT
You put your left foot in, you take your left foot out, you put your left foot in and you shake it all about. You do the hokey pokey and you turn yourself around, that's what it's all about. Hokey Pokey! That's about how most people try to do Hollywood – halfway. They dabble in this, then they dabble in that and then they wonder why nothing's showing up for them. Hollywood can, truthfully, only be done one way. All the way. I've found (from experience) that halfway effort yields halfway results. If you're really serious about being a star, then go for it. Put your whole heart and soul into it. If it doesn't work out, you can always go back to working at the Blockbuster Video Store around the corner from your house. And remember, be kind, please rewind.

WHY HOLLYWOOD'S GREAT
Screw poverty. People don't want to labor in minimum wage jobs, working with people they can't stand, slaving for bosses with the IQ of toast, doing work they detest for the rest of their lives. Nobody wants that. That's why people want to be in Hollywood. That's why I want to be there. Because it's the land of milk and honey. And I happen to like that combination for some reason. You get to hang out with fairly intelligent life forms, make tons of money and drive fancy cars. Oh, and get stared at by people who want to be just like you. That's the allure of Hollywood. That's why you want to be there and the sooner you embrace that, the better off you'll be.

Face it, Hollywood is not about creating world peace. It's not about providing a safe, cozy haven for orphans in Africa. It's not even about making great cinema, but it sure beats delivering packages for UPS. No offense to the men and women of UPS, especially those with the 90210 route.

You're probably saying, "Not me. I want to become a Hollywood 'fill in the blank' because I want to make great movies that change the world."

Note to self. You have a better chance of snagging the state of Florida from George W. Bush in the 2004 presidential race. If you want to change the world, you're in the wrong business. Hollywood is about entertainment and if you're serious about your career, it's time you got with that.

Nobody goes to the movies for life changes. Nobody. We go to the movies to be entertained and, on occasion, to see Brad Pitt's or Denzel Washington's butt – but most of the time it's to be entertained. Repeat after me. We go to the movies to be entertained. We go to the movies to be entertained. Good. Remember that. And remind me of it when I start yakking about world peace through film and other nonsense.

AGAINST ALL ODDS

Let me play arm chair statistician for a minute and ask you a question. Why is it that, out of roughly every 1,000 actors, producers, singers, filmmakers, directors, and writers who set out to make it in Hollywood each year, only about five actually end up making decent livings in the business? Because many of them underestimate how difficult it is to get work in an industry town. You're better off becoming famous in your own hometown and then moving the show to Los Angeles. Instead, lots of folks get sucked into the allure of the party scene they see on E! but eventually leave bitter and burned out, returning to teach Metal Shop at their high schools. It's not pretty.

YOU WANNA GO WHERE NOBODY KNOWS YOUR NAME

Every wannabe's had this experience. You go to an event, maybe a club. You walk up, thinking the burly bouncer at the door knows who you are. After all, you did do that cheesy local furniture commercial that runs everyday during *All My Children*. And you were interviewed on the NPR gardening show a couple of times. And if you listen really, really hard, you can actually hear someone whose laugh sounds just like yours in one episode of *Who's Line Is It Anyway?* So, why can't this guy with the shoulders recognize your face?

It's rough when nobody knows who you are, but look at it this way: Even though your chances of being bombarded by mobs of young girls or boys are slim at this stage in your career, your chances of being stalked are equally miniscule. But the biggest bonus of being a relative unknown is that you get to screw up royally without the *Hollywood Foreign Press* or the *National Enquirer* giving a damn. So, cheer up. Enjoy your anonymity while it lasts because if you follow the sound advice in this book, you won't be an unknown for long.

BEFORE YOU SPEND THAT $21.95

Think about this. You already bought (or stole) 20 books on filmmaking, singing, producing, directing, acting, or screenwriting. Unless the one you're contemplating buying was written by James Cameron or Polly Platt, what's the point? They all say about the same thing. Okay, so, this one's really, really different, right? Maybe it is. But chances are, it's not. Chances are it's got a cool jacket cover with a snazzy title (sorta like this one) and it speaks to you. It's the one that's gonna change the complexion of your career. And besides, you say, what's $21.95 for a soon to be Oscar-award winning filmmaker? I'll tell ya. Twenty-one ninety five you could have spent on getting some decent letterhead instead of the crap you're sending your query letters out on, that's what.

Do this. Grab every "educational" book you've bought in the last year or so. Look through each one and tell me that 80% of the contents in one can't be found in the other 37. I rest my case.

THINGS YOU COULD'VE BOUGHT WITH THAT $21.95

So, you just wouldn't listen, huh? You bought it anyway. Had to have one more book on your shelf. Have I taught you nothing? You don't need more books! You need to spend your money on improving your craft. Here are just a few suggestions for how you could have spent your $21.95. Five minutes of acting class. A sliding scale session with your therapist, whom you keep saying you don't have a crush on. A tank of gas for your 1991 Toyota Camry. Anything. But not another book! You'll learn.

AN INTERVIEW WITH A FORMER GO-GO DANCER

JULIA MICHELS
VICE PRESIDENT, CREATIVE AFFAIRS | 20TH CENTURY FOX MUSIC

FH: You've got the coolest job but you didn't start at Fox, right? So, take me back.
JM: When I moved to L.A. I wanted to get into the music business. The first job I got wasn't even in the music business, however, in the building where I worked there was a placement agency for the entertainment industry. It was a temp agency, but they also did full-time placements. After the third or fourth time, the guy in the agency office said, "Okay, go on this interview, it's an agency that represents film composers." So, I went to the interview knowing nothing about film composers, but I was familiar with two composers they represented, Danny Elfman and Stewart Copeland, two rock guys. It was a long interview but I wound up getting the job.

FH: Shut up.
JM: Yeah, and I got to be the assistant at this boutique agency for two years. I made all the demo tapes and I learned film music really well. Shortly after I got there, one of the composers wanted to start a record label. So I decided to leave with him to start this little label called Baby Records. We signed three acts and over the course of the year developed one of them. Only thing is that I needed to make money. So, he said why don't you be my music editor and then he spent three months showing me how to cut music. I did a Showtime movie. Remember that show, *The Parenthood*, it was on the WB? I edited that show. At the end of the year it kind of dissolved because the guy who'd started the label wanted to be in one of the bands so, he then went back to that original agency.

FH: The one with Elfman and Copeland?
JM: Yeah, I went back there and they hired me as a junior agent. I started making deals for composers. Left there, was independent for a while, then I started working in a composer's studio, Basil Poledouris. He taught me all about the studio stuff and allowed me to continue doing my own stuff. So I started coordinating soundtracks. People would call me and ask me to put together the music for the soundtracks they were distributing. Out of the blue, I got a call from Capitol Records

saying "our soundtrack person just left and we have a deal with Miramax. It's a three-month job and we need someone to do the movie, *Scream 2*." I said "Okay, I'll do it." I knew nothing about the record industry at that point. Even though it was supposed to be a three-month job, I decided to turn it into something more. So I started sending all of my contacts in the film business our music like Everclear and The Dandy Warhols, Meredith Brooks. All of a sudden that job turned into a two-year job. I became the director of soundtracks. I did something like 12 soundtracks when I was there and it was great. I had a great time. The label was really fun because it was all about the music. Capitol was such a landmark; I got to drive into Capitol tower everyday. Very cool. Then I'd done three Fox movies – *Hope Floats*, which sold almost three million copies, *There's Something About Mary*, and *Never Been Kissed*.

FH: *Never Been Kissed* is one of my favorite movies. I drive my friends crazy imitating The Denominators. Remember the nerds, the math geeks? Love 'em.
JM: I do. That was a fun movie. Those were all Fox movies. So Fox sorta became my second family even though I was still working at Capitol. I loved my job. Then one day I got a call from Fox saying "We're gonna hire you." And I was like, "For what?" They said, "We have an opening here for a film music executive because one of our people is leaving." I said "okay."

FH: What else are ya gonna say?
JM: I signed a four-year contract at Fox and I'm in my fourth year as a music executive. Going from the composer agency to the recording studio to the record label gave me all the knowledge to do what I do now, which is to oversee all the music in a film from start to finish.

FH: What a journey. So, when you walked through the doors for the first time at the temp agency, what did you expect to get out of it? What did you want to be?
JM: Actually, I didn't know anything about the music business. So I had no idea what I wanted to be. And I never would have said "I want to work at a composer agency" because I didn't even know what they did. Most of America goes to the movies and hears the music in the background, but doesn't realize that someone actually writes the music, then goes into a recording studio with a 90-piece orchestra that plays to the picture.

FH: It's amazing. It's something to watch.
JM: It is. So, I feel so lucky.

FH: So, what qualifications do you need to be a music supervisor?
Licensing of course.
JM: Yeah, the ins and outs of music licensing, publishing, marketing,
soundtracks, radio promotion, etc. You have to have contacts in the business. Management contacts, label contacts and besides all of that, you
have to be creative and love music. And love finding the perfect song
for a scene. One third is excitement, a third being a fan and a third having the knowledge of what to do. You can't just have the knowledge and
be successful. I'm in my job also because I'm a music fan.

FH: Why did you dig music so much?
JM: I don't know. Who knows why I cared? Maybe being a dancer, a
cheerleader, a gymnast, I was into the music and the beat and how music
was cut. Just a passion for it. You gotta have knowledge and passion otherwise it's hard to survive this business. There are a lot of good days,
bad days. A lot of crap. Hard work. And if you're not loving the music
in the end, you won't last.

FH: C'mon, dude, a bad day? You have one of the most enviable jobs
in the business. You're the reason I cried in *Remember The Titans*,
when the coach's daughter was talking about how disappointed she
was that her dad didn't get in the Hall of Fame! There was some
James Taylor song playing, what was that song? Oh, *Fire and Rain*. I
know that's not your movie but the point is, it was the *song* that
yielded maximum emotional impact in that scene — for me. I digress
a lot. So, what makes for a bad day?
JM: [*Laughs*]. Let's see. A bad day is when you're trying to clear a
song, get the rights and we hear that it's unclearable, we can't get it.
And it's not so much that it's a disappointment to me, but then I have
to go back to my director, who's in love with the song and tell him he
can't have it.

FH: They don't understand the work involved, the process.
JM: Right. They just say, "Well, you have to get it. We have to have
this song." And you're crying, "But I can't." It's just not a good day
when you have to deliver some bad news to the filmmaker.

FH: What are some of the reasons songs become unclearable?

JM: Well, a bigger band like a U2 or even the estates, say for Frank Sinatra or Judy Garland, have say over what they give their music to. So, you have to send script pages that describe the scene. If they feel that it's not appropriate or even if they just don't want to be associated, then they say "sorry, we don't want to give it to you." That happens mostly in teenage sex comedies. Sometimes people don't want their songs associated with some cheesy scene. It doesn't happen very much, but when you've been in the business for a while, you know the tough ones. The Rolling Stones. The Doors.

FH: Boo hoo! Well, let's say there's a Judy Garland song and you want it in your movie but her estate doesn't want it in your movie, can you hire someone to sing the song?

JM: Good question, you're so smart.

FH: Thank you. Can I get that in writing?

JM: In some instances you can do that if you can't clear a master recording. You hire a singer to cover the song, period. You betcha, you can do that. And we also do it when the license is too expensive. If the band wrote the song, you're out of luck. Sometimes when you do a cover, it might work fine in the movie but if it's not the greatest rendition you might not put it on the soundtrack.

FH: So, what's been the hardest thing about being in the business?

JM: The hardest part about the business is the lack of integrity sometimes, the untruths and the manipulation that people feel they need to do to get what and where they want to get. And not so much people stepping over you, but more negotiating in what you're doing. You're calling about something grand, you're making a deal with people and they're telling you that they don't have other jobs and then I find out from another studio that they're negotiating on other pictures and it's like, just tell the truth.

FH: What made you leave Chicago to come out here?

JM: Really, truthfully?

FH: Yeah, since truth's what we're talking about right now.

JM: I wanted to dance in music videos. I wanted to dance with Paula (Abdul), Janet (Jackson) and Madonna. And that's why I came out here. To dance.

FH: Hence the first job as a go-go dancer.

JM: I started to go on auditions. I was teaching aerobics and then I broke my foot. That's when I said I'd be in the music business. If I can't dance, I'll be in the music business. But never in my wildest dreams did I think I'd be the vice president of music at Fox. Never. It just happened.

FH: Yeah, but it happened because you put yourself in positions for it to happen. That's what a lot of aspiring folks forget. It's not about forcing something to happen, it's about doing the work, quality work and then putting yourself in situations for positive things to blow by. Okay, so what were the reactions you got from friends and family when you said, "I'm going to California to be in music videos?" [*Laughs*].

JM: They thought I was crazy. My friends were out getting married. I don't know that they thought I'd stay that long. When I got out here I was so poor I was sleeping on my friend's couch, getting my car impounded, all of that. It was hard. Moved in with my boyfriend so I could pay my impound fees. It's taken about 11 years to get where I am today. It feels like it's gone by really fast.

FH: So how were you dealing with the poverty? What kept you saying, "I can do this?"

JM: Good people, friends, and family.

FH: Ever want to go home?

JM: No. Never. I had friends out here and we just supported each other. We all worked at the same health club. I mean, I went from being a valet to a desk person to aerobics teacher to a trainer. It was my support. Without them I would have been so lonely, so beaten down.

FH: On to more important things. Craziness. Madness. Mayhem. Casting couch escapades.

JM: Luckily I don't have a casting couch story, but this director tried to pick me up by saying "hey, you got a good face, why don't you come to my hotel tonight and audition for a movie?" I said "What?" He gave me his card. I said, "Can I bring my boyfriend?"

FH: You killjoy!

JM: Exactly. He said, "I prefer to work alone." I told my boss, because one of his friends was composing the score for a movie for this same guy. My boss couldn't believe it. I mean, this guy wanted me to come to his hotel to do a reading and I wasn't even an actress! But you know, you'll run into those kinds of people. At first I'd think that they were really interested in doing business with me, but then I'd find out that it wasn't my band they were really interested in, it's my…

FH: Bed! That's crazy. So, ya got a lot of women mentors?
JM: I do. I'm fortunate. There was a woman, Liz Heller at Capitol Records, who was my boss and she was the number two person at Capitol. She was tough on me but she also believed in me. She was the one who taught me how to survive. I remember one day I walked into her office. I learned that you have to admit your mistakes, because if someone starts screaming at you and you say, "you're right, it was my mistake," it ends the conversation. What else are they gonna say?

FH: It diffuses the drama, that's for sure. Is it really as cutthroat as everyone says? I've spoken with producers, directors, etc., and my sense is that the competitive dynamics that are present with actors, writers, and other creatives, don't really exist in the area in which you work? Is that fair to say?
JM: Well, yes and no. I'm in a position where people come to me. In my other jobs, I had to sell composers to people and I was in competition with other people. I have a job where everyone wants his or her song in a movie. They want their bands in our movies, so I get the phone calls. I don't buy any soundtracks. And the only competition I really ever see is if I want a band that's doing another song for another movie studio. That's not a real big deal because there are 50 million other bands out there.

FH: What a great life. What's down the road?
JM: I'd like to produce someday, but then I see filmmakers fight with the studios all the time. Music is just one part of the film. Producers have to answer to the chairmen of the studios, where execs may want to change only parts of the producers' movies. That's where I see all the fights and back and forth. I've worked in some situations where I was working with someone on a movie where we haven't gotten along. I mean, it's rare but it has happened.

FH: That's gotta be a special brand of hell.
JM: It is. It's hell. Everyday, you say "I have to call this person" and you don't want to, but you have to, because she's producing the film. But three quarters of the way through something usually clicks and it turns out okay. But until then, it's hell. You decide, "I'm going to figure out how to deal with this person and we're gonna make the best film we can make."

FH: What in your life, if anything, prepared you for this journey?
JM: I'm an athlete and so are you, so you know that sports are a great classroom for life. Working with people you may not like... everyday [*Laughs*].

FH: What have you drawn from it?
JM: I think I have really good adaptability skills. I don't know where I got them. Maybe because we moved around a couple of times. Different schools, maybe, but as a gymnast I was a little sheltered from the rest of the world. Then I had a career-ending injury and it was so traumatic. I thought my identity was gone because I'd never seen my life without gymnastics. I thought I was gonna be like Mary Lou Retton. I was going to be an Olympian.

FH: Have your mug on a Wheaties box.
JM: Yep. When that happened I was forced to look at my life differently and actually get out of bed in the mornings. When you're a junior in high school and you lose the one thing that sort of defines you, it's traumatic. Realizing that there's more to life than the one thing I was concentrating on. I discovered that it's important to be happy with what you're doing or leave. I've left jobs because I was miserable in them. I just had faith that something would work out. You have to go to the happiness.

FH: Walk toward the light!
JM: Right. Go to the happiness.

FH: Is the happiness in the Hollywood scene at the parties?
JM: At first, yeah. You say "Oh my God, there's so and so" but after a while these people are coming to meet you in your office. I'm used to it now but every now and then it hits me. Like a while back my assistant yelled out to me, "Irene Cara's on the phone!" And I said "what?" Irene Cara was in *Flashdance* and *Fame*, two movies that defined my childhood. What a geek, I know. I knew all the dances.

FH: I know all the songs.
JM: After we spoke, I called my best friend and said, "Irene Cara just called me!" The fan in me comes out.

FH: That's cool. Clearly you have to be here to do what you do but how do you respond to the "you don't need to live in L.A. to be in the biz" mantra.

JM: I really think the Hollywood attitude is "out of sight, out of mind." I've had independent music supervisors who think they can live somewhere else and still get lots of work here. Not gonna happen. There's always that person behind you — who lives here, next in line to steal your job. Sometimes that keeps you going.

FH: Why are people so unrealistic about success here? How to get it, how fast it comes, yackety smack. They think once Hollywood gets to behold their amazing talent that they will be the next Denzel Washington or Tom Hanks or Julia Michels.

JM: I'll tell you why, and I learned this from my coming out here to dance. You go from being the best at what you do in your own little hometown or school, or wherever, to a place where everyone was the best at what she did and it's completely overwhelming. When I came here, it was the most humbling experience. You look around and you think these people are better than you are. All of them! For one thing, you have to have that drive to get here, but you get hit immediately, because everybody here is trying to be somebody.

FH: But it sounds like you have it all. Good friends, good relationship, awesome job. How about throwing 1.5 kids into the blender?

JM: Oh my God! You'll probably talk to me in two years and I'll be pregnant, but I applaud the women who can do career and children. I don't know how they do it.

FH: Best advice?

JM: Like who you are everyday because if you go home at night and hate who you are it's gonna carry over into other areas in your life. Be happy waking up with yourself because at the end of the day, you go home with yourself. It sounds kind of cliché, but it's so true. If you've done your work in a way that you believe in, even if you're beaten down, you know you've done it the right way and that's the most important thing.

FH: Advice for the newbies out there?

JM: Don't expect your overnight success to be, literally, overnight. Don't expect to come here and have people telling you how wonderful you are. Don't expect to be signed the day after you get here. Know that you have to love what you're doing everyday. If you don't love what you're doing, get out of it.

OPPORTUNITY = PREPARATION + TALENT

You'll hear me say it again and again. I don't believe in luck. I believe in being prepared for those defining moments that are bound to show up in your life, if your approach to achieving your goals is setting clear intentions.

One of the first skills you have to hone on this journey is extemporaneous speaking. Learning to communicate, on cue, on a very basic level with people you don't know and who are giving you only 30 seconds to make your point — who you are or what your story's about. They say that public speaking is one of the most common fears known to mankind. If that's the case and you're in that group, you are in a vat of you know what because your success, at least early on, will depend solely on how well you communicate on paper, on the phone and in person.

If you're not a great orator, that's cool. We're not talking about turning you into Dale Carnegie or Oprah Winfrey. We're talking about storytelling. That's what selling yourself is all about: telling your story. If that skill is not something that comes naturally for you, there are ways to improve.

> √ Take a storytelling or public speaking class
> √ Join Toastmasters, an informal (but official) extemporaneous speaking club
> √ Form a group of your friends in the business and practice making presentations and telling stories

Eventually, you'll want to take your skills to a level where you become good at pitching — the art of telling a story to an audience or buyer, generally with the intent to sell something.

THE PITCH BITCH

Take the most prolific writer in the world, place her in front of a class and ask her to pitch her script and guess what you're likely to see in her eyes? Sheer terror. In one of my recent pitch workshops I had 30 people from different backgrounds — actors, writers, producers, filmmakers — with one goal: to become a pitch bitch. That person who can stand before any size audience, tell a compelling story, and get the sale.

My classes are always filled with writers who are trying to sell scripts. Actors who are trying to land roles. And producers who are trying to secure financing for film projects. Each seminar is always filled with a few people who have never spoken in front of a group. There are always a few people who admit that their idea of pitching is memorizing their scripts.

Now, before we talk about how to become a pitch bitch, it's probably a good idea to talk about pitching in general. Nobody's born a pitcher but the skill may come more naturally for some than others. Not to worry, anybody can learn to pitch, but it takes practice and you have to like it. You can't just say "I want to be a good pitcher" then kick and scream the whole journey. Won't work. You have to like it.

READY TO BECOME A BITCH?

Good. Now that you know what a pitch is, we can talk more specifically about how to deliver a powerful one. First, there is no set time length for a pitch. It's whatever time it takes you to convey the essence of your story in a way that those listening can understand. It can be 30-seconds long or it can be 30-minutes long.

And while there's no magic formula for how to get a buyer to say "yes," there are some basic principles I've used in my pitches and workshops that have resulted in sales.

First, write down the high points of the story.

If you're trying to sell yourself, write down significant career events or awards. If you're pitching a story or script or show, pick two to three key points that really sell the essence of the story.

Second, decide on the 'moral' or 'theme' of your story.

Every script has a main theme. The film *Tootsie* is about an out of work actor who lies and cheats his way to on-screen success only to find out later that the real way to discover your best "self" is to be who you are from the start. That's one of the themes of *Tootsie*.

When you're pitching a property, like a script, it's the story that's central to the pitch. But let's say I'm trying to get signed by a big agency like William Morris. My theme would be that I'm a versatile talent who's covered sports, entertainment, lifestyle, and news programming. A broadcaster who will be a hugely successful, nationally syndicated talk show host unless I change my mind. Those would be the selling points in my meeting with them. I highlight the things I've done in those four TV areas, choosing maybe one "high point" for each category. By signing me, William Morris would get a well-rounded, talented (good looking) on-air personality who has excelled in numerous areas of broadcasting. My theme is *versatility*.

Third, fill in your high points with two to three secondary points.
Those are the minor events that string the story from one high point to the next. You would structure your pitch to hit the secondary points that put you closest to the most critical high points. In other words, if you were pitching the movie *Remember The Titans*, you wouldn't need to go through all of the football practices to pitch that movie. Instead, you'd set the stage by telling the buyer something like this.

> *The year is 1971. And even though the official Civil Rights Movement has ended and integration is a reality, a southern town of blacks and whites is still about as separated as oil and vinegar. And it's about to get worse when Boone, a black football coach, is hired to replace the beloved white head coach who's led the team to past championships. Now, Boone, a somewhat self-righteous but good-natured tough guy, arrives along with the school's first crop of black athletes and immediately challenges the boys to become one team, one heartbeat. His first task, ironically, is to get all of the players on the same bus. An event that leads to Boone's first major showdown, not only with the old coach (who's now his assistant) but also his white, superstar defensive player and team leader, not to mention the legion of parents who have come to send their sons off to preseason training camp.*

Boom! In one paragraph (about one minute in oral time), I've conveyed the essence of this movie. The people listening to this one snippet GET where this movie's going. They don't know the ending yet, but they know there's gonna be some racial tension, probably lots of it. They know that either this team is going to come together or stay separate. They know that the audiences watching this movie are going to be challenged to look at their own lives and attitudes about race. The theme of *Remember The Titans*? United we stand, divided we fall. A universal message. I didn't need to go into, "And then this happened, and next, that happened...." A pitch is a broad sketch of the whole story. Keep it moving, keep it exciting and keep it on point.

Fourth, start off with punch.
Once you've identified the major points on which to hang your story and the secondary points leading up to the major ones, you're going to write down five (5) different possible beginnings.

> Beginning #1: A compelling statement. (Drunk drivers should be executed)

> Beginning #2: A provocative question. (Should drunk drivers who kill be executed?)

> Beginning #3: A time frame. (It was 1960 at the height of the women's movement)

> Beginning #4: An engaging event. (A loud shot blasted through Bob's bedroom)

> Beginning #5: A quick exercise that leads you right into your pitch. For example, in one pitch I held up an object and asked the audience members what they saw. Once all of the responses were in, I demonstrated that people see, sense, and perceive based on who they are, where they're from, and their own pictures of the world. I held up a pair of scissors and some people saw a sewing tool and others saw a deadly object.

Fifth, end with a bang.
It does you no good to engage your listeners at the beginning, to keep them with you through all of the rocks and rills and then finish flat. A lousy ending could ruin the whole pitch.

So, now you're going to find a way to end the story with your theme. Yep, you're going to end the story with "what the movie's really about." If you were pitching yourself, this would be the part where you'd say, "What I'm really about is earthy, jazzy music. It's what I grew up on, it's who I am, it's what I do best."

Here's a sample ending of a pitch for the movie _Tootsie_. It's near the end of it.
> ...it's only after Michael unmasks in front of a live TV audience, that all of his co-stars, including Julie, the woman he's in love with, realize just how good of an actor he **really** is. It's so quiet on the set you could hear a teardrop fall on cotton. He stands there in

his dress watching Julie slowly walk over to him, not knowing what she's gonna do. Everyone else is looking at Michael up and down, up and down, checking out his vital areas because they simply can't believe he's a man. Julie faces off with Michael and then Bam! Socks him in the stomach and walks away. Weeks later Michael sees Julie after she's leaving work and gets up the guts to strike up a conversation with her. She tries to ignore him but she can't. She loves the guy even if he did betray her. Michael's repentant. He knows he was wrong and he finally tells her that lying is no way to gain trust in a relationship, but that it took becoming a woman for him to become a better man.

Now, that was a very basic exercise on how to set up a pitch, you'll have to come to one of my workshops to get more advanced tools! Until then, here are a few things that will help you to become a better pitch bitch.

Number 1: Nothing takes the place of passion. If you're not passionate about what you're selling, nobody else is going to get excited about it either.

Number 2: Know that the first sentence sells the next one. In other words, don't waste any words, make them all count because the more persuasive your first sentence, the more likely I am to listen to your second, and third and so on.

Number 3: Keep the energy up. Even if you're telling a story that's tragic or sad, you can still have good energy. Don't bore people to yawning.

Number 4: Don't be on autopilot. There's a good chance the people you're talking to will want to chime in and ask a question or comment; that's why I don't recommend memorizing a pitch verbatim.

Number 5: Know the story inside out. Don't memorize, know it. If you know it, you won't be thrown off by potential distractions such as an assistant entering the room, a phone ringing or a train passing by. Know the story.

Number 6: Know when to shut up. Sounds harsh, but if I don't say it that way, some of you will keep talking way past your "yes." One of the things I learned early in my sales career with Procter & Gamble was to zip the lips once a buyer said "yes." If the person you're pitching to, says, "love it, print it," that's your cue to end the pitch. Don't utter another syllable. You've done your job. You got the deal, way to go.

Number 7: Always have a post-game conference with yourself. After you've celebrated and used all of your "anytime" minutes calling your friends to share the good news, take a step back and assess what you did well and potentially, what could have been better about your pitch. Remember what I said earlier: if you got the deal or the part, you did a good job. This is not about perfectionism; it's about repeating what works and deleting what doesn't.

So, as you assess your pitch, see if you can remember what your audience responded to. Was it the phrase you coined at the end of the pitch? Was it the rhetorical question that gripped them in the opening? Do you want to lose the joke that nobody laughed at? Probably. You get the picture. Even when things go your way, always take time to refine your skills. The more you do, the better you get at pitching, the more sales you make, deals you seal, and roles you land.

One final suggestion: record your practice pitches. First, tape yourself using a Dictaphone or Mini Disc Player, or whatever you use for audio recording. When you listen to yourself without accompanying pictures, you can concentrate on the mechanics of delivering a phrase effectively. You'll know which words to punch. Where voice inflection is needed most. Audio taping yourself also gives you a sense of how you sound over the telephone. It may provide insight into what people hear when you call their offices.

Next, you'll go for audio and video. When you videotape yourself, it's more about body language. You don't throw the audio out the window, it's still important. But the addition of being able to use hand gestures, facial expressions, and body movement gives you an added dimension that could mean the difference between getting the job or getting a pass.

HOW TO GIVE GOOD PHONE

Writers write. Filmmakers film. Producers produce. Directors direct. Singers sing. Actors act (some of them). That's why most of them suck at giving phone. Yet this is perhaps the most important skill you can develop as a wannabe. So, why aren't any of these "experts" telling us this? I'm convinced they don't want us to break in. Face it, you're not going to get a meeting with Polly Platt first time out of the gate unless you know her manicurist, which you don't, and that's my point. So, you've gotta learn how to make the phone work to your advantage.

Let me give you an example. It's 5:05 p.m. today and I'm sitting at my desk working on this book when my phone rings.

"Hello, Ms. Harris, this is Rachel with MCI, how are you this evening?"

"Good. Busy, Rachel, what's up?"

"I was wondering if you would be interested in a special we have going right now...."

Ehnnnnk! Click. Bad phone. Very bad phone. Why? Because Rachel's not listening to me. She may be hearing me and that's only because her ears are working, but she's not *listening*. What did I say to Rachel? I said, "Busy."

It would have been good for Rachel to ask, "Would there be a better time to call to tell you about this special that could save you $50 next month. It expires at 8:00 p.m. tomorrow?"

Had she listened to me, she would have heard me say that I was busy; she would have been able to come back with something as clever as the line I recommended she use on me.

This is what happens with lots of beginners and let's be real, veterans, as well. People, in general, just don't give good phone. Lucky for you, it's a skill that you can learn. Here are some techniques to help you.

Tips for Giving Good Phone

Get out of the gate smoothly.
When the person answers, actually listen to her. If she says, "Billy Jean's office," don't comeback with "Billy Jean?" Most Hollywood execs don't answer their own phones that way — if they answer their own phones at all.

Be cordial, energetic, but not too eager.
Your goal is to stay on the phone for the next 30 seconds. So, be friendly but not giddy unless, of course, you get George Clooney on the line, then go for it.

Have a plan.
As a rule, you get about 10-15 seconds to get someone's attention. If you screw up, you're probably not going to get your full 30 – 60 seconds. So, practice what you intend to say and time yourself, keeping in mind that you may hit it off with the person on the other end and be granted more time.

Stick to the formula.
What formula? This formula. "Hi, I'm Suzy Filmmaker, I just completed a feature about green gorillas who are living in a commune with a tribe of Native Americans and I'm interested in sending it to you for distribution consideration."

SOME RESTRICTIONS APPLY

Did you read the small print on the last product you bought? You know, that blah, blah, blah under the "Some Restrictions Apply" heading? Probably not. Most of us don't. But not reading that itty bitty writing at the bottom of the page could cost you your first real Hollywood deal.

Wanna know why the majority of people who set out to break into Hollywood don't succeed? Because they won't or can't follow simple instructions. But people won't tell you that. They'd rather say, "We're not taking submissions." When what they really mean is that they're not taking *yours*.

Three years ago I was looking for films to shoot, so I got the crazy notion that I would conduct a screenwriting contest and choose a script from the pool of amazing writing I would be so fortunate to read. I called it the Fantasy Screenwriting Contest. Boy, did that turn out to be a nightmare.

I received about 75 entries from all over the world, far more than I bargained for. It was the best and worst thing I ever did in my career. I'd always heard agents and managers talk about how awful the scripts that came to their offices were. I didn't believe them.

After I read about four scripts, I understood exactly what they meant. And I also understood why most screenwriters are such failures. The contest was listed on a couple of filmmaking and screenwriting Web sites with very specific instructions. I even provided directions for how to submit a screenplay, something most contest coordinators don't do.

Within a week, the scripts started pouring in. And guess what? Of the 75 submissions, maybe five of the writers followed the instructions. Five! That's pathetic. And it won't cut it in Hollywood. I had people sending me scripts without covers. Others sent scripts in binders. Some poor soul even sent me a 140-page script when the contest rules clearly stated that scripts were to be no longer than the standard 120 pages. I don't have to tell you where his script landed... but I will. In the recycle bin after I shook my head at it for about 10 minutes straight.

So, let's talk briefly about script formatting, in case those 30 books you own don't cover it. Feature film scripts are typically 90 to 120 pages. If you're new to the game, don't go under 90 or over 120 pages. I don't care how good you think the script is, don't violate these rules. And if you do, don't say I didn't tell ya so.

"I'd rather be smart than be a movie star."

— *Natalie Portman, actress*

FRAN'S GOLDEN RULE #2:
YOUR HEART WILL GO ON

Okay, so you've put in a year with this last screenplay and your cousin Buford, the plumber, thinks it's really good, even though he's never read a script or been to a movie theater. You send it to the big Hollywood producer you met at the Annual Toenail Clipping contest while he was shooting a movie last winter in your hometown. He reads it and two months later his assistant calls you to deliver some strong medicine. They're passing on the script. It's not right for them. What do you do? You sit silently on the phone trying not to cry or cuss. After all, Cousin Buford loved it. Instead you politely thank the assistant and hang up. Over the next three weeks you barely manage to get out of bed. Your dog Phoebe's wondering what the hell's come over you, you used to be so much fun with the Frisbee and all. Only now you're just a shade of that fun-loving, Frisbee-throwing diva. All because one producer didn't agree with Cousin Buford's coverage. Now, does that make sense? No. Heck no!

Here's what you do. You get your bestest (yes, bestest) thank you card out of your desk and you send it to the producer, thanking him for giving you a good read. After you've mailed it, if you still feel like it, go ahead and cry a river. Then, a few days later, you dry your eyes and begin the search for another opinion on your work. Remember, it's a subjective business. One producer's dread could be another's delight.

SO MANY FIRST IMPRESSIONS... SO FEW CHANCES TO SCREW UP
Listen, we all know that clichés bear at least a morsel of truth, that's how they become clichés. And this one's no different. You only have one chance to make a first impression and if you're dealing with someone who doesn't believe in second chances, your first impression could be your last. But there's a secret to making good first impressions: be a good, decent person. See, most people make the mistake of "trying" to make a good first impression. If you "are" a good impression, you'll make a good impression, capisce? In other words, if it's in your natural rhythm to be kind, energetic, genuine, and courteous, it will be almost impossible for you to make a bad impression. Some of you may think you're not making a good impression when what's really happening

is that you may not be a good "personality" fit for the person you're meeting. We all have those people with whom we click almost instantly, right? Now, count on your hands and toes how often that has happened to you. You probably have limbs remaining, don't you? Why? Because there are only so many perfect matches out there. So, rather than trying to lather up someone you really want to be in business with, be friendly and sincere and let your work do the selling.

DEJERKING 101

Let's get this out of the way right up front. Are you a jerk? A certified arse? Don't know? Okay, let's do a quick inventory. Answer the following questions right now or if you're hung over, do the exercise after you've had a few cups of joe.

In the last week have you...
- Done something that you knew offended someone in your life (intimate or stranger) yet you haven't apologized?
- Been rude to the telemarketer who calls you every night just as you're sitting down to eat your Spam sandwich?
- Been perpetually dishonest, unfriendly, or otherwise cold, even to kids?
- Yelled at the person tending the drive-through-window at the fast food restaurant near your house?
- Cut off a senior citizen in traffic?

If you answered yes to two or more of these questions, there's a real good chance you're a bonafide jerk. And if that's the case, you will have a hard time getting your career two feet off of the ground. Nobody wants to be in business with a jerk. Especially an *unproven* jerk. Oh, sure, Hollywood's full of jerks, some widely known for their jerkability, but these jerks are in very powerful positions. Positions that other people have to come in contact with. Which has nothing to do with you, by the way. You still need to be a good person to get anywhere in the Wood.

"What can you do" you say, *"I've been this way all of my life?"* It's simple. Stop it. I don't have any 12-step program referrals for you, only some sage advice. Stop it. Hollywood will not welcome you and your attitude, so either pursue another career or change your evil ways. Or get some therapy. You'll need it down the line anyway.

THE ULTIMATE SHOWBIZ TOOLBOX

Okay, where was I? The business of show. Right. I ranted briefly about your need to embrace the business side of showbiz, now I'll get more specific about some strategies for "Inc."-ing yourself. There are a few things we all need in our arsenal to begin this journey. These things need to be on board from the start and then updated regularly. Some of the items are specific to certain industries and you'll be able to figure out what's for you and what's not.

Resumes

Everybody needs a resume that accurately reflects his or her talent and skills. For producers it's often called "credits." I recommend that you go online to find some samples. The most important element on any resume is accuracy. Don't lie about anything. Don't say you're 5'2" if you're really 5'8". Don't say you were the lead in the film if you were a non-speaking extra. Don't say you directed the play if you were the assistant to the assistant costume designer. You get the point: crime does not pay.

Think I'm pulling your leg? Here's a snapshot from our dear friend, Coach George O'Leary's yearbook.

At some point in his life, George O'Leary, a high profile NCAA football coach, decided that he would beef up his resume by adding an extra graduate degree. Merrily he rolled along until he applied for, and got, the head coaching job at Notre Dame University in 2001. That's when a pair of glasses did some poking around and found that this guy had not earned this fictitious graduate degree. When confronted with the findings, the coach claimed to have forgotten about the entry (uh huh).

What happened next should serve as a lesson to all potential lawyers, er, liars. Not only was this coach crucified in the media, but he also suffered severe public humiliation and, essentially, was forced to resign from his position at Notre Dame. His transgression had a lot of folks inside and outside the sports world shaking in their boots. And I guarantee you, prescription medicines and White Out sales went through the roof around this time.

So, take a tip from Coach: if you need to lie on your resume then maybe you're not really suited for the job.

George O'Leary was human. A human being with a common dilemma. One that has probably faced us all at some point in our lives. You want the job but you're not (or you think you're not) completely qualified "on paper." In other words, you could do the job with your eyes closed but you lack the official training or pedigree that would normally go with the position, right? Been there, got the DVD. So, how do you handle this obvious outage on your resume? You focus on your *skills* rather than your education or previous job titles. But more importantly, be honest. You may not get the job, but at least you won't be looking over your shoulder for the rest of your career.

Also, you should continually update your resume and make sure it's tailored to the position for which you're applying. For example, I keep a file that has four different resumes in it — actor, director/producer, writer, and broadcaster. When I get a bite for a TV job, I send the broadcasting resume. When someone's looking for a producer, I send out my credits.

Another thing. Go to extreme measures to keep your resume to one page. People will appreciate your ability to convey your brilliance economically. You do not need to list every single credit, job or role you've ever landed. A good rule of thumb is to keep your resume within a two to five-year span. Keep it relevant and don't take us back to your high school days when you were secretary of the Key Club, unless that time period falls in that two-to five-year span.

Business cards
Your business cards are a quick way to disseminate your information to people. Some actors or models put their headshots on their business cards. I think that's a good idea. It's a mini headshot and much easier for people to transport than an 8 X 10 photo. Some producers list sample credits or shows on their cards. Writers list their books. Be creative. With the plethora of software programs out there, you don't have to spend a lot of money for quality business cards, but make sure the information is accurate and well presented. I also advise people to put two phone numbers — office and cell — on their cards. That way if you happen to be in transition, there's always an alternate way for someone to reach you. Be sure to proof before you print.

Headshots
A close-up photo (normally an 8 X 10 black and white) showing your best attributes. Not those. The G-rated attributes. Expect to pay at least

somewhere between $250 – $500 for the photo shoot and another few hundred for duplication. Do not continue to use the same picture year after year, especially if you change your hairstyle. Got a new look? Get new pictures. You can't use the same headshot you were using in 1995 because when people respond to your headshot, they want to know that the person coming into their offices is the person on that picture. You'd be surprised how many people send out old pictures. So, if you're wondering why you're not getting any jobs, it could be because you look like you're stuck in that '80s show.

The flip side of not looking dated is not overdoing it. You don't wanna look like you're on your way to the Grand Ol' Opry or a Tammy Faye lookalike convention (sorry, Tammy, but the lashes are not working for me). Headshots are business tools, they're not calling cards for a beauty pageant. Remember, your picture needs to look like you. So, avoid heavy makeup and big, greasy, shiny hair. If you can swing it financially, get someone to do a professional makeup job and hire a professional photographer. They're both worth it.

Clippings
Although clippings tend to be staples for freelance writers, archived articles of music, performance, movie, theater, or film reviews are great tools for anyone in the business. And they are essential for your media kit, which I'll talk about next. Be sure your copies are crisp and clean, free from soda stains, potato chip oil, and stray pen marks.

Media Kits
A must have for the professional who's got game. A press kit, also known as a media kit, is a simple, organized collection of you and your work, usually for the purpose of getting you "press" or "media" attention. It's what's will be sent to media outlets, for instance, in preparation for my *Crashing Hollywood* book tour.

A media kit can vary in its contents but it typically includes:

- a 4 X 6 black and white or color photo of you (or your band, as an example)
- a clean copy of your product's cover (CD label, book cover, etc.)
- a current press release
- articles or clippings written about you or your product

- a quote sheet: a list of quotes from other people about you or your work
- a fact sheet that might list upcoming appearances, releases, etc.
- a question sheet, a one-page list of good questions to ask you about your work

Web site

Don't let anyone sell you a $3,000 Web site when there are simple, effective and quality options for less than $25 a year or more professional packages for $30 a month. Do your research to find the best alternative for you. If you have thousands of dollars to spend and you want a Flash site with scrolling text and other features, go for it. Just know that there are other economical options for those of you who want to invest your money elsewhere. In fact, you can go to my Web site, *www.talltreeproductions.com* and sign up for a similar package at a reasonable price.

As a rule, you want to tailor your site for your particular talents and skills. A producer's Web site, which may include links to trailers, viewing schedules and project lists, may be more extensive than, say, an actor's Web site, which may only have photos and resumes. There are no set rules, really, just make sure your Web site is an extension of who you are and make sure that it's professional.

Here are a few design tips to get you started:
1. **Keep it simple.** No need to make your site a maze. People like to click and go. They don't want to work too hard. If your site's too difficult to navigate, people will leave. Yes, they will.

2. **Keep the color scheme simple.** All of you neon-loving people are killing me. I went to a site the other day where the background color was solar pink and the text was yellow. It was the most painful experience of my life. Don't go crazy with the colors, it's too hard to read. If you want to experiment with colors, buy a paint set. Try to stick with background colors that are gentle on the eyes — white is best. Use font colors that work on white — black or blue are best. Yes, you can highlight areas using other colors, just don't overdo it.

3. **Don't go koo-koo for ALL CAPS.** Do you know how much I want to strangle those people whose Web sites are written

entirely in capital letters? Again, a string of all uppercase letters is terrible on the eyes. For the love of popcorn, don't do it!

4. **Spell check.** Sure, there's bound to be one, maybe two errors on your site, but if your site starts to look like it's written in Polish, you've got a problem. Try writing your site's text in a word processing document so that you can run a thorough spell check before transferring it to HTML or text and uploading it to your site. Even after you run spell check, I recommend giving your text to a few good editors because Spell Check is human, too.

5. **Pictures take time.** So do graphics. If you want to show your visitors all of your pictures from your last trip to Hollywood, that's fine, but just know that it's going to take time for the site to open, which may mean that some visitors will get impatient and leave. If you insist on using lots of pictures, make them small, no bigger than 2" X 2" or thumbnail size.

6. **Always capture visitor information.** At minimum you should have a small box on your site that says "Sign My Guestbook" or "Sign Up For My Weekly E-zine." This is an excellent way to build a database of future customers or clients.

7. **Engage your visitors.** Host contests, ask for feedback, give something away, anything to keep your fans coming back to your site and connected to you. Why do you visit your favorite sites? Because they offer something that you like. Same thing here. Give people a reason to come back.

Reel, Trailer, Demo Tapes
used typically by broadcasters, producers, directors, singers, musicians, actors.

Demo tapes, also known as reels, are audio or videotapes of your work. Trailers, of course, are two- to three-minute highlights of your films. A singer or musician's demo is simply a sample of his or her music, probably on a CD. They are short, powerful snippets. I like to call them "The Best of" collections. These should be professionally produced and should represent the absolute best of who you are and what you've done. They are electronic resumes, in a sense. Remember, people just may base their hiring or booking decisions on what they see or hear in your reel. Be sure it screams pro and not amateur. You can also put your reels on DVD or CD, but just be sure the person receiving your materials can view them in the format in which you're sending them.

I'LL HAVE THE SCREENWRITING SALAD... ON THE SIDE

I don't believe in luck. I never have. If anything happens that I wasn't expecting, I don't think luck had anything to do with it. It was just time for it to happen. That's why you have to always be prepared for "your time." And more importantly, that's why you have to always *be preparing* for your time. Some people say, "I sell computers but I'm a writer on the side." Well, I don't know many people who are happy with their passion being a side dish. How do we typically treat side dishes? They don't get our full attention, do they? They're almost like an afterthought.

In fact, the other day I had lunch at the Cheesecake Factory and ordered a grilled cheese sandwich with French fries... on the side. I ate all of the sandwich and two fries. See, what I mean? On the side. Won't work. Make your art your main course and watch your life change before your eyes.

AN INTERVIEW WITH A FUTURE GRAMMY AWARD-WINNING MUSICIAN

RACHEL MACINTYRE | MUSICIAN & SINGER | BELU

FH: How long have you been singing?
RM: I've been singing since I was about 10 years old, I'm 20 now. Everything from jazz to pop to country. I studied opera in college.

FH: Really? And what kind of band do you sing and play in?
RM: We're a rock band. [*Laughs*].

FH: The one thing you left out. Had to be.
RM: We play a lot of clubs in Austin. Right now we're finishing our album so we can shop it to labels. Hopefully be able to do music full time, eventually.

FH: How long have you been on the circuit?
RM: It's a start-up project. We've been together about a year. We're totally committed, we all work full-time jobs and then after work, go and sit in the studio for about five to six hours. Maybe we get three hours of sleep at night. As long as the album gets finished. We're considering moving to L.A. because that's the best thing for the band.

FH: Four to five band members, a couple of girlfriends and boyfriends all under one roof? Where are ya gonna live?
RM: We're all moving into an apartment together so we can save money for U.S. tours, even Europe. Right now I'm living on $5 for the rest of the week. That's the sacrifice you make. This summer we're going to take a West Coast tour and try to arrange some showcases while we're out there. I haven't been there since I was four. We'll see what's what. If all goes well, we'll be out there by August.

FH: What's your plan? Do you have a booker?
RM: Most of us have been in enough bands to know what we're doing. Once we get the album done and get settled, we'll get some of those things, agent, booker. For right now, we don't need the overhead.

FH: What kind of feedback have you gotten on your music?
RM: We have someone in England who loves our music and wants to set tours for us all over Europe. We have contact with someone at RCA. We get good vibes from people on the radio station when our stuff gets played. Lots of good feedback from a lot of different places. Again, we gotta get the album made.

FH: You're kinda alternative, sorta rock, sorta jazz, sorta...
RM: Eclectic and I think that's why they like us so much in Europe. That's why we want to possibly move to L.A., to see how people in other cities respond to us. There's only so much you can do in Austin. I mean it's great to play all of these bars, but what's the likelihood of the president of Sony walking into the club one night when you're playing?

FH: Not very.
RM: Right, so we want to expand. We applied for South By Southwest, but we haven't heard back yet.

FH: Everybody's got a band, what makes Belu different?
RM: Well, this may sound conceited, but we feel like we're in the top 2% of the bands trying to get out there and make it. We've heard maybe two, three bands here that we feel can compete with us.

FH: That's in Austin. Now, when you get to L.A. the stakes are higher. How will the little band from Austin, Texas handle all of the perceived competition?
RM: Try to stay confident. Try to remember what makes us special. The reason bands don't make it, is because they quit. If we can just keep going, maybe the bands that are just as good as ours will eventually drop out of the race.

FH: Ya think?
RM: That's what we're hoping anyway.

TOP FOUR REASONS PEOPLE DON'T MAKE IT IN HOLLYWOOD

First, they have no plans.

If you fail to plan, you plan to work for near minimum wage for the rest of your life. Don't be blinded (or seduced) by the bright lights of

Tinseltown. Success in Hollywood has a price. And no matter how entic-ing and exciting the potential payday and media attention, you won't get there without a plan. Sure, you may ultimately strike gold if you sputter around in the wilderness. Even the Israelites eventually made it to the Promised Land. But I don't know one person who wouldn't mind cutting her travel time to any destination in half if she could. I mean, would you rather fly to New York from Los Angeles in an hour or the standard, five? That's what I thought.

Second, their plans are unrealistic.

An elephant has a greater chance of walking through the eye of a needle than you have of going to Hollywood and becoming a big star right off the bat. I'm not raining on your parade, I'm trying to prepare you for one universal truth: making it in showbiz is more likely to be a marathon, not a sprint. If you are in that 1% of the population who become literal overnight successes, bravo! Call me, I'd like to write your biography. It doesn't happen that way for most people. Even though I applaud you for your positive attitude, I also encourage you to develop a plan that takes longer than instant oatmeal to execute.

Third, they fear (or can't handle) rejection or straight talk (direct feedback).

Face it. Some people base their whole existences on what other people think of them. Sure, we all want some level of approval or validation. But when your need for either of those things paralyzes you, it's impos-sible to succeed on a large scale. I'll probably say it several times, but you must detach from other people's opinions of you to make it in Hollywood. Now, let's examine the word "detach." It doesn't mean that you'll bowl people over with your "I don't care what you think" attitude. It means that you'll simply disengage from their opinions. It means that you'll have no emotional investment, whatsoever, in their opinions or decisions. If we responded to every rejection, dismissal, or negative review, none of us would ever amount to anything. Yes, feedback is important to our growth. We need it. Just remember, you don't have to buy into every bit of input you get.

Fourth, they lack confidence when it comes to their art, talent, projects, etc.

You? Lacking confidence? Never! Well, maybe not you, but your friend, the singer with mad skills who won't utter a note in front of anyone but his cat, Whiskers. He's the one we're talking about in this section. Or your cousin Esmeralda, whom you think would put most of these so-called A-list actors to shame, but who won't even audition for the Annual Bingo Talent Extravaganza. She's the one I'm talking about.

It takes confidence and lots of courage to go on auditions, send your script to a director or approach a producer about viewing your film's trailer. But sooner or later, it's your confidence that will determine your altitude in the business. You can get away with low levels of confidence in Sedona, Arizona, but if you're planning to eat at the grownups' table in Tinseltown, you need to be sure of yourself.

Lack of confidence is much more noticeable than we think. When I audition actors for my plays, I can immediately identify the little red engines who believe in themselves and their talent. Sometimes a casting agent will give a part to a more confident candidate even though others are more talented. I don't know what it is, but confidence is magnetic. It's contagious. So catch it!

THE MIGHTY OGSM?
Before we move on to "Act II: Playing The Game," I gotta make sure your game plan's tight. Allow me to introduce you to the ace in my arsenal: my **OGSM**.

An OGSM is a planning tool designed to help you achieve your goals. It's a simple, yet effective way, to help you crystallize a road map for your career. And guess what? It works!

Let's look at each letter.

O = Objective.   *The big picture.* If you allowed yourself to dream the impossible dream, what would it be?

G = Goals.   *The nuts and bolts of your objectives.* The specific targets that will help you fulfill the big picture.

S = Strategies.   *The steps you'll take to make sure you hit your targets* (goals).

M = Measurements. *How will you know that you got there?* How will you know that you hit your marks on the timing that you set for yourself?

Developing an effective OGSM might take anywhere between 20 minutes to an hour, depending on how deeply and extensively you want to go with your career. Here's a sample from a fictional B-list actor's chart.

OBJECTIVES (BIG PICTURE)	GOALS (SPECIFIC TARGETS)	STRATEGIES (HOW I'LL DO IT)	MEASUREMENTS (EVALUATION)
To be an A-list actor by 2005	To co-star with 5-7 A-list actors over the next 2 years. To land the leading roles in 1-3 studio films each year leading up to 2008	Be signed by a larger agency by the end of 2003 Get an A-list mentor Hire a mega-publicist by the end of 2003	Number of films I did with A-list actors Number of leading roles I land Amount and quality of publicity I get as a result of publicist's efforts

Here's the key to making this tool work for you. Take it seriously. Print your completed OGSM and hang it on your wall. Get a wallet size one to have with you at all times. Revisit it at least once a quarter to make sure you're on course for achieving your goals and nailing your time-lines. Remember, Jim Carrey wrote himself a $10 million dollar check years ago and look what good it did him. He's now a member of the elite $20-million-a-movie club.

ACT I CHECKLIST

√ Are you sure this biz is for you? Has anything in the previous section made you give your decision second thoughts?

√ Have you decided on your company name? Does it represent you in a way that makes you proud?

√ What did filmmaker Sean O'Brien say was one of the biggest lessons he's learned in his independent filmmaking career thus far?

√ What's one key to giving good phone?

√ Can you identify one quality of a jerk?

√ If you don't get a "yes," does it mean you've made a poor impression?

√ What item in the Ultimate Toolbox would you like to give your immediate attention?

√ What's one of the top four reasons people don't make it in Hollywood?

√ Fill in one line of your OGSM below.

Objectives	Goals	Strategies	Measurements

ACT II

PLAYING THE GAME

"What's a man's first duty?
The answer is brief: to be himself."

— *Henrik Ibsen*

FRAN'S GOLDEN RULE #3:
DETACH FROM OUTCOMES

This is one of the hardest things for any of us to do. What does it mean to detach from the outcomes? It's simple. It means you are going to do the best job you can do, when given the opportunity, then you're going to let go of whether you actually get the part, the deal, the movie, etc. It doesn't mean that you don't care about your career or that you're not going to think about it. But it does mean that you will not get caught up in the "will I get it?" madness. In other words, when you're truly detached from the outcome, you do the work and let the Universe handle the rest.

HOW TO GET 'THE' MEETING (AND ACE IT)

During the course of writing this book someone asked me, "How in the world are you getting meetings with all of these people in Hollywood?" It's a fair question. After all, I do live in Texas. But so do Sandra Bullock and a slew of other stars. It's not about where you live. It's about how wide you cast your net. It's about how good of a net-worker you are. I'm an excellent networker. It's not a gift, though, it's something I've learned over the course of my adult life. And now I teach other people how to do it.

See, getting meetings in Hollywood is only hard if you know absolutely no one. Most of us know at least one person who at least *thinks* he or she is somebody. Chances are, that person actually *knows* somebody. And all you need is one person to know somebody, the right somebody, to get the meeting you want. One person!

But wait! Before you start asking people to hook you up with other people, let's take a long look at your game plan. How are you going about getting meetings? Are you writing query letters or making cold calls? No wonder you're not having any success! Cold writing and calling is the least effective way to get through to the people you want.

The best way to get a meeting is a referral. And guess what? Any solid referral will get you a meeting. It's not that hard. Trust me on this. Your job is to build your solid list of referrals. We'll talk more about networking later.

For now, let's say you're a comedian who wants to meet Chris Rock because you've got this great idea for his production company. Well, you probably won't get a meeting with Chris Rock right off the bat, so what you aim for is a meeting with Chris Rock's *people*. "People" is an important word in Hollywood. Ultimately, I want to sit in front of Spike Lee and talk about having him direct one of my projects, but in the interim I need Spike's story people to like my script enough to discuss it with me. If all goes well with the *people*, it will only be a matter of time before I'm talking to Spike. Got it? Get to the people of the person you want to meet, first. Build those relationships and then getting the ultimate meeting will become easier.

Now, one sidebar. This is not about *using* people. This isn't a pass to be an ass. This is about business. It's not called show friends; it's called show *business*. So, if you go about building relationships in a disingenuous fashion, you'll crash and burn, because people will feel used and that's never a good thing. So, rethink your game plan. Sure, it can be discouraging when you call Sean Combs' office, leave a message and never hear back from them. That's happened to me dozens of times. I just keep plugging away because I know this is normal and I know that one day soon, my calls will be returned.

One final word for those of you who see yourselves as nobodies: stop it. If somewhere deep in your soul you don't think that you really "deserve" a call back from some big wig's office, you're undermining your own success. You're sabotaging your own efforts. Worthiness is a big part of extreme success. The more unworthy you think you are, the further behind you fall in the game. You're *new*, not nothing. In the scheme of human evolution and existence, the people you admire in Hollywood are no higher on the food chain than you, but, and this is a big but, he or she is in a position to help you fulfill your dreams. That's why I call them Dream Fillers. You want to get a meeting with dream fillers. Once you finally get the meeting, it's your job not to turn them into dream *killers*.

Before we go any farther, let's identify the major players in your game plan. This one we'll divide into four categories. (1) Dream Fillers, (2) Assistants to Dream Fillers, (3) Friends of Assistants to Dream Fillers, and (4) Wannabe Friends to Friends of Assistants to Dream Fillers. Try to place names under each column. At first, you may only know people in the fourth category — that's fine. What you're doing here is building a network. If you're committed to the game it won't take you more than a year to have a list of names under all four categories.

Dream Fillers: These are the people on the top shelf. The people who can green light movies, sign you to record deals on the spot or put you in their next movies without consulting a casting director.

Assistants to Dream Fillers: These are the people who want, and could probably do, the Dream Fillers' jobs. They're second in command and, typically, very well respected by the Dream Fillers. Their names aren't usually listed in the trades, but if you ask around you can probably get their names, numbers or e-mail addresses.

Friends of Assistants to Dream Fillers: These people are in the business, but not necessarily directly connected to the same area of the biz as assistants. For example, I have an acquaintance who's the assistant to the president of a production company and most of her friends are assistants to Dream Fillers in the music and TV business.

Wannabe Friends of Assistants to Dream Fillers: These people are everywhere. There are probably some of these folks within a block of where you live. These people are those who don't really know Dream Fillers, but they have been in the same restaurant or gym as Dream Fillers. Now, don't underestimate these people, they're sitting on mounds of information. They often know the comings and goings of people who are close to the Dream Fillers, so don't be afraid to strike up a conversation with them.

Here Are Some Suggestions for How to Land (and Ace) Your Meeting.

#1: Work on your craft before you tell anybody about it or try to get people to help you get a meeting.
Notice I didn't say that you needed to "perfect" your craft, I said it's a good idea to work on it and work hard at it. Perfection doesn't exist. If you call yourself a perfectionist, you're wasting your time; you'll never be perfect 100% of the time. Instead you'll spend your whole life striving for something that's non-existent, which is really stupid if you stop and

think about it. So, forget perfection and think authentic. Think real. Think of how you can get the most out of your God-given talent and work ethic.

Once you're good at what you do, you'll find that it's not that hard to get meetings. Once you learn how to leave good impressions with everyone you meet, people will gladly give you referrals. The trick is in being ready to shine when it happens.

#2: Make a list of the people you want to meet.
Take out a sheet of paper and devise your "Top 10 Hit List." These are the people you'd like to have play a part in your success story, in one way or another. Now, these are not people whom you want to meet with so you can drool and dribble all over them, these are potential stakeholders in your career. To be successful in this business, ya gotta get out of the star-struck mode and get into reality. Your idols were once rookies too, so don't put them on pedestals. The more touchable they are, the more attainable your own goals. Once you have your list, get on the Internet and do some basic homework on these people. How did they get started? When did they get their first big breaks? Success is as success does. There's a good chance that you can use some of the same strategies to achieve your goals.

#3: Know the players in your area of the industry.
These people may include some of the people on your Hit List but most likely, they're a different group of people. Harvey Weinstein of Miramax, for instance, is considered a power broker in Hollywood because he can get a movie made just by breathing. If you're an actor, is he someone you want to meet? Not necessarily, but it's still a good idea to know a little something about him because he's a mover and shaker in *your industry*. Who else moves and shakes in your world? Be on top of it.

TIME OUT WITH A PLAYBOY... SORTA

RICK VAN METER | PRODUCER

FH: It was fun to find out that you're also writing a book. Is it an interview book about producers?
RVM: Yeah, I decided to write it because I was constantly being asked what producers do. So, I started setting up interviews. The first ones I landed were Scott Mosier and John Daly, who are both in California.

FH: So, you came out here just to do those two interviews? Who, besides me, comes to L.A. with only two interviews scheduled?
RVM: I know, but I may get to interview somebody who produces for the TV show *Just Shoot Me*.

FH: There are other interviewing books, what makes yours different?
RVM: There's really nothing out there on producers. There are books about how to become a writer, how to become a director, nothing about becoming a producer. I did find something about how to produce a low-budget feature; those kinds of books are a dime a dozen, but in terms of how to really become a producer, no road map. I'm going for the gritty stories about how they got started, because I didn't have that guide when I started. I read biography type books, like Robert Evans and I read it cover to cover.

FH: So, your favorite question. How did you become a producer?
RVM: I went to school and I did some independent commercials. I answered an ad in *Variety* for a production manager job, which was for Playboy TV and I really had no idea what a production manager did, the full scope of it. So, I bought a book, *How To Production Manage*, highlighted it and read it overnight. I interviewed for the job and went back for three more interviews. What kind of sealed it is that I was good with computers, I knew how to do all of the technical stuff. I stayed at Playboy for three years, but I quit because I didn't see any potential to do much more than what I was doing. So, I quit and went to San Francisco to sort of take a breather. Soon afterwards, I started this TV show with this guy. The concept's there, very low budget. A little bit like *The Insomniac* with Dave Attell meets *Cheers*. It's a low, low budget show where we brought in musical acts, singers, comedy sketches. It's fun. Now we're shopping it.

FH: But now you're back living on the East Coast.
RVM: Yes, I moved to New York to be with my girlfriend. We were doing the long distance thing and I just decided that the time was right to make some changes.

FH: A lot of people would come to L.A., plant a tree and stay out here. If this is where the business is, why leave?
RVM: Well, I don't want to work my way up as a P.A. A lot of people do that and that's a great way to go for some people. My buddy right now is a P.A. for Nickelodeon and he knows in two years he could be a coordinator and in two more, a manager and so on and so forth. But I've always been trying to carve my own path, with the San Francisco show, the book, leaving Playboy and starting my own company. So, I've always been trying to get to the top in a different way. If I have to take the little jobs here and there that sometimes aren't even related to the industry, then I'll do that if it means I can get into a producing job somewhere.

FH: You're actually doing it, you're producing. I know there's value in being the runner or gopher on a show, but I've always been more interested in doing the job I want to do.
RVM: Exactly, you don't learn how to produce if all you're doing is buying a producer's sandwich from Greenblatt's all day or booking her flights to Europe. I feel that to become an assistant to a producer is very beneficial, but learn what you can and then move on. You can't get seduced by the money and the glamour, but it's hard *not* to. I was getting sucked into it because I was paid well at Playboy. I was doing the Hollywood scene and going to the parties. But then you realize that doing it for the money won't last. It's about following your goals and dreams.

FH: So, everything you describe sounds very appealing to some people. How did you not get sucked into it? Where's the antidote?
RVM: Well, I literally went from working at Kinko's or whatever I was doing, to working at Playboy TV. So now I'm going to the Playboy mansion, going to parties, getting a limo on the weekend for fun. It was all very attractive. Then I started talking to people and I'd say I work for Playboy TV and then I'd send my resume to them. The responses kept coming back like, "Oh, well, what else did you do? Just Playboy?" I started getting turned down.

FH: They weren't feeling the bunny?

RVM: No. But then I realized that I was much bigger on feeling good about what I do for a living. And I started seeing my job for what it was. I had to step back and start looking for something else, for better or worse.

FH: Tough decision?

RVM: Yes and no. I knew I was done at Playboy, but then the investments in my first attempt at a production company fell through. But the funny thing is that when I moved to San Francisco I had friends and family, so I stayed there and everything worked out. I had gone to a bar to interview someone who wanted to do a TV show. Now we're in a position to show it on FOX Sports in a barter situation, three times a month. It's a good product.

FH: That's cool. What's your ultimate goal? What's the carrot that keeps you trying stuff?

RVM: Ultimately I want to run my own production company. TV, film, it doesn't matter. I like walking into a theater and seeing people respond to what's on the screen. I'd like to do something one day where I'm partly responsible for that. I did standup when I was younger and it was great. The raw response you get from entertaining people, that's what keeps me going.

FH: You think you'll move back out here?

RVM: I think so. I've been on the East Coast for three months and I'm definitely not an East Coast person. When I first moved to Los Angeles, I drove a Peugeot, which is French for piece of shit. It went 0-60 in two days. Didn't have a working speedometer or radio and it was really awful. One day I went over to some place on Sunset and I pulled up for valet and the guy pointed to another garage about a block away saying, "Park down there. We'll cover it but you can park there." I mean, I looked suave, had a good-looking girl with me, had money in my wallet, but I was driving a Peugeot and they said, "I don't think so." It's all about style out here.

FH: What's your honest response to that, when you come from a set of values that says work ethic, diligence, and being a good person count? So, how do you put those qualities into the Hollywood blender, where all of the external stuff is supposed to be as important?

RVM: You have to work really hard at it. You have to get people to like you for who you are. It's like that guy in high school who wasn't that great looking but he had a great sense of humor and everybody liked him. They didn't care that he came from the wrong side of the tracks, they loved him. So, be forthcoming about who you are but don't change who you are. Alter things here and there. Like brush your teeth if you don't, but do not change yourself for them. That's how you're gonna succeed.

FH: A lot of people lose themselves out here. They transform into whatever they think they need to be to achieve some short-term goal. And then they lead these lives of quiet desperation... ooooh, I think I lifted that last part from somebody legendary.
RVM: That's the truth out here. It's a walking movie. Everyone's always on. Everyone wants to be discovered. It's the City of Angels. City of Dreams. City of Lost Hope, in my opinion, because a lot of people come out here and fail. You really have to be grounded. If you feel yourself starting to slip, leave. If only for a short time. Take a break.

FH: It's amazing that you left, because most people I've talked to have taken the out-of-sight, out-of-mind approach. So it was pretty brave of you to take off, given how competitive it is.
RVM: Well, part of me thought it was going to be a temporary move. Then the New York thing came about and I really don't think I'm hurting myself by moving to New York. If anything, I am creating more branches in my tree to success.

FH: Yeah, it's not like you moved to Abilene, Texas. How do you deal with poverty? Yeah, it's an assumption on my part but I think it's a fair one for most people trying to make it in this business. At some point, you're eating rice and beans three times a week!
RVM: Oh, definitely. You have to be smart about finances. If you don't come from a well-off family and you came out of college with debt, you have to scale back. You need to look good and drive good, but you don't have any money to do that. You have to be smart about it. Choose your events wisely. Let people invite you to special events, those are the ones worth going to because somebody special's gonna be there. Don't be like a little panting dog waiting to get in. Be casual, play nonchalant. Don't say, "I'm an actor, I've done this, I've done that." Even if you risk the chance of their not being interested, it's better to be casual about what you do. Tell people but don't force it.

FH: It's such a turnoff when people reel off their resumes at the grocery store. Subtlety is a lost art. People think they need to shove their cards down your throat or carry scripts in their back pockets. Relax.

RVM: Well, I think the easiest thing to do is remember a person's name. If you don't drive the Beamer, it's okay. Get a reliable car. You don't want to be broken down in L.A. I did the bus system here once — for about a week. What are you laughing at?

FH: I'm laughing because I still can't remember how I met you.

RVM: I know. You're on my e-mail distribution list.

FH: I have your business card.

RVM: But I have no idea either.

FH: So, this makes this interview extra crispy. Thank you. Last thing. Advice for peers and wannabes?

RVM: Yeah, I think following your gut is the key. The other thing is never take on too much. There are so many little things that you need to learn, but the most important one is this. Unless you have a photographic memory, make sure you write everything down because somebody once told me that if it's not written down, it doesn't exist. I don't know how many times as a P.A., I would be listening to a conversation but not writing anything down, and then I'd forget what was said and it just got worse after that. So, always leave a paper trail.

KNOWLEDGE IS WHAT?

It's not who you know, it's what you know, right? Wrong. At first, anyway. In the beginning, sorry to say it, it's all about who you know. If you think about it, in a business and town that's built on relationships, it has to be about who you know. Once you're in that first meeting or in that first job, it switches immediately to what you know. Who you know may get you in the door, but what you know will keep you in the game. At least in Hollywood. Never lose sight of this important fact. As a matter of fact, why don't you highlight that line.

THREE DEGREES OF SEPARATION

Know this. Today, right now, you are no more than three people away from the person who can change your career. Your job is to make an impression with your work, first. Sometimes Hollywood can seem like it's this far, far away land that can't be accessed by anyone who's not already in the industry. Unfortunately, that line of thinking keeps a lot of people from their dreams. The only thing that's keeping you outside of Tinseltown is contacts. And by the time you're done reading this book, you'll know exactly how to find the three people who stand between you and your ultimate dream.

EXPECT THE BEST

Ever met someone who was always expecting the worst? *My agent's getting me a meeting with Clive Davis but it'll probably fall through. We're planning to release my CD in December but I bet something comes up.* And so forth and so on. The bane of most human existences is negativity. What about you? Are negative people or self-limiting belief systems in your way? If so, shake 'em. Tell the people in your life to get with the program or get lost. And then, go to work on your own negative thought patterns. They're your worst enemy, not the receptionist who won't put you through to Jodie Foster.

Sometimes in Hollywood, the only thing you have going for you is your belief in yourself. If you're feeding yourself a bunch of "can'ts" and "won'ts," don't expect great things to show up in your life. It's not psychobabble, it's the truth. People who are phenomenally successful expected it to happen. What about you? What are you expecting to happen with your career? If you expect the carpet to be pulled from underneath your feet, don't be surprised when it happens.

Here's what I've found to be true. I call them my Fab Five. If you work hard, honor your craft, treat people properly, maintain a sense of humor, and network smartly, amazing things show up in your life almost on cue. But all five of these things have to be active at the same time. Just working hard won't really do much for your career if you're not also always building your Rolodex. Laughing at the madness won't amount to much if you're not also honoring your art. Your biggest challenge is to create harmony between all five pieces of your orchestra. Never forget the Fab Five.

DR. FEELGOOD

Sometimes surgery's necessary. In the fall of 2000, one year after I officially launched my screenwriting career, I met screenwriter William

Broyles, Jr. at the Austin Screenwriters Conference. I'd read the festival updates online and had done some preliminary research on all of the speakers, especially the writers, because we never really hear a lot about writers, only actors, directors, and producers.

When the screenwriting conference started, Bill was one of the round-table leaders in one of my sessions and I got a chance to talk to him about one of my projects. We chatted for a few minutes after class ended, then we set an appointment to talk further over coffee. But before I could get out of Bill's presence he gave me two very important gifts. He asked to read one of my scripts and he said, "You have to meet Sheila." I smiled. "Great," I said, not having a clue as to whom Sheila was or why I should meet her. "She's worked with me on my scripts. Look for me later and I'll introduce you to her."

That meeting marked the acceleration of my writing career. Sheila became the first script doctor I had. Like lots of screenwriters, I had no formal training when I started dabbling in screenwriting in the fall of 1998. By all accounts, there's really no formal training for someone who didn't earn a masters of fine arts in screenwriting. Many scribes discover their passion for screenwriting long after they've graduated college. I studied journalism in undergraduate and graduate school and somehow stumbled into screenwriting because I love movies and thought I could be good, one day great, at it.

Once I started writing though, I couldn't get enough of learning about it. I bought books, took classes, chatted online, joined groups, subscribed to magazines, and networked like nobody's business. Testing waters is basically part of what you have to do to find out where you stand as an artist. Mix and mingle with other artists. Get some feedback from real professionals, not just the arm chair quarterbacks who say they know what they're talking about. That's why Bill's recommendation meant so much to me. And that's why Sheila's feedback was critical to my development as a writer. She analyzed, critiqued, and dissected my work in a way that forced me to look in the mirror and ask myself one important question. How badly do you want this? My answer was a resounding *really badly*, knowing fully that my answer would guarantee one thing and one thing only: one hell of a rollercoaster ride.

But I also knew that once I boarded the Hollywood Express there would be some acceptance, some rejection, maybe lots of rejection, along the way and that I didn't have to become a slave to either. And once Bill Broyles introduced me to Sheila, there was no looking back, as far as I was concerned. I was in the game.

Now, why's that story important to you and your career? A number of reasons. One, as a result of one decision (to attend the conference) I had a beeline into Hollywood. Bill Broyles, for those of you who don't really read the credits at the end of movies, is one of Tinseltown's most prolific screenwriters. One of his most recent films was *Unfaithful* but he also wrote *Cast Away* starring Tom Hanks, and many other great flicks.

Two, I went to the Austin Screenwriters Conference with my OGSM in hand. I had clear goals and strategies walking into the Driskill Hotel on the opening Thursday. One goal was to get at least one A-list writer, director, or agent to read my script. I set my intention, put in the work, and was ready when the opportunity presented itself in my roundtable discussion. And it happened. Bill Broyles asked to read one of my scripts and Mickey Freiberg, a literary agent, asked to read another script!

Now, you may be saying, "well, anybody couldn't have struck a conversation with somebody." And you're right. But I'd be willing to bet some hard earned money that fewer than 1% of the writers at that conference had any kind of meaningful contact and follow up with anybody. Why? Two reasons. One, no plan. And two, weak skills. I surveyed 10 writers from the Austin conference and found that all of them fell into two categories: (1) either they didn't have a script ready to show or (2) they had a completed script but were too afraid to show anyone because they weren't sure if it was ready to show.

SLIME SHADIES

Unfortunately, because there are so many wannabes in the world, there's also a growing number of slime balls ready to take your hard earned pennies, if you're not careful. One friend told me that someone quoted $1,500 for a screenplay consultation. $1,500? Are you nuts? That's criminal. I can't possibly justify paying anybody $1,500 for a script consult unless he or she can guarantee a sale — which probably won't happen — so forget it.

Another wannabe e-mailed me saying that someone in her hometown was offering a service through which this "professional" would shop an artist's demo for a fee and then take a percentage of the deal, once it was made. I can't say whether this is a legitimate business or not. All I can say is that I wouldn't do it. Most reputable managers are willing to put in the time it takes to get an artist in front of a label executive, with the understanding that they'll be compensated when deals are struck. This is how the business works. Of course, there's more than one way to skin a cat, just be careful and always ask questions.

Here are a couple of things to watch out for.

- Agents who charge you to read manuscripts, scripts, book proposals, etc.
- Agents who charge to rep you. Most agents typically receive a percentage of the deals they secure on your behalf.
- Scouts who charge you a retainer for finding a job for you. Scouts are typically paid finder's fees by the agencies they work for.
- Anyone who asks you to audition at odd hours (late night, early morning) or in odd places (their hotel rooms, homes).

If you do decide to work with those who charge fees before they do anything, be sure to get a list of clients or references.

WHERE SHOULD WE MEET?

For the most part, if you're meeting executives, the meetings are most likely to be at their offices. That's cool. Don't be intimidated. It's just bricks, cement, and mortar — and a little plastic, maybe a lot of plastic. If you happen to be in a position to suggest a place for the meeting, ask the executive where she'll be around the time of the meeting. If she's going to be in the Valley (Burbank, Van Nuys, Studio City, etc.), then have a few places ready to suggest. If the exec suggests a place, don't be afraid to ask for an address, if you're not familiar with the establishment. It makes no sense to be a know-it-all or a show off by saying that you know where a place is, when you don't. Once you get the address, that's when your homework comes into play. This will also help you to plan the rest of your meetings.

Once you have a meeting place set with one executive, then you can begin to plan all of your other meetings in that area. In other words, strive to see all of your Valley people on one day, all of your Beverly Hills people on one day, all of your Hollywood people on one day, and all of your Santa Monica people on one day. This is in an ideal world, of course. But you'd be amazed at how easy it is to make your schedule work, with a little preparation.

Now, if you can't get everyone in the same area on the same day, that's when you work in day *parts*. You'd put all of your Culver City meetings in the morning and all of your Valley meetings in the afternoon, giving yourself plenty of time to get from one area to the next. Never, and I do mean never, underestimate the time it will take you to drive 15 miles in Los Angeles. What might take 10 minutes on one day will invariably take 45 the next. Don't tempt the traffic gods, people. Plan well and save yourself the high blood pressure medicine.

TIME OUT WITH BIG MO

MAURICE GOLCHIN | ACTOR

FH: You're an actor, but does that mean you act or you work?
MG: It could encompass a lot of things. Right now, it's good because I actually have some work. We're all actors. When things are good, we're working, but a lot of the time, we're just looking for work. I have some commercials that are running and that's keeping the lights on at my house right now.

FH: When did the acting bug hit you?
MG: I was six years old and I didn't have so much as a sense of "I want to do that." It was more I "can" do that. It was a series of events. I started out as a child model in New York City and then I went to a commercial audition. I booked the job and started from there.

FH: So what keeps you acting?
MG: It's the only thing I've ever wanted to do. Like I said, I don't think I'm qualified to do anything else. If someone really wanted to play ball even in the minors, it's hard to give that up.

FH: Thousands of people move here every year with the goal of becoming movie stars. Are those numbers ever daunting to you? You're up against a lot of people for parts.
MG: I have a sense of the competition, but it's an interesting thing you just said. You said people come here who want to be actors. Actually, I am an actor, but I want to be working. I really think there's a difference between those who are actors and those who come here saying they want to be actors. If you don't think of yourself as an actor, the goal of landing work is much harder. You have to see yourself as an actor. So, yeah there's a lot of competition, but a good segment don't think of themselves as actors so, really, they're just sort of in the way. Here's a good example. If you ask those who "want" to be actors what they do for a living, you'll get "I'm a waiter" or "I tend bar" or "I temp." They don't want to say they're actors.

FH: Why?
MG: Fear! You have to operate with a certain amount of bravery. There's a lot of throwing caution to the wind when you try to find work in this business and it scares people to hang it all out there. They try not to bring any undue pressure on themselves. I get it all the time. People say to me, "What do you do?" I say, "I'm an actor." They say, "Oh, my God, what have I seen you in?" That's my least favorite question — "What have I seen you in?"

FH: Have I seen you in anything?
MG: Look, I say, "don't look for me on the cover of TV Guide anytime soon," but if you've got a Blockbuster card, you can go rent something I was in. I was in a very, very bad movie from Paramount in the mid-80s and here was the problem with *Fighting Back*. It was a serious drama about a South Philly vigilante. An Italian South Philly deli owner who's sick of the crime in his neighborhood, who takes care of business. The guy they got to play this part? Tom Skerritt.

FH: *Picket Fences'* Tom Skerritt?
MG: Exactly.

FH: *Top Gun* Tom Skerritt?
MG: Precisely. Smarmy southern doctor in *M*A*S*H*. Great actor, but you do not get this guy to play the South Philly Italian deli "ey- oh" guy! The film tanked.

FH: Did it have a theatrical release?
MG: Oh yeah. Me, my sister, my mom, and about eight other people were there on opening night. But I got my credit, I played a neighborhood kid who had a heroine problem and that's how the bad element gets into Tom Skerritt's home.

FH: Oh, you had a role!
MG: I had a good little part. That wasn't even my first role. It was a 1982 Movie of the Week for NBC, opposite Bette Davis.

FH: Shut up.
MG: Yes. How blessed I am. Forget about actors my age, any actor would love to be in a movie with Bette Davis. It was great. I played the product of a mixed marriage. My father was black and my mother was white. So, let's get the Middle Eastern kid, he can pull it off. And you know there was some biracial kid actor out there going, "that little son of a...."

FH: How'd a Middle Eastern kid get to L.A.?
MG: I was going to go to college in upstate New York and the summer before I was supposed to leave, I looked at my mother and I said I'm gonna save you and the state a lot of money, and myself a lot of college loans. So I moved to Los Angeles. I was 17, turning 18, at the time. I had to do a lot of growing up before I could pursue my career in earnest. Overall, I think I made the right decision. There have been times when I've thought maybe going to school to study theater might have helped but, basically, I think this is a job you have to do. I like it here. I manage to not get caught up in the scene.

FH: During the course of the last 12 or 13 years, has there ever been a time when you felt like waving the white flag because it wasn't happening?
MG: I've been discouraged before, but I've never internally resigned to give up acting. I've been a SAG member since 1982: There were times when I was living here, doing other work, outside the industry, but when it came time to pay my dues, I did not want to relinquish my membership.

FH: That's quite a commitment. SAG membership's not cheap.
MG: No, it's not, but it's a resource I felt I needed.

FH: What's been one of the most challenging things to deal with as an actor?
MG: Getting opportunities. I once heard a poet say "all I want is an opportunity to have an opportunity." I thought, wow, that's it. It's supply and demand out here. More actors than jobs.

FH: So representation is key to getting those opportunities? As a broadcaster, it's certainly a lot easier to get my tape seen when I'm repped.
MG: I was just talking about this. I see agents as a necessary evil. Just because somebody's an agent doesn't mean he or she is any good at being an agent. It's a constant struggle, because agents want to get 10% of a lot. If they could rediscover Julia Roberts, they'd do it. They don't look to nurture new talent; bigger agents look to poach established talents. It takes commitment to nurture a new actor.

FH: Who has time for that? That's their mentality. But how do you propose to get anywhere without one, given the sheer numbers of acting vultures out there?

MG: Very brutal truth that says you have to be repped in some capacity. Tom Cruise doesn't need an agent; he needs a lawyer because now people throw work at him.

FH: It's such a Catch-22 because no established agent's gonna take you on, but what new agent's gonna get any play when she calls to get you an audition? So, how do you maneuver around with that set of factors? Given the choice of an established agent who agrees to take you or a hustling, pimping new agent, which one do you want?

MG: Yes. [Laughs].

FH: Yes? [Laughs].

MG: Right now I'm looking for someone with a pulse! Quite honestly I tell people who ask me what I'm looking for in an agent, "I'm looking for the same qualities I look for in my mother." Those who will believe in you like they believe the sun is hot. They'll go to the top of any mountain to get you the job. They just need to believe in you. I don't care if they're new or Ed Limato, one of the biggest agents in town. They need to believe that you're a viable commodity, not even the greatest actor in the world. They just have to believe they can sell. I have to believe I'm the greatest actor in the world.

FH: In the meantime, what tricks are you employing to get those jobs?

MG: I have very specific protocol. You have to know that mailing your pictures somewhere ain't the way. Forget it. You have to messenger them there if you want them to get your package immediately. You have to know that when you call, the person you want to talk to is not going to answer the phone. Have the sense to know that today's assistant may be tomorrow's casting director. You want to come off as someone who knows how things work. Follow up with people. When you meet people, follow up. Learn how to stand out with people. I doubt that anybody in this town gets a thank you card from an actor and says, "Oh how nice," but you know what? It's one more way for me to be in front of them. They'll remember you.

FH: You DO stand out that way. I tell people that all the time. You may not get the job, but if only 1% of the rejectees send thank you notes, you're among that minority. Maybe next time, it's that one little extra effort that gets you the part or the meeting.

MG: Yeah, I haven't booked one network job this year, but I've thanked people for bringing me in.

FH: Yep. What are some of the mistakes you see your peers making?

MG: Having expectations. Thinking that being good supercedes everything. It's also a business and how you behave says a lot. One famous actor got away with a lot of ridiculous behavior for a while and he got away with it because he was a commodity. I've seen actors without that level of success behave that way.

FH: What are your goals? Or is it whatever shows up, shows up?

MG: I have a double-sided goal right now. Book some work, get an agent. I can't think much beyond that. I'm a runner and every now and then I look up and see where I'm going, but that's not what I normally do. I normally keep my eyes at a 45-degree angle and watch where I'm going. That's kind of how I approach my career.

FH: How do you handle the down times?

MG: Love and support from friends. I handle "professional" pretty well. A hell of a lot better than I handle personal rejection, that's for sure. I'm living thousands of miles from my roots so, out here, I've had to put together a de facto family — my friends and I count on each other. I have two friends who are part of a directing team. They're funny, they're good at what they do, but they haven't been able to get a deal.

FH: So, when you see that — honest, ethical, hardworking people not working — how do you respond?

MG: It's not a sign. It's not an omen about being in the right business. There's enough room at the top of the hill for everyone to be there. It's not the head of a pin. Whoever wants to get there, can get there with some dogged determination and some dedication to craft. If you don't get this one, there's something else.

FH: Ask George Clooney, who, I think, was in about 15 failed TV pilots. Wasn't he like the wealthiest out-of-work actor, back then?

MG: Right. Garry Shandling got told "no" on at least seven different occasions by the owner of one comedy club. He also told him he'd never be on television. This person said to him, "you're just not telegenic and your stuff's not that funny." Seven different times.

FH: Don'tcha love it? Who gives anybody the right to tell someone that he or she doesn't have what it takes to be successful? And you know what's funny? Struggling musicians, writers, artists, filmmakers, actors, whoever, have no clue as to the amount of rejection endured by now-hugely successful celebrities. All of them still get passed over for parts.

MG: There's no such thing as on overnight success. It just doesn't happen. Homeboy Clooney was hitting a pilot every season. And finally did a pilot for *ER* and....

FH: There you are.

MG: It's all a stepping stone. Get work, keep working.

FH: There's another route to success in Hollywood. Pucker up and kiss the right asses.

MG: Listen, schmoozing is a part of any business, but it doesn't have to be disingenuous.

FH: Sincere butt kissing is desirable? [*Laughs*]. As writers, we're told to see movies, read scripts, etc. As an actor, how do you get better?

MG: Act. I want to act for many different reasons. I want to feel useful. I want to get better. It's like Tom Hanks' career. He's gotten better with each project. Could the Tom Hanks on *Bosom Buddies* go from there to *Philadelphia*? No, but he worked and got better. He became the person for that role over the course of his career.

FH: Best advice you could give to an aspiring actor?

MG: Think of the thing you can't live without and try to live without it for a short period of time. Jones for a while and then go back to it. Then ask yourself, "Is that how I'm going to feel about acting if I quit?" If you know you can't live without acting, just do it.

FH: So, are you saying that if there were no possibilities for you to be paid for acting, that you'd still do it?

MG: Somebody's grandmother asked me once, "Maurice honey, acting's such a hard job, what happens if you don't make it, what are you going to do?" I said, "you know I thought about it recently and I have to think that between now and the next life, if it doesn't work out, I'll be a plumber because those guys..."

FH: ... are always working.

MG: As far as I know, I get one shot at this, I've got one life. I am born to make manifest the glory of God inside of me; I believe I can do that as an actor.

FH: Amen, brother.

HOW TO SEND A GOOD MEETING SOUTH, PRONTO

Imagine yourself in a meeting, pitching what you think is 2004's next action blockbuster. It's a futuristic film with lots of fire, crashes, and explosions. You can see Ah-nold playing the lead. The two Dreamworks executives sitting across from you appear to be fairly excited about your story. They listen intently, nodding and even smiling, on occasion. You finish and one of them says, "What if we made your main character Scottish?" The other one chimes in, "Or, or we could make him part Italian, part Russian." The other one pipes in, "Yeah, yeah, and he comes over to avenge the death of his father who was killed in a war started by the Americans." •

What are you going to do if this happens? Most new people would do this. They'd jump in and the first thing they'd say is, "That's not really how I see the story." Uh oh. The two executives who, two minutes ago, were juiced, are now wearing a scowl that rivals anything that The Wicked Witch of the West ever shot at Dorothy in *The Wizard of Oz*. Instead of sitting on the edge of their leather seats, they're now reclining. Instead of shooting ideas at you like a machine gun, they're silent. And what are you doing? I'll tell you what you're doing. You're hoping somebody, somewhere is about to throw you a bloody life jacket because you are sinking like the Titanic, fast and furiously. And you don't even know why. All you said was "that's not really how I see the story." Well, that was plenty.

Before you started pitching you'd been tabbed an up and comer, but guess what you'll be labeled when the door hits you in the butt? Difficult. All because "that's not really how you saw the story." Your job is to give the buyers hope. Hope that they can make the movie "they" want to make using your script as a template. That's how it works for new people. A-list writer/directors may be able to walk into a studio and say, "This is the movie I wrote. This is the movie I want to make." You don't have this luxury. Deal with it.

You scored the audition, the pitch, or the meeting, a difficult feat. Don't blow it because you want to see "your" movie made or because you have a vision for how a character should be played. That's not the most important thing. The most important thing is to keep the conversation going. Say it with me. *Keep the conversation going.* Keep your name in the hat. Many an artist has killed his dream by being too opinionated before he had a right to be. Remember, you're there to do a deal. The more deals you do, the more creative license you will achieve. The more power you have over your career. Until that day though, sharpen your communication skills, learn to listen strategically and resist the temptation to shoot down a studio head's ideas even if you hate them. Remember, it's a conversation, nothing's decided yet.

THE WINDOW OF COMMUNICATION

I'm gonna share something with you that you probably haven't seen in any other book about breaking into the business: *communication tools.* Yep, practical things that you can do and say that will increase your chances of keeping every single door open and all conversations flowing. When you're trying to break into the biz, you have to learn how not to alienate people in conversations. Why? Because people like to do business with people they *like.* People like to do business with people who are at least pleasant to deal with. And most importantly, the more advanced your communication skills, the better you'll become at negotiating. And the better you are at negotiating, the more successful your career will be. In the immortal words of the venerable Bleek, played by Denzel Washington in Spike Lee's *Mo' Better Blues,* "mo' better, make it mo' better."

Now, I'm not suggesting that you become a "yes" person, not at all. I'm recommending that you develop the skills that make you respectable and more than bearable to do business with. This will take practice.

People aren't born with great communication skills. They learn them. And while I know that you can become a masterful communicator, it's not an easy process, primarily because most people enjoy talking more than they enjoy listening. But guess what? The more you talk, the less you know about the other person. The less you know about the other person, the less likely you are to have insights into what makes her say "yes." So, let's move on to the two components of effective communication: listening and reflecting. If you were expecting listening and talking, keep reading.

Listening, not just hearing, is your hole in one. If you can learn to tune into what the buyer's saying and not saying, you'll have more effective meetings, better auditions, and smoother relationships — professional and personal. Yep, these things work in intimate relationships, too!

Reflecting means volleying the conversation using clarifying sentences and phrases based on what the other person has said, while incorporating your own ideas. It means never adding a value statement or negative slant to what's been said.

Now, keeping the shade open on communication is no easy task. It takes a lot of practice, but once you get the hang of it, it'll become very natural for you. And more importantly, it'll mean better results in your career.

Here's an example of someone who's keeping the conversation open. We enter this meeting in progress.

Scenario #1
BUYER: I know you want money for your script but we really don't have a lot of cash right now… would you be willing to take deferred payment? We really want to make the film.

YOU: I appreciate that (*acknowledging the buyer's enthusiasm and interest*). I worked really hard on the script and I want to see it get made, too. Have you found a distributor yet? (*getting key information*)

BUYER: We're talking to two different ones.

YOU: Really? Do you mind sharing which ones? (*good idea not to say "who?" but instead to ask if they "mind" sharing*)

BUYER: No, not at all. Miramax and Paramount.

YOU: Wow! That's great. So, they already gave you the go, huh? (*good way to find out if the deal is done*)

BUYER: Yep. I mean, we've still got to find another $3 million, or so, to produce it, but I feel like we're right there with a couple of investors. We just need the right script.

YOU: That's exciting. So, are you still accepting submissions? (*finding out if there are other scripts they might make besides yours*)

BUYER: We've got a few more to read but we really like yours. We'll make a decision by Friday.

YOU: That's great. I like your ideas for the film too, especially the twist on the ending, that was cool. Well, I'd like to make a suggestion. Since you've still got a few more scripts to read, how about us chatting on Friday, once you've had a chance to really look at everything? How's that sound? (*giving the buyers room to be included in the conversation*)

BUYER: Sounds good. We'll call you on Friday.

Now let's look at the same conversation with a writer who doesn't have the skills to keep the window of communication open.

Scenario #2:
BUYER: I know you want money for your script but we really don't have a lot of cash right now, would you be willing to take deferred payment? We really want to make the film.

YOU: Well, I'm not gonna just give my work away. (*Are you defensive or what?*). I worked really hard on the script and I want to see it get made, too, but I know everybody says the right thing when sitting in front of you. I don't know how much I trust what people tell me in Hollywood.

BUYER: I understand. Look, we're not trying to steal your work or not see you get paid for it. We just don't have the money. (*now, they're on the defense*)

YOU: Didn't I just read that you optioned a script the other week? (*you're challenging their integrity*)

BUYER: Yes, you did.

YOU: But you don't have the money? (*this is like saying, "you're lying"*)

BUYER: We optioned the script for $10. (*they're really ticked now*)

YOU: Oh. (*your foot's in your mouth*)

BUYER: Look, we really like your script but maybe this isn't a good fit. (*uh oh, you've turned them off completely*)

YOU: Wait. No, I've just been burned a couple of times and I just wanted to make sure everything was on the up and up. (*you're sinking in quick sand and can't get up*)

BUYER: Uh huh. Well, let us get back to you on that. We still have a few scripts we're considering. We'll be in touch. (*no, they won't*)

Now, take a step back. Reread these two scenarios, if you have to. They are real. These are not fictional stories. They happen every single day. If you think communication is overrated, I encourage you to examine these two case studies. What do you think happened in each case?

Scenario #1: The writer got the deal... and some very respectable option money because the producers really liked the script and the writer; they wanted to go the extra mile to show the writer that they were sincere. The film got made.

Scenario #2: The writer got squat... and left a very bad taste in the producers' mouths. He's still shopping that script.

My fellow wannabes, you've been warned. That's all I'm going to say. If you don't learn how to be respectful in conversations, you won't get a lot of deals, I don't care how talented you are. Well, you say, my agent or attorney's going to do all of my deals. Not when you're new, because you won't have an agent or attorney. *You'll* be your agent. So, it behooves you to learn how to talk to people and represent yourself.

Down the line you may not have to be a part of these conversations, but you'll still need to be an effective communicator to work with people. Communication. Learn it. Love it. Live it.

Here Are a Few "Good Meeting" Suggestions:

#1: Body language.
Sit with an open body position. This invites openness from the other person or people in the room. No arms crossed over the chest.

#2: Look pleasant.
No frowning. You don't have to be in a full frontal smile, unless it's natural for you, but you can't wear a frown and invite good energy and positive vibes. If you're a pensive, serious person, do a few facial exercises before your meeting to relax your facial muscles, so you appear to be alive. If you're a goofy, airhead type, tone it down a little — you don't want them to think the lights are on but nobody's home.

#3: Watch your cadence (rhythm of speech).
If you talk too fast, you appear nervous. If you talk too slowly, you put them to sleep. A natural, even pace is what you're shooting for.

#4: Employ vocal variety.
That's right. Sometimes it makes sense to talk louder on a certain part of your story. In other places you may talk softer, faster, or slower.

#5: Useful phrases.
When you want additional information about something that's been said: *"Can you share a little bit more about...."*

When you're clarifying what you've heard: *"So, what I'm hearing is...."*

When you want to know if someone knows what you're talking about: *"Are you familiar with...?"*

#6: Avoid window-closing words or phrases.
- You're not making sense (try, *"I'm not sure I understand...."*)
- You didn't make yourself clear (try, *"Let me make sure I heard you...."*)
- You're not listening to me (try, *"Maybe I didn't make myself clear...."*)

- Have you ever heard of… (try, "*Are you familiar with…?*")
- That's not telling me anything (try, "*Can you say a little more about…?*")
- I disagree (try, "*I'd like to share a slightly different perspective….*")

Practice these phrases in your everyday dealings with insignificant others, department store personnel, waiters, whomever, and you'll start to see a difference in how people respond to you.

TIME OUT WITH THE KING OF SCREAM

JAMES DUDELSON | PRESIDENT & CEO | TAURUS ENTERTAINMENT

One of Jim's distinctions is that I heard him before I met him. While inter-
viewing the incomparable Veep down the hall, I heard Jim screaming about
something. "You'll meet that voice later," I was told. That was only one of
the reasons I got along with the Taurus people so well. They also had
candy in the break room. Boisterous leaders. Warped senses of humor.
And they produce horror movies, too? I was in hell and glad to be there!
Not to mention that Jim's a musician and his office had amplifiers and
guitars all over the place. It's amazing we actually finished this interview.

FH: Okay, so you got in the business because your father was in the
business and stayed because you love it, but this is a tough, tough gig.
How do people do it?
JD: You just do it. If you love it, you do it. I directed this movie about
a year ago and I cast this talented actor. Last night, we were at a club
and he's the waiter there. He's talented. And hasn't gotten the breaks
yet. He did well in my movie, he got another movie but then things just
fizzled out. And he's waiting tables until he gets another break. When
I first moved out here a lot of my friends were teenage has-beens —
they'd all been in TV series and they were making lots of money and
they thought it would never end. Then it all went away. They can't get
arrested. With their egos they can't get jobs at Nordstrom's or Macy's
and it's really sad. I remember when I used to hang out with them,
when my son was young and he'd say, "Dad, all your friends are teenage
has-beens." And there's nothing they can do. What's really sad is they
think it's never gonna end. You got a series, you're making great money
for three to five years, and then it's over.

FH: But you know what, Jim?... they have to see talented people
around them out of work, depressed, losing their money... I guess,
it's sorta like professional or elite athletes....
JD: They think it's never going to end.

FH: There's this sense of invincibility that kind of comes with being
at the top of your game. It's scary.
JD: They're not preparing. It's like a baseball player who thinks "my
talent never ends."

FH: The talent well's never gonna run dry.
JD: Yeah. I'm always going to be fast. I'm always going to be able to hit the ball or throw the ball 90 miles an hour. And nobody banks for the future. The first thing they do when they start making money is buy the car. Then the house. Then the party's over and then it's "wait a minute, how am I gonna pay my mortgage, how am I going to pay for that car?"

FH: Even though you've had your success as an independent, would you ever consider being bought out by a large company?
JD: I enjoy it the way it is. Autonomy to do what I want. I've got to be more careful because I can't afford to make a mistake — one mistake puts me out of business. So, I move very cautiously on projects.

FH: You acquire projects?
JD: We develop a lot in-house. We look for finance. You have any money? Want to finance a movie?

FH: Not with me. Left my checkbook in Texas. Can't finance your movie but I'll write one for you.
JD: Everybody wants to write a movie, I need the financing. It's getting tougher and tougher. A lot of people used to invest in movies, but then they put a lot of money in stocks, tech stocks, and the stock market went bad and they lost their money. They used to invest in film and at least they'd get their names in the credits.

FH: If I say I want to be in this business, the business you're in and I declare that I want to be a producer, what do you say to me?
JD: I say you got a million dollars, you're a producer, you got a half a million dollars, you're an associate producer. I'll give you an example. I was asked to speak, the first and last time at this conference of independent filmmakers. It was about 15 years ago. And everybody wanted to be a producer. Everybody graduated college. One kid, can't remember his name, but he raises his hand and he says, "I'm making a film about migrant farm workers in the Southwest." And I said, "Who the f___ cares?" He says, "Oh, it's gonna be great." I said, "What's the budget, half a million, three million?" He says, "$400,000." I said, "You got your family to invest?" He said, "Yeah." I said, "And then what? You sell it to PBS for $10,000 and you got a $390,000 deficit." That's not a business. Go out and make a porno, make some money. I also look at this as a business in which you have to make money. I made a lot of films in the

'80s; some of the critics said they were some of the best films made. I went to Cannes three years in a row with some of the films I was involved in — they didn't make any money! It's not just about making great documentaries; you also have to make a living.

FH: So how did your relationship with Showtime come about?
JD: Just over the years with friendships. You talk ideas, sometimes they buy them, sometimes they don't. I mean, I go on pitch meetings, in fact, I'm always going to a pitch meeting.

FH: You take 'em, pitch meetings?
JD: I used to sit in on them.

FH: What's the common flub of pitchers, the ones you've seen in your office?
JD: They don't understand the business. Because everybody who comes in here launches into "and it's gonna make so much money." Immediately I say, "Get out of here. Do your research." The percentage of movies that actually get made and make a lot of money is very small. You make a movie and if you're lucky enough, it makes money. So, sometimes I tell these producers, how about getting an exclusive television deal or video. They say, "No, it's gotta go theatrical!" And if it does go theatrical, of course it's going to lose. All the money they make in the ancillary markets pays for that deficit from the theatrical. To release a film today is expensive.

FH: How do you make money, then?
JD: You don't! You know who makes the money? The distributors always make the money, because they're in the first position.

FH: Right. So, how do you stay in business?
JD: It's called mirrors. [*Laughter*].

FH: How are we sitting here? You're doing something right.
JD: Well, we also sell internationally, television, video. So we have different areas. But it's really tough. I remember the first, well this last film that I made, I could have gone theatrical. I got offers from two studios. I knew it was not a theatrical movie, I knew it would lose money. But they didn't care because whatever they lost in theatrical they were going to recoup out of video and television — that's where the money was. So, had I gone with them they'd be taking my dollars and I don't

have that big of an ego. I made an exclusive network deal — that was all my money. I made an exclusive video deal. Then I sold it internationally and I made money. But most people who make films want to see them in the theater. And I understand that ego, "it needs to be on the screen." But I need to see money in my bank account. And it's amazing how many people just don't get it. They just don't get it.

FH: Best advice for a wannabe or new person?
JD: Get a real job and pursue this on the side.

FH: Move out here?
JD: Move to California?

FH: Yep.
JD: I think you have to be in California. You know, you network, you're meeting with people.

FH: Bumping into people.
JD: Yeah, I mean I'm still networking; I'm still meeting people. And there's always new people moving in and also the business is getting younger.

FH: Best advice anybody ever gave you about getting into the business.
JD: Get out of the business. [*Laughs*]. Get a real job.

FH: You didn't take it. Why didn't you take this advice? Hard headed, stubborn?
JD: I love the business. I enjoy the people. I get rejected a lot. I mean, it's like anybody else, when you're pitching a project and you think it's just so good. It's really good. And they smile and give me the courtesy nod. But once I leave, they're probably laughing. You call 'em back, they don't take your call.

FH: How do you deal with that?
JD: You deal with it. You move on. There'll be other deals and you just remember why you're in the business. Hopefully, it's because you love it. And that takes you through the difficult times. Most people get out. That's one way of dealing with it. And look, this business is not for everyone. These kids come out of film school and they think they know everything about everything. They don't know shit. But you can't tell them that. Or when you do, they still think they know shit. This is a business you have to do. I'm not saying film school is a waste of time....

FH: Yes you are.

JD: Okay, I am, sort of. But what I'm really saying is that the entertainment business is a hands-on industry. Have to be in it to really be in it.

FH: Sounds like the $25,000 a year tuition for film school may help you with the industry glossary, but that's about it.

JD: That's about it. Because to make it in this business you have to learn it up close and you have to be willing to take the bumps and the bruises that come with it. Otherwise, go home. Go be a schoolteacher.

ANY MEETING IS A GOOD MEETING... AT LEAST AT FIRST

In June 2002, I had a meeting with two executives from a growing, but already high-profile, Hollywood network. I had gotten this meeting through a friend of a friend and I was psyched because I knew I had some good ideas to pitch to them. I'd spent one full day researching the company. I stayed up until 3 o'clock in the morning, watching the network so that I could be genuine when I said, "I like what you're doing, and I've been watching your shows."

One thing to note about preconceived notions heading into meetings: throw them out the window. I've found that meetings rarely go the way you expect them to, so it's best to be prepared for anything.

Next, and this is really important, so highlight it — the meeting starts with the *pre-meeting*, which starts the moment you encounter anyone connected to the company with which you have the meeting. This includes the valet, the elevator attendant and of course, the receptionist in the main lobby. Don't make the mistake of thinking that the meeting starts when the executive walks into the "pitch room." Some executives rely heavily on their support staff to learn about wannabes. You're expected to be charming to the executive's assistant, you'd be a fool to be rude to him or her. But what about the supposed "little" people? A lot of wannabes have missed out on jobs because they were rude to doormen. Don't make this mistake. It could cost you your career.

Back to my big pitch. I was scheduled to meet with two executives, but one was just getting out of another meeting, so I got to have a little one-on-one time with the first exec, whom we shall call Kat. The meeting started with some important chitchat about the weather. Yes, the weather. This is one time that I'm not being sarcastic.

I'm from Texas and anytime people know that, one of the first things they say to me is, "You don't have a southern accent" and next they ask, "So, how's the weather in Texas?" Consequently, I've become adept at ways to talk about the weather in Texas in a way that's neither boring nor fake. Texas summers can be brutal and I don't mind saying so. If nothing else, executives feel grateful that they live in Southern California after my weathercast.

But seriously, icebreaker conversations are critical. It's not so much about the topic as it is how you handle the topic. Don't view chitchat as wasted time. It's precious time. See it as your chance to warm up executives; to get them to find out more about you and possibly want to do business with you. Chitchat hour is the one shot you get to set the tone for the meeting. So, be ready to talk about anything — shoes, frozen foods, volcanoes, and little league sports — for about 10 minutes. Yes, 10 minutes. Sometimes you will be meeting with several people at once and not all of them may arrive on time. What are you gonna do while you wait for the others to arrive? Stare at the wallpaper? Read the *Popular Mechanics* magazine on the table? Don't you dare!

You're going to talk. And, we hope, in an intelligent and witty fashion. So, Rule #1, become a master at idle chitchat, it's the key to a good start in your pitch meeting. Now, let's get clear on the aesthetics of idle chitchat. Idle chitchat is not synonymous with lame conversation. It's not bs-ing the executive to the point of projectile vomiting. It's honest, sincere, preferably light conversation. And those who are good at it will never have trouble getting people to stay on the phone with them or to consider meetings with them (provided you're also talented). Learn it, become good at it and you will reap the benefits.

Back to the meeting. Kat, the first exec to arrive at the meeting, was a cheerful, pleasant woman with warm eyes. I knew we'd hit it off. I stood when she came into the room, walked toward her and introduced myself.

Let's review what just happened. When you visit someone, you are the guest. When she enters the room, it is good manners to stand and move toward her with a warm (not flimsy) handshake. Then, take your seat, the meeting just started.

After we talked about the weather and my trip to L.A. and yes, the other companies I'd pitched, Kat mentioned that the other executive, we'll call her Linda, would arrive shortly. I never asked Kat about Linda's whereabouts, I let her offer the information because here's the deal: the pitching doesn't start when you want it to. It starts when they're ready to hear what you have to say. In the meantime, don't get impatient and don't get bored. Always be, or at least appear, energetic and interested in every little detail of the conversation.

Five minutes later, Linda walked in and apologized for keeping me waiting. I got up and repeated the greeting ritual: smile, stand, walk toward, shake hands, sit. Fortunately, Linda was as easy to vibe with as Kat; I was now feeling particularly inspired. I told them a little bit about myself and then one of them said, "So, whatcha got?" The pitch just officially started.

I was sure that my first idea would excite them. It was a multi-segmented, fast-paced show that was perfect for their demographic — or so I thought. I'm flowing and going when Kat interrupts, "Do you have other ideas to pitch?" I said yes.

"Great," she said. "You seem like the kind of person we can be direct with, so let me just say that we've had several people pitch us similar ideas, and while your idea sounds like a fun show, it's strays a little bit from what we're trying to focus on right now."

Now, three key things to take from what's already happened in my meeting that you can use in your meetings. One, always have two to three ideas to pitch. Two, always be the kind of person people can shoot straight with and three, ask clarifying questions, so you can pitch future ideas that are more closely aligned with the buyer's wants and needs.

After they'd finished explaining why they wouldn't be buying my first idea, I asked a few clarifying questions and was able to get some valuable information about the current climate and needs within the company, as well as what kinds of shows they might be looking for in a year or two. Good stuff to write in my journal and to keep in mind for my next meeting with them… because there will be more meetings with them.

Recovering from being "shot down" is a skill you must learn early in your career. Even as an actor, I've had directors or casting agents interrupt me mid-stream to ask me to do a monologue a different way. So, you have to have great recovery skills, especially during a pitch meeting. Finally, Linda and Kat gave me the "go ahead" nod and I moved on to my second idea, a show about finding the next great talent. It was called *American Beauty* and I was sure this network would love it. I was partially right. It was closer to what they were seeking than my first idea and I could tell they liked it because they asked lots of questions about how the show worked.

Curiosity is a sign of interest. If you're pitching and they're just sitting there silently, counting the stripes on your tie, you're in deep trouble. You've managed to put the executive in a deep hypnotic state and this is never a good thing, unless you're pitching a movie about the power of hypnosis. And even then, I'd be worried about bringing them out of it.

For the next 15 minutes the three of us threw out ideas about *American Beauty* and how it could work. I was feeling like there might be a sale at the end of the tunnel until they looked at each other and said, "let us think about it for a few days." My stomach dropped.

I have not found those nine words to indicate present buying behavior. Common buying phrases include "… I'll call Bob (your agent or attorney) today" or "Love it!" Those are strong buying words. Anything else is up for debate and typically means "no sale."

So, what do you do when you feel like you've pitched yourself and your ideas extremely well but the fish just aren't biting? It's simple. You graciously say something like, "Well, thanks for the meeting, I really appreciate the opportunity to share some of my ideas with you." You pick up your belongings, smile as broadly as you did at the beginning of the meeting, shake their hands and leave saying, "Have a great week."

That's it. No groveling, no begging, no promises, no last ditch attempts to "find something they'll like." Your charge is to keep the window of opportunity open for future meetings. If you've shown initiative and creativity, you'll get more meetings. The thing to focus on at this point in the meeting is your exit. It must be smooth. Be friendly and professional to everyone you see on your way out. Thank the people who gave you the nametag or water, wish the bellman a good day, and tip the valet.

Once your car pulls onto Wilshire Boulevard you can bawl your eyes out if you so desire. But not one tear should flow before the end of your meeting. And remember, the meeting doesn't officially end until you are off the company premises and at least four blocks away in the Ralph's grocery store parking lot. I hear they have great powdered donuts.

MOST LIKELY TO GET A DEAL....

Succeeding in this business is not about being popular or well liked by everyone you meet. Think about it this way. Only one person has to like you, or your work, for you to be on your way to phenomenal success. Just one. Even if you get 10 rejections, if one somebody digs you, your career's launched instantly. In fact, if you think about it, it's how every single person's career started. People told Madonna that she'd never be a singing sensation. George Clooney starred in pilot after pilot after pilot until he finally landed a recurring role on *The Facts of Life*. Yes, George "GQ" Clooney shared the screen with Tootie.

A television exec took one look at Oprah Winfrey and knew she was much more than a television news anchor. Brian Donlon, who was president of sports at Lifetime Television when I retired from the WNBA, flew to Austin to meet with me about joining his team. Our meeting took my TV career to another level because he offered me a job on the spot. In other words, one person saw something in each person's talent and took a chance. Somehow we've lost sight of this spoonful of truth. It only takes one person to like you. Don't forget that.

In 2002, I had a 60% success rate, which means for every 10 scripts, pitches or other kinds of proposals I submitted, I was only rejected four times. That's not bad. Would I want a 100% success rate? Not really, because although I'd be insanely rich if everyone bought everything I created, I wouldn't know just how amazing the word "yes" sounds because I wouldn't have a "no" to compare it to.

MAKING LOVE TO REGGIE

Most of us give rejection too much dominion in our lives. Rejection can't stop you from having anything you're willing to work to achieve. It can delay your arrival, but only you and your self-limiting belief system can fully stall the train. When I first started writing screenplays I wanted to hear how much people liked my scripts. I got over that real quickly and soon discovered that even if someone likes it, it doesn't mean that it's going to get made. So, I adjusted my desires a little. Now,

I'm all about writing something that people like enough to make because if they want to make it, they like it. Every time I send out query letters, I remind myself, "I don't need 10 production companies to like my script. I need the right producer or director to commit to making it." This small shift in mindset has drastically changed the way I respond to "pass" and "it's not right for us" or "I think the characters need to be flushed out a bit more." I put all of the feedback into a hat and weigh it out. I'm not devastated by the people who don't like what I write and I'm not ready to sell the farm when someone calls to talk enthusiastically about my latest screenplay.

Likewise, as a broadcaster, I don't need every producer who looks at my reel to think I'm right for the part of the hot reporter on his show, I just need one of them to see my hot-ability. And it's the same for you. Stop wanting all people to like you. They won't. Even if you're ultra talented and super sweet, everybody's not going to like you. I won the presidency of my senior high school class by a landslide, but there were still about seven people out of the 632 who didn't vote for me, who probably couldn't stand my guts. I didn't need them to vote for me to scoop the president's seat. I needed the majority of my insanely brainwashed classmates to think I was right for the job.

So, chill a bit. If the producer's already staffed her show, move on. If you didn't get the lead in the low-budget movie, revel in your co-starring role. There will be other shows, if you keep at it.

LET IT SNOW
There's one sure way to knock yourself out of the running for a job in the biz. Flake out. Show up late for auditions. Specialize in drama. Forget to send a requested script. Call Julia Roberts Kyra Sedgwick (even though the resemblance is amazing). Ask the fiftysomething female exec if the good-looking boy toy on her arm is her son. And so forth and so on. Flakiness happens. It happens to the best of us. At some point, most of us have dropped the ball. That's life. But when it becomes perpetual, it's bad form.

So, if you're one of these people who is "known" for being late, I suggest you become known for something else before you venture into showbiz. Yes, we hear that superstars show up when they feel like it, *if* they feel like it. Pretty soon, people get tired of the b.s. and pretty soon those same superstars aren't asked to sing at the Super Bowl anymore.

We all have flaws, but being late for a meeting, showing up stinky and then overstaying your welcome, will not win you many brownie points in Hollywood.

MEET THE SNOW FLAKES

Here's the cold hard truth, you can't flake out on people. Again, like being a jerk, this is one of those qualities that I suppose you can let out of the closet once you've made it, but until then, your ship has to be tight.

I've got a great flake story to share. In fact, I've got two flakes to share.

Flake #1:

I've directed four plays and in all but one of those productions, I had at least one flake. That one person was on drugs, or something, and didn't know how to manage the day to day of being an actor. In this particular play, this individual called to say that he wanted to drop out because he didn't feel like he was really capturing the essence of his character. I thought he was doing fine. Granted he wasn't the star of the show, but he was giving effort and that's really all a good director can ask for. Anyway, this actor called me the week before opening night to tell me that he wanted to drop out. Even at this late stage of the game, he was still actually replaceable, but I felt I needed to impress upon him the importance of protecting his reputation. If he became the "Guy who bails the week before opening night," the word was going to spread like herpes, and I told him he didn't want that. Maybe he did. He quit anyway.

Flake #2

Now, I'm not big on gossip but I'm gonna tell you this anyway, because you seem like the kind of person who can appreciate a good word of caution. On another ensemble production, I had a woman drop out for no apparent good reason. There were conflicting reports circulating among the cast as to why she left the show. One was that she found out that several of the cast members were rumored to be gay. The other was that she'd had a death in the family. I didn't really care which it was, but since I rarely pass up the chance to share my opinion on anything, I told this new actor that the last thing she needed was to let her personal position on gender, race, sexual orientation, or any thing else, interfere with her ability to do her job. And that if she became known as "The Woman Who Quit Because She Was a Bigot," it would probably not have a positive effect on her acting career. She assured me that, in fact, she had had not one, not two, but three deaths in the family over the last, oh, week and that, in fact, was the reason she needed to leave the show.

Now, call me crazy, but that's a lot of death in a span of a week. And since I'm not one to mess with the other world too much, I had my say and accepted her explanation… just in case it was true.

WHAT DO YOU DO WHEN THEY FLAKE OUT?

Do the suits ever screw up, forget or ignore you? Absolutely. But what are ya gonna do? I'll tell you what you're not gonna do. You're not gonna handle a studio exec the same way you'd handle your significant other, or a friend who ignored you. If your partner left you standing in the foyer of a restaurant for half an hour, you'd be pretty ticked, right? And you'd probably let him or her know about it in very certain terms. Unless you're one of those people I saw on *Oprah* a few weeks ago. I think they were called Doormat Deluxes. In which case, you'd simply lie down and let this person pass. But when those who have the power to change the complexion of your bank account overnight flake out, well, you tend to handle them slightly differently. You're still ticked, but you don't tell them that.

Now, you'll be happy to know that when you're dealing with reputable people, flakiness is rare. That doesn't mean they don't have last minute things come up. But I scheduled 23 meetings (by phone or in person) in Hollywood in 2002 and not one of them was canceled. A few were moved around, but none was completely cancelled. Furthermore, across all 23 meetings, I probably waited a grand total of 45 minutes. In other words, people, reputable and professional people, typically don't stand people up, casually disregard or cancel appointments for no reason. If you make it onto their calendars, they perceive that there's at least a crumb of value in meeting with you. It's up to you to prove them right… or wrong.

AN ANONYMOUS EXECUTIVE GOES
ONE-ON-ONE WITH FRAN

VICE PRESIDENT OF AN UNNAMED PRODUCTION COMPANY
FIRST JOB IN THE BIZ | ASSISTANT AT KOPELSON ENTERTAINMENT

FH: Why/how did you decide to get into the entertainment business?
VP: When I was a kid, I watched *Entertainment Tonight* and I loved when they would show clips of the celebrities entering the red carpet for a premiere. I wanted to be a part of that. But I didn't actually decide to pursue film as a major in college until my junior year, when I was forced to declare a major.

FH: What was the one perception you had about being in the business that you found out was inaccurate?
VP: Celebrities are glamorous. Women could rise above the glass ceiling.

FH: What do you wish someone had told you prior to your diving in?
VP: "Remember, it's just a job."

FH: Who are/were some of the people you admire (d) in the biz and why?
VP: I admire any writer or filmmaker who doesn't sacrifice the story or vision for money.

FH: What's been the most difficult aspect of being in the biz?
VP: Time spent indoors.

FH: What do you think you'd be doing if you weren't in the biz?
VP: Playing outside.

FH: Ever slept with someone to get a job? How'd you feel the next morning?
VP: No, thank God.

FH: Share one hard knocks lesson you learned.
VP: If you f--- up, admit it right away and don't lie. Lying will snowball beyond control and your boss WILL FIND OUT! This town is too small.

FH: Share one pattern or mistake you see newbies make (e.g. not understanding how the biz works or not taking a mailroom job, if it gets them in the door).
VP: Not respecting the low level people (assistants) they are getting direction from. Those little people are soon agents and producers and are in a position to hire you (or not). I have seen AFI and USC Peter Stark Program kids waltz into internships and make fools of themselves. They have this allusion that no one else knows as much as they do. First thing I learned: those kids who spent hundreds of thousands of dollars on film schools know jack shit. The kid who has been an assistant to a producer, who was working at McDonalds' before getting hired knows much more.

FH: If you had the chance to start your career over, what, if anything, would you do differently?
VP: I would have taken more chances. I would have produced my own film earlier in my career.

FH: How do you handle rejection?
VP: "It's their loss."

FH: Best advice given to you?
VP: Keep your mouth shut and make sure your job is only 10% of your life.

FH: One or two pieces of advice for wannabes.
VP: Write thank you cards. Work harder than you are expected to. Proof read and page count even when you are not asked to do so. You couldn't make more of an impression than finding a typo in a letter that is going to Sherry Lansing or Denzel Washington. Follow your gut.

PEOPLE WATCHING

In one of my latest scripts, one of my characters says, "You can learn a lot by just paying attention." Sounds simple but you'd be amazed at how much information is right in front of your eyes if your antenna's working. Instead of being the one who monopolizes the conversation at your next gathering, be the one who stands in the corner watching everyone else. Especially if you're at a Hollywood party.

Now, some people would tell you to burst onto the scene and make sure everyone knows who you are. Squash that. There's plenty of time for that. You need to know who owns the room and there's no way you can know this if you're busy talking without commas and periods.

Look around. See who's kissing up to whom. See who's surrounded by two big bodyguards. Get their names. Don't be afraid to ask who people are or what they do.

> **"The golf course is the only place I can go dressed like a pimp and fit in completely."**
>
> — *Samuel L. Jackson, actor*

I LOVE BARBECUE BUT....

It's 11:30 at night, in late 2001 and I've been on the set of the motion picture *The Rookie* since 11:00 that morning. I'm an extra in the "barbecue scene." That morning, when we checked in, we were told that the "barbecue" scene would be shot early in the afternoon, which, if you've ever been an extra on a movie, you know could mean anywhere from 11:30 in the morning to 5:00 in the evening.

But now it's 11:30 at night and, at this point, I don't care how cute Dennis Quaid is, I'm ready to go home and watch my taped *Entertainment Tonight* shows from the past week.

Mind you, all of the other cranky extras are holding up the wall, flirting with each other, telling me that my scene is a critical scene and that there's no way it'll be cut, so I should stick around. I figure they're just punchy or drunk, because I've never seen these people before in my life and I'm starting to wonder why they care so much about me staying for some dumb barbecue scene.

I know extras are not exactly the seams in the jeans but a 13-hour-in-advance call time is a bit much, even in Texas. I can tell the night is long because I'm starting to yawn and tell really bad jokes. All of a sudden, there's some rumbling among the lowlies. "We're next," I hear. I'm hoping so, since by then, it's cold as hell. I know this because I'm wearing a halter and a mini skirt, courtesy of the casting director who thought I'd look "smashing" in it. Which I did, but that had been at 11 o'clock that morning. It's past midnight and the temperature has dropped at least 30 degrees.

So, anyway, they call for my scene and this really grumpy second or third AD-type guy comes over and tells me that "all you need to do is grab the plates like this and carry them into the next room." Seemed simple enough. "Okay, let's do a trial run," he said. "Go."

I grabbed the four plates, which weighed about as much as two small watermelons, and off I go.

"No, no, no. It's gotta be faster than that," he said rudely. "What's your name?"

"Fran."

"Again, Fran," he demands. I nod politely.

The camera on the rolly thingy starts approaching me and all of a sudden I feel this immense pressure. Like the future of all bit extras rests squarely on my shoulders. I gotta get this take, I say. Like I'm a real actor or something. So, I grab them and he says, "Better." Screw you.

The director director says, "We got it. Let's get another one. Aaaaaand action." The rolly camera thing comes by and I grab the four plates on my arms and walk past Dennis and his boys. This we did for six or seven more takes. I don't know who was screwing up but it wasn't me. I've never carried dishes so well across the room in my life. But I decided that day, because, by now, it was 1:00 in the morning, that I was never going to be an extra again, that if being an actress was in my cards, then I'd have to be a star, because the extra thing had, in 13 hours, played out.

By the way, my scene was not cut. And when The Rookie opened, I screamed like a sorority girl when the "plate" scene came up on the screen.

AN INTERVIEW WITH A DOT COM PIONEER

LESLEY BRACKER
INDEPENDENT PRODUCER & FOUNDER OF *WRITERSCHANNEL.NET*

I first met Lesley online, I think, in 1999 — the year I officially became a screenwriter. I'd written my first script and was hungrier than a polar bear for information that could take me to that elusive next level. My basic Internet search took me to a site where I found online classes. Every week, for a while, I paid $89 to sit in an online class with studio execs, writers, agents, and producers. At the end of the class, we'd get to submit a query letter to the special guests. Not bad, if they requested your script, but pretty soon the 89 bucks became quite an expense coupled with the $15 a script copying furor I'd begun. But before I dropped offline, I had the pleasure of having Lesley give me feedback on one of my query letters. I got great marks, which only fed my sickness and desire to become a "real" writer. So, here it is, three-and-one-half years later and we're sitting face to face at Pete's coffeehouse in Santa Monica, which she pre-e-mailed me about, telling me it was better than Starbucks. A fact I still can't substantiate because I never got past Pete's apricot croissant.

FH: So, here we are. But how did you get here?
LB: It started in 1994. I was getting sent a lot of scripts, I'd just been at ICM as story editor and I would still get a lot of screenplays from new writers. I was offering notes and professional coverage for people at a time when nobody was out there doing anything like that. It was a great deal of work, so I started to charge for it. I set up a place on the Web to offer that service. And in '94 there was nothing like it. I was doing notes for new writers all over the world. Before, writers would write in a vacuum. They would base structure and format on movies, never having access to screenplays or books on screenwriting. And so the writers started wanting to know how I'd break down a script, and what a reader looks for. So, we would pick a movie, we would break it down together, and they could see the structure of the screenplay. Remember, also, this was before there were a lot of books out there about three-act structure. This was before any of Syd Field's popularity. This predates a lot of that. So I started to invite agent friends and executive business friends to

come do these structured class nights and answer questions about the business. Then, writers started to ask the execs about the craft itself, which they couldn't really answer, so we started to invite writers to the class. It became a three-night class all held by Screenwriters Online.

FH: So, with the slew of sites out there claiming to be the second coming for us screenwriters, what separates *WritersChannel.net* **from the others?**
LB: I know, there are a million of them. The Writers Channel is a real honest to goodness community.

FH: I've seen your site, it is different. What kind of research did you do?
LB: I just knew from my own experience, from noticing how students from the Screenwriters Online classes were getting to know each other personally, from the chit chat before and after the class. I noticed they were reading each other's work. I remember 12 people coming together in the mid '90s and we thought 24 people was a crowd. Now it averages about 60 every other week, seven years later.

FH: I don't know why, but that amazes me.
LB: It is amazing how it's grown. The thing I was noticing is this need for people to hang out. And I was noticing private messaging during class. And how well they were getting to know each other. Oh, and the other thing was whenever they would come to town, they'd call and say "let's meet, have drinks." I realized then, that there was no home on the Web for what was happening or no center point for writers. I knew I wanted to create a community, so I put out a letter to anybody I'd worked with over the years asking "If you could create a community of writers, what would you want to see." And the number one thing that came back was mentoring.

FH: Really?
LB: Mentoring. There wasn't one site out there that offered mentors. The Writer's Guild has an e-mail mentoring service.

FH: I've used it. Not bad. Got some interesting feedback, all of it honest, some a little cynical.
LB: So you know. The response is slow and you don't know to whom you're writing.

FH: When you were doing Screenwriters Online, what was one of those glaring new screenwriter things that stuck out like a fly in milk?
LB: Well, the most common thing is a writer taking at least 20 to 30 pages to lay the foundation for the script and introducing us to the characters. In most cases, it could have been done in three pages, three to five pages at most. Another glaring problem is the writer understanding that a movie is visual — which requires writing visually. There are so many cues you can give your audience about your characters simply by setting them up visually. Instead, you have a lot of expository dialogue. Characters saying "I came from Alabama, I grew up without shoes on my feet." When you could just have Julia Roberts in the first scene barefoot, speaking with a deep southern accent and there you have it. And no offense to Alabama, but this visual cue tells us everything about her background and who she is. There's no need to include it in dialogue and not only does it waste valuable pages and time, but there is no drama in having a character TELL us who she is, you must SHOW us.

FH: And what about the angst that people feel about writing query letters? Many a writer has died of query-itis.
LB: Here's the thing about query letters. It's interesting, they've gained importance because the Web has made them important. It was never, ever a way into Hollywood before the Web. As an assistant in various jobs in the '80s, I would see them sporadically. It was a way in legally, because it created a paper trail. It's always been true that you just can't...

FH: ... submit blindly.
LB: Right. No unsolicited submissions, that's always been the rule. Here's the deal, there are legalities. I mean, it's like those pitch festivals that are popping up all over the place. Didn't exist before. But Hollywood's a business, a real business, therefore you have to set up a system to navigate the legalities that exist in that system. The query letters, organized pitch fests, both help to protect both sides to a certain degree.

FH: So how do you navigate in a system that doesn't really seem to want you to have access?
LB: Lots of ways. Go to conventions, conferences, where they have established managers, agents, producers in attendance.

FH: That means you really need to learn how to pitch.
LB: Here's the other thing about pitches. If you catch that person's attention with your one paragraph pitch, which isn't that different from a query, you're in a situation where people get to ask you questions and start thinking in terms of the movie...

FH: ... they wanna make.
LB: Right and they get to ask you questions, you get their creative juices going. And the next thing you know, they're saying "send us the script."

FH: Since you've created this haven for writers, seemingly from all over the world, the question most out-of-L.A. writers want to know, myself included is...
LB: Do you have to live in L.A.?

FH: Bingo.
LB: You don't. You don't have to live here. The thing that is a plus about being in L.A. is that this is where the meetings take place. But if you can spend two weeks out of every few months here, then you're fine. I do not know one executive or one agent who's biased against someone who doesn't live in L.A. In fact, there's a little mystery about you if you don't live here.

FH: So, what about getting an agent? What are my chances of bumping into an agent at the WritersChannel site?
LB: Well, last month I had an agent on from ICM, but there wasn't anything that he felt that he could really sell.

FH: See, that's what writers don't understand... really, it's that we don't like it... we don't understand why an agent won't sign us when we've written something we think is the next best thing, but the market is not hot for.
LB: You can't take it personally. Agents make it their job to know the marketplace well. They look for things they can sell. That's just the reality. In the smaller agencies, the boutiques, they can afford to maybe take on writers and nurture them through the writing of a promising script. The other problem is that a lot of first time writers come up with these huge stories for their first scripts. These elaborate sets, sci-fi plots, tons of locations. So, when I work with a writer on a pitch, I try to break it down to the most basic elements. You cannot sell a spec script, in most

cases, that's a very expensive movie. Once in a while it happens, remember that there are always exceptions, but most all agents will tell you that they will not take on a script by an unknown writer that would cost $100 million to produce. One of the best pieces of advice I can give first time writers is to write a personal story. Every big writer from Scott Frank to Ed Solomon, wrote small personal stories for first scripts. The heart comes through and those are fairly easy for an agent to sell because those screenplays with heart tend to show off the writers' talents best. After you've written that script, you can go and write *Contact*.

FH: So, now you're a producer?
LB: I've always wanted to be a producer. I kept reading these great scripts, passing them on to other people until, finally, a friend and business associate and I decided to partner up. My first job was as an assistant to an executive at WB. I was in my early 20s. I was gathering info and learning everything I could about every job.

FH: Okay, last question. Best job to take.
LB: I think any job that doesn't really drain your creativity. I know a writer who says that being a bartender was the best thing he ever did because he got to hone his dialogue, really listen to how people speak. Dialogue is really important. He felt he got more. If you want to get into that business, sometimes being a writer's assistant is a good start. Any way into the industry so that you can get to know the business better, is a good idea, but writing is what's important.

WHO ARE YOU WEARING?

All wannabes long for the day when they get to walk down that red carpet and be asked The question. *Who are you wearing?* I mean, if you're a devout Joan Rivers clone, you probably think that what you're wearing is the most important thing in your life. It isn't. Besides, I don't take my fashion tips from people who get paid to hate whatever I'm wearing. Clearly, some people do think your clothes are important. At least one of my screenwriting instructors did a few years ago.

"This is very important," she said. I grabbed my pen and listened intently. "Wear black pants and a white shirt to your meetings. No exceptions." I looked around smiling. I thought she was joking. My classmates began jotting down copious notes. "Are you serious?" I asked. "You're not serious, are you?" But she was. "Oh yes," she said, "There's a definite uniform for writers in Hollywood and it's black pants and a white shirt."

I'd never heard this and furthermore, I found it hard to believe that we actually had to subscribe to this strict a dress code, just for a meeting. Were we in prep school? I've found it to be one of the biggest misconceptions about breaking into the business. Like in any business, there are things you should do and there are things you shouldn't do, depending on your particular industry. I've found Hollywood to be a place that's fairly open, when it comes to dress codes, but just in case you've got a big meeting coming up and you want to avoid having a Clothes Crisis, here are a few things to keep in mind.

Fashion Tip #1: Do not dress to impress, you'll end up being stiff and unnatural, which means the best you won't come through.

Fashion Tip #2: Do not dress to seduce, you'll end up looking like a loser and your reputation will be forever tainted. You'll have a hard time trying to undo this kind of reputation.

Fashion Tip #3: If you're applying for a creative position (writer, singer, dancer, producer, director, etc.) do not dress like you're going to a corporate job interview — blue suit, starched shirt, shined shoes.

Fashion Tip #4: Lose the low cut blouses or jeans with the butt cheek cut out of them. It's not chic, it's tacky. Don't do it.

Fashion Tip #5: Wear comfortable shoes. Sometimes you may park in one place and have to walk yards to the actual meeting. Or, sometimes, execs will want to take you for a tour. You don't want your dogs to be barking across the Universal lot.

Fashion Tip #6: Flaunt your unique style, but try not to be flamboyant. In other words, if your style is along the lines of *Moulin Rouge*, tone it down, at least at first.

DO YOU SEE WHAT I SEE?
When people first meet you, what do they think? Sloppy? Confident? Shady? Funny? Don't know what people think? Don't think they think

anything? Think again. They think something. You may not know what they're thinking, but they're thinking something. If you wanna know what your reputation is, all you have to do is ask. First, I want you to take out a sheet of paper and draw a line down the middle of it. On one side you're going to write the heading, "What I Think People Think About Me When They First Meet Me." On the other side, write "What People Think When They First Meet Me."

What I Think People Think About Me...	What People Think of Me...
intelligent	stuffy
funny	funny
friendly	aloof

Next, you're going to fill in the right side. So, take a deep breath and ask a few friends if they can remember what they thought of you when they first met you. Compare your notes with their responses to monitor the accuracy of your self-perception. This exercise will help you to identify which qualities you want to accentuate and those you want to tone down or eliminate from your personality, altogether. Here are some ways to improve your first impressions.

Warm up. Go to a room and get ready to shine. Defrost. Don't be stiff. You're not a mannequin, you're a budding star. If you look like rigor mortis has set in, you won't get lots of jobs, you'll get lots of people standing over you saying Hail Marys. People would rather talk to engaging people. If you were given the chance to chat with a vivacious, energetic soul versus a stone-faced person, which would you choose? The energy bar, right? Of course, you would. So, maybe you're not as bubbly as Goldie Hawn, that's okay, but you can't be as cold as my man, Lurch, from *The Addams Family*, either, and expect to generate heat for your work.

DO YOUR HOMEWORK

If you're going to be in this business, then be in this business. Know your industry inside and out. If you really love it, study it. Know the current players and know their histories. Why? Because this knowledge will give you an edge in conversations with other people in the business and it will help you improve your craft. Where can you find this information? The Internet is a great place to start. Next, read industry trade publications or magazines. Join an industry group, attend events and network with people who do what you do.

A DIEHARD LOS ANGELES SPARKS FAN GOES ONE-ON-ONE WITH FRAN

NAN DIACOVA
VP | LEGAL AFFAIRS | WBTV
FIRST JOB IN THE BIZ | PRODUCTION ASSISTANT

FH: Why/how did you decide to get into the entertainment business?
ND: Obsessed with films... ok... I saw Bette Midler in *The Rose* in 10th grade and knew a career in medicine would never happen and I was off to Hollywood, in search of Bette. I really didn't care about fame and fortune. And I did finally meet her in a very noisy bar, in which I'm sure she didn't hear a word I said.

FH: What was the one perception you had about being in the business that you found out was inaccurate?
ND: Everyone was rich.

FH: What do you wish someone had told you prior to your diving in?
ND: You will not be rich.

FH: Who are/were some of the people you admire (d) in the biz and why?
ND: Annette Benson, casting director. She guided me and trained me and never worried about me succeeding, and taking her job. She always wanted me to succeed and did everything she could to help that happen.

FH: What's been the most difficult aspect of being in the biz?
ND: Getting respect... it's all about the résumé. Unfortunately.

FH: What do you think you'd be doing if you weren't in the biz?
ND: Doctor.

FH: Ever slept with someone to get a job? How'd you feel the next morning?
ND: No, damn it!

FH: Share one hard knocks lesson you learned.
ND: Given a dark room and a director next to you, a hand will appear on your lap.

FH: Share one pattern or mistake you see newbies make.
ND: Giving up too soon and going back home.

FH: If you had the chance to start your career over, what, if anything, would you do differently?
ND: Nothing... it was an experience.

FH: How do you handle rejection?
ND: "Says who, you? Don't think so." That's my response to rejection.

FH: Best advice given to you.
ND: Hang in there and it will happen if you really want it.

FH: One or two pieces of advice for wannabes.
ND: Don't let anyone tell you that you have to do it a certain way just because he or she did it a certain way. You can get there on your own path.

FH: Open forum, freelance — add whatever else you want to add.
ND: Life is short. People love to see people fail. There'll always be someone somewhere who'll say you can't do it because you don't have enough of one thing or too much of the other. Just nod your head, move on and find people who aren't scared to see you succeed and take their jobs... they are out there... keep looking.

> "How does Keanu Reeves work with Coppola
> and Bertolucci and I didn't get a shot at that?
> Know what I'm saying?"
> — *Charlie Sheen*

'TWAS THE NIGHT BEFORE SUCCESS

It's the eve of your big day. You've landed the meeting or gotten a special audition time. Now, you basically have two choices. You can take
your tired butt down to the Exxon and fill up the Hyundai or you can
convince yourself that you can get up the next morning to do it. Which
do you choose? Option B. And boy, do you regret it. Because the next
morning, here's what happens. The exec's assistant calls. Guess what he
wants? To see if you can meet earlier. Of course you can, you say as
you look at the clock, wiping the sleep slobber from the side of your
mouth. It's 8:30 in the morning and the meeting's at 10:00 in Burbank,
which wouldn't be a biggie, if you were staying with a friend who lives
in, say, West Hollywood, but you're not, you're staying in Venice. Now,
you've not only got to get gas but you've also got to get to your meeting an hour earlier. This puts you in a state. Bad form. Don't do it. You
want to be like a new dollar bill heading into your meeting.

I once heard a motivational speaker say, "Never let your hand get below
the half tank mark." I thought, yeah, right, like I'm gonna pay attention
to that useless piece of advice. Then I started to notice something.
Little emergencies started to happen throughout my workweek. A
meeting would go over time and the hour and a half I thought I'd spend
getting lunch and gassing up the Franmobile, would be spent backed up
behind Granny in the Buick Skylark on the freeway.

I'd look at my gas hand with the orange light flashing. Only it wouldn't
just flash, that would be too easy. It would start talking. "You just
wouldn't listen, wouldja? In the last day you've passed by a Texaco, an
Exxon and a Sak 'n' Suds. Now, look at the mess we're in. You're never
gonna make it to the meeting because I'm about to conk out on ya, just
to prove a point."

This goes on for the next 10 minutes and now the orange light is constant and I know that I have a choice. I can either risk life and limb to
get out of the left hand lane and make my way to the nearest exit to
get some petro. Or, I can push the limits of my faith and hope that my
car — which has never driven 50 miles on empty — will somehow do
it on this day because I'm supposed to be on the Fox lot in 20 minutes.

THE DAY I SWEAT MORE THAN NIXON

True story. I had one meeting on this day. One meeting. I wake up, go to the gym, have a great workout, then head back to the house to get ready for my afternoon meeting, which is in Hollywood. I have the address and phone number of the place I'm going to. I even open my Thomas Guide (map) and glance at the area where the meeting will be held. Doesn't appear to be too far away so I bag plotting the course from my doorstep to the meeting. Instead, I decide that I'm going to see what Map Quest has to say about how to get there from my friend's house.

Next, I log onto the Internet and punch in the appropriate factors. Address. Destination. Stuff like that. It spits out door-to-door directions from where I'm staying to the studio. I don't bother to double check the route using the Thomas Guide because I figure *MapQuest.com* had done all of the work for me.

I get in the car and head down the Interstate 10 freeway. Only now, I notice that it looks like I'm going into some areas that look nothing like any I've ever seen, so I decide to call the office where my meeting's taking place. "Oh," he said. "You're about 30 minutes away. Take I-10…." My jaw drops. Thirty minutes away would have been fine if my meeting weren't in 15 minutes. So, I turn around, cussing about how idiotic it was not to look at the map and off I go down the Interstate. The whole time I'm driving, I'm reminding myself how late I'm going to be. It's bumper to bumper traffic and I have no idea how far away I am from my meeting.

The receptionist at the exec's office says that the exec is still in a meeting, so I'd probably be fine. That wasn't good enough for me. I need to slap myself around a bit more, just so I know that I'd made a grave mistake. By now, I'm sweating like Albert Brooks in that scene in the film *Broadcast News* and I can't get my heart to calm down to save my life. So, I call my friend. Not just any friend, but a friend who used to live in L.A. and who knows that area like the back of her hand. She assures me (every three seconds) that I'm going to make it, that I'm actually very near my destination. Of course, I don't believe her because when you're in that "I'm so stupid" state, you won't let any reasonable thoughts into your brain space.

"I'm gonna stay on the phone with you until you get there, okay? Where are you?" she says.

"I'm so goofy for not looking at the map!" I say.

"It's okay, you're going to make it, where are you?" she asks.

"At Gower and, and, I can't see the cross street, I'm never gonna make it...."

And this goes on for another 10 minutes until I finally tell her where I am.

"One more light and you're there," she says.

I figure she's lying just to get me to stop convulsing, but she isn't. One more light and I pull into the security checkpoint.

"I'm here. Thank you, thank you. Thank you. I owe you my first born."

She assures me that isn't necessary. I hang up and guess what? I have exactly one whole minute to spare. And, get this. The executive is still in his meeting when I sit down to watch *The Road Runner* cartoon in the waiting room. I am relieved.

The moral of the story? Never tick off your friends who live in L.A. You may need them to get you to an appointment. Okay, for those of you who may think I'm being serious — the real lesson is to use the map.

The other moral of that story is to make sure your cell phone is always charged. Now, imagine the stakes had I not had my charger with me! Talk about tense. If my battery had been low while I was lost, I have no doubt that I would have needed some serious sedation. So, remember, on the way to meetings and auditions, your job is to keep your blood pressure low.

HERE'S YOUR CHECKLIST FOR THE NIGHT BEFORE THE BIG DAY:

1: Be sure you have everything you need for the meeting. A resume, demo, whatever you're supposed to take. If you don't know what you're supposed to take, ask.
2: Verify the address and be sure you write the address and phone number in the same place. Take this with you. It does you no good to leave it on the pad next to the phone.
3: Get gas.

4: Charge your cell phone.
5: Practice your pitch, audition, etc.
6: Do something fun.
7: Go over your route to the meeting.
8: Do some last-minute Internet research. Find out what's gone on in the company in the last few days.
9: Get a good night's sleep. Don't party all night and try to wing it the next day.

OTHER THINGS TO DO THE DAY BEFORE:

1: Call to confirm the time and place of your meeting. Most executives' offices will not call to confirm with you. Some will, most will not. It's not their job to call and confirm, it's yours. First, you want to be sure you have the assistant's name. When he or she answers the phone, say hello before you move on to anything else. Then say something like, "I was just calling to confirm our 10:30 meeting and to make sure I have the address, it's 1234 Your Place Ave." They will confirm or correct and that's it.

2: Do some updated company specific research. I already said this at least once, but know your industry. No exceptions. If I haven't said it already, subscribe to at least one trade publication or at minimum, visit its Web site several times a week or join its newsletter. Most importantly, if you have a meeting with someone in the industry, always do some last-minute research. Find out if anything good or bad has happened lately to that particular company or within that particular area of the business. It could change the complete complexion of your meeting. I know this from experience.

Two years ago my agent set up a meeting with a development executive at Big Ticket Television. They were excited to talk to me and I was thrilled to have landed the meeting. The day before our meeting they learned that a television show they were very high on, and one they'd planned to launch nationally that fall, was not going to happen. Not enough market clearances. The executive was really bombed, I mean, he was tanked about it, but he took the meeting anyway.

What was I there to talk to him about? A future talk show. Do I need to tell you how that meeting went? Here I am, a new person, known nationally only in the sports television arena, trying to persuade an executive who's just had a nationally syndicated show with a known personality, canceled, to think about the possibilities with me. Oh yeah, that meeting was a blast.

Fortunately, my agent had prepped me with the cancellation news that morning; it hadn't hit the wires yet. So, there would have been no way for me to really have this information prior to the meeting without my agent (another good reason to marry a good agent). Could I have done anything differently, had I known this the day before? Sure. I could have brought a card or something to go above and beyond the usual, "I'm sorry to hear about your show." So, stay on top of your business and you will be ready for the unexpected.

WHO'S NEWS?

Sometimes you'll spend months courting a particular executive at a company only to find out weeks later that that individual is leaving the company. This is another good reason to read the trades and stay on top of your industry. There's always a revolving door with personnel. Don't sweat it. In some cases, the assistant for that VIP will remain in his or her post, so with hope, you've remembered to develop a good relationship with that person.

In one of the newsletters I receive via e-mail, there's a section that tells readers who've made recent personnel moves in the business. Always have access to at least one trade magazine or online subscription in your area of the industry. Some of them can be pretty expensive, so if you can't afford a subscription, you have some options:

Subscribe to their weekly e-zines. An e-zine is basically an online magazine or newsletter. These are often free. They're not as extensive as the print version, but at least you'll get some updates and breaking news stories.

Split the subscription with friends. There are some fantastic trade publications on and offline. *IndieWire.com*, *Ifilmpro.com*, *The Hollywood Reporter* and *Variety* are all great. If the subscription price isn't in your current budget, consider splitting the cost with your friends in the business. It's well worth it. And you really can't be in the business without knowing what's going on at all times.

Visit key Web sites often. Bookmark your "work" sites or put them on your favorite lists.

HANGIN' OUT

There's an art to hanging out in H-town. First thing. Gotta know where to hang out. If you don't know where to start, grab your pad and pencil and watch one of the top entertainment news programs, they're always good for dropping a few names.

You know what I did just for you? Just for you. Just for this book, I went beyond the call of duty. I got no satisfaction whatsoever from this little excursion. I went shopping and dining on Rodeo drive and some other places where I know celebs like to hang out. I learned a few things. Namely this. If you really want to know how to work a hangout, here's what you have to do.

Step 1: Decide where you're going to go.

Step 2: Make sure you have cash and (yes, and) a credit card with at least a few hundred dollars of available credit.

Step 3: Once you settle on a target location area, get on the Internet and find three to four places within the zone that you can visit. You're going alone, by the way.

Step 4: Plan on taking something to read or write and plan on spending at least four hours in the area. Your activities will include a meal, coffee, shopping and just hanging — walking around, window flirting and maybe drinks, depending on what time you go.

This technique is useful in any setting, but let's say you decide to have lunch at a hot spot, which doesn't have to be expensive, by the way.

The waiter comes over and you order. Make small talk, be friendly. Notice who comes in. Get to know the buses, waiters, managers, and valets. If you can afford it, go regularly for about a month, or so. Pretty soon, they start knowing who you are and what you do. Pretty soon they start expecting to see you there. Ordering your *regular*, sitting in *your* spot. Starting to feel *me*?

Okay, pretty soon, the people you want to be in business with start recognizing you, too. You follow me? Pretty soon you'll find yourself talking about sports, film, music. All of a sudden, you're in conversation with a mover and shaker. Remember your Dream Filler chart? Time to add another entry.

AN EXTRA SPECIAL CORRESPONDENT
GOES ONE-ON-ONE WITH FRAN

JERRY PENACOLI | ENTERTAINMENT CORRESPONDENT FOR *EXTRA* (WARNER BROS./TELEPICTURES)
FIRST JOB IN THE BIZ | PRODUCTION ASSISTANT AT NBC TELEVISION NETWORK IN NEW YORK CITY

FH: Why/how did you decide to get into the entertainment business?
JP: The "why" is more boring than the "how," but here goes. It's not an unusual story. I was the kid always performing -– for my parents, for my teachers, for my friends. When I was on my way to college, I told my parents I wanted to study drama and be an actor, and they said "over our dead bodies." So I studied broadcast journalism instead. I figured (and my parents concurred) that working in television would still satisfy my desire to "perform" but, with hope, would be a little more consistent and secure, and according to my parents, more respectable. Boy, were they wrong. As for the "how" — when I was a sophomore at the University of Bridgeport (majoring in broadcast journalism, with a secret second major in drama, shhhh don't tell my mother) I "auditioned" for a brand new internship program at NBC in New York. It consisted of a meeting in New York with several of the personnel people (I don't think the term human resources existed back in the dark ages) and a couple of producers. I got it.

On alternating semesters (and in the summertime, when they actually ended up paying me for my menial labor), I commuted by train from my dorm in Connecticut to the big, bad city (what was I, 19?). And in the three years I was there, I worked with the likes of Barbara Walters (I wrote her questions for a syndicated talk show called *Not for Women Only*) and Tom Snyder (who was anchoring local news at WNBC while hosting a late night chat fest called *Tomorrow*). At one point during a strike, I was enlisted as a scab — what did I know? — to run teleprompter for Tom Terrific, who told me I looked like his younger brother. While at NBC, I befriended a lot of people in news, both local and network, and programming. I even dated the daughter of one of NBC's star directors — I was learning fast. One of the VPs of the network was involved in the Society of Professional Journalists (SPJ/SDX) and so was I, as student representative on the National Board for the entire eastern quarter of the country, so we had that bond. He pulled some strings, and I was able to sit in John Chancellor's chair — he was Tom Brokaw at the time (yes, this WAS the dark ages) — and I read five minutes of news that I wrote.

At the same time, I was interning at the ABC affiliate in New Haven, CT on the weekends — I was an overachiever, still am — and I put together a "package" on the longest running card game ever in Connecticut. Married the two pieces onto a tape, and upon graduating, peddled those frickin' tapes all over the country. After enough rejection letters to wallpaper a grand ballroom, I decided to take a more "grassroots" approach. I drove to Florida (my brother and his wife had a spare couch on which to crash)... and literally began knocking on TV station doors. Finally, this tiny, little station in Jacksonville, Florida thought I would be an asset to its five-person news team. I mean, there were only five people in the ENTIRE news department. I could go on, but this is your book, not mine. Let it suffice, that when I got that job making $175 a week — that's gross, and it WAS gross — I was the happiest man alive. I was in the news biz, but when you get right down to it, I was in SHOW BIZ!

FH: What was the one perception you had about being in the business that you found out was inaccurate?
JP: Refer to the last line in the previous question. I was told I was getting in the news business, but in reality, it was show business. It took me a long time to realize it, though. I was young and idealistic... who isn't when they first start out?

FH: What do you wish someone had told you prior to your diving in?
JP: That you don't just have to do or be ONE thing in this business... that you CAN reinvent yourself, and that in order to survive, you HAVE to know the art of, what's it called these days... multi-tasking?

FH: Who are/were some of the people you admire (d) in the biz and why?
JP: Early on, I had no idea the people I was exposed to would go on to become huge icons in the business... Barbara Walters, Tom Snyder... they were just the folks I worked with every day... I admired them then, and still do. Fast forward to the mid-90s. I'm now living and working in Los Angeles at E! Entertainment Television, and shortly before I arrive there, a guy named Greg Kinnear leaves his little show *Talk Soup* to pursue a career in acting. He had always been a TV guy, as far as I knew, so to see him go from that, to starring in movies, made me both excited and in awe. I've always admired him for making such a huge, yet smooth transition. Up until that point, I had done some small roles in New York soaps, and lots of theater stuff in both Connecticut and New York, but that was it. When I came out to L.A., and this is key: I was told I could do BOTH the TV reporting/hosting AND acting! I was in shock! I managed to get a recurring lead role on an NBC soap *Santa Barbara* — and I thought "WOW, this is easy." Boy, was I wrong.

FH: What's been the most difficult aspect of being in the biz?
JP: Trying to find the extra 10 hours you need in a day to get it all done, and manage a happy life, professionally and personally.

FH: What do you think you'd be doing if you weren't in the biz?
JP: I'd either be a teacher, or a professional pianist.

FH: Ever slept with someone to get a job? How'd you feel the next morning?
JP: Yes, in fact I f----d my way to the top! (only kidding) What do you think, someone's actually going to answer this question? (P.S.: the answer is "no").

FH: Share one hard knocks lesson you learned.
JP: There are so many, I couldn't share just one. But generally speaking, the best lesson learned is realizing that everyone in this business (especially in the "talent" end of it) is considered dispensable. It isn't until you reach a certain level in the biz, that you start to feel a little more confident, but even then, there's always someone in management (whether it be a studio or a network) who will make you feel like there's someone waiting in the wings for your spot.

FH: Share one pattern or mistake you see newbies make.
JP: The biggest mistake I've seen newbies in the biz make has to do with overall attitude. A lot of young people feel that it's NOT necessary to pay dues, that their stars will shoot to the top, they just know they will. And yes, that happens, but rarely — and not usually without having to sleep with someone in order to make it happen. If I hadn't learned (at that five-person news department in Jacksonville) how to shoot, write, edit, and report, all in a one-man-band situation, I'm sure I wouldn't have had the success and the respect that I have today in this business (or at least the success and respect I *think* I have... humor me, will ya?)

FH: If you had the chance to start your career over, what, if anything, would you do differently?
JP: I would have "gone for it" despite my folks' reservations, and concentrated wholeheartedly on acting, from day one. I've been lucky enough to have been able to mix the two careers simultaneously, out in Hollywood. So, while I interview the stars on red carpets for *Extra*, I can still guest star on dramas like *The District* and *J.A.G.* and land lead roles on sitcoms like *Ellen* and *Wings* — and even hold down a recurring principal role on a daytime serial *Days of Our Lives* (for 10 months playing Deidre Hall's boss). I'm lucky I have a boss here who is very supportive of my acting endeavors, and will make sure I have the time off when I need it. But I also work a lot of weekends and amass many "comp" days, so when I get cast in a role in an Indie feature like *Separate Ways* with C. Thomas Howell, I'm able to take the 12 days off in order to shoot it.

FH: How do you handle rejection?
JP: I used to go on auditions and have that traditional "post-audition depression" that so many actors have, but then, after awhile, a switch flipped in my brain, and the skin got thicker, I guess. After auditions, I just gave it up to the higher power. A funny thing happened, I started booking job after job.

FH: Best advice given to you.
JP: "If you want to be on TV, BE ON TV!" This was told to me by that VP of news at NBC (when I was in college) after I waffled upon being asked what I REALLY want to do in this business. Of course, being Italian-Catholic, I was brought up to be modest and humble, and I

thought if I had said I wanted to be on television, he would have thought I was conceited (I know, what a dork I was). But that one piece of advice drove me to pursue not one, but two careers.

FH: One or two pieces of advice for anyone entering the business.
JP: 1.) Be whatever you want to be, and 2.) Keep your life in balance, while driving yourself crazy pursuing whatever it is you want to be!

> "I arrived in Hollywood without having my
> nose fixed, my teeth capped, or my name changed.
> That's very gratifying to me."
>
> — *Barbra Streisand*

HOW TO STAY OUT OF HYGIENE HELL

One friend said to me laughing as she read this section, "I can't believe you have to tell people this stuff!" I laughed, too, but I interviewed tons of power players for this book, some on the record, some off. And the stories they told relating to hygiene are enough to make the hairs on any wannabe's head stand at attention. Hey, don't shoot the messenger! I'm trying to look out for you. Here are a few watchouts:

LEAVE SPOT AT HOME

C'mon. I don't really care that you and your 60-pound Golden Retriever, Yosef, sleep in the same bed, but nobody wants to see his dog hair all over your clothes in an audition or pitch meeting. I don't care who says you shouldn't judge a book by its cover, people do. And they always will. So, make sure your cover is clean and presentable. If you have a dandruff problem, pick up some Tea Tree or Head & Shoulders shampoo and treat your scalp. If your flaky scalp is chronic, at least be sure you dust off your shirt, blouse, or jacket before you enter the building. I've had people show up at my auditions smelling like they just left Pets Mart. Not good. Unless you're auditioning for The Discovery Channel's *Animal Planet*... as a dog.

DO I HAVE BROCCOLI IN MY TEETH?

If you do, guess what? Nobody but your mother's gonna tell you. Always make a run to the restroom before your meeting to check the pearly whites.

Nose. A quick glance won't do it. Grab a Kleenex and excavate, my friends. Even if you don't see anything, there could be a few latent boogies in the old nostrils. We don't want them to show up in the middle of your big performance, do we?

Teeth. Catch me any day of the week and I will always have a travel size canister of floss and toothpaste in my back pocket. It's like a part of my uniform. No exec wants to look at a speck of pepper or a sliver or chicken lodged between your teeth. Nobody. Floss after lunch.

Nose Hair. Trim it, please. I had a high school chemistry teacher who had so much nose hair, I thought he was growing dreadlocks. Snip and clip, please.

Ears. You guessed it, same chemistry teacher had so much hair in his ears that, well, you get the picture. It's gross, don't wanna see it.

Altoid, anyone? Nobody wants to be remembered as the artist who had bad breath. The good news is that an Altoid will kill anything within a mile of it. Stock up.

What's That Smell? This was probably the most complained-about hygiene-related topic I heard. "Why are you coughing?" I asked the nice executive. "Because the person who was in here for a meeting before you apparently bathed in a bottle of Tommy Hilfiger cologne," he replied.

And here I was thinking it was particularly smoggy that day in Los Angeles.

People, listen up! Lay off of the fragrance. It's killing bugs within a 15-mile radius and it's driving execs batty, too! A splash of Mackie might not bother anybody, but when you exterminate your body with it, it's truly a turnoff. Apparently you don't know that your perfume is choking innocent executives. Trust me. One tiny splash is plenty.

THE WAITING GAME

Here's a fact. You'll drive yourself crazy pursuing your Hollywood dream if you're impatient. Here's another fact. You'll spend most of your climb up the silver ladder waiting. Waiting on phone calls, waiting on callbacks, and waiting on decisions to be made. That's how the business works, take it or leave it.

If an agent takes your script home for a weekend read, don't expect it to be read that weekend. If you give a casting director a headshot for an upcoming movie, don't expect him or her to have an answer about the part within 24 hours. The entertainment industry is a multi-billion-dollar industry, which means jobs are at stake. Careers are on the line daily. Sometimes decisions are made on the spot. Most of the time, however, they are not.

Here's a snapshot of the lives of lit agents, just as an example. Monday through Friday they spend all day on the phone in meetings or making deals. After hours, they take clients, producers, or people they want to be in business with, to dinner. They get home by 11 o'clock, or so. On the weekend, they typically read scripts. So, imagine this. Good agent takes home about 10 scripts. If they get to five of those, they're a bad mother-shut-yo' mouth. It takes at least two hours to give a script a good read. A weekend is only two days. So don't start foaming at the mouth if an agent has your script for three weeks, but you haven't heard from her. Three weeks may feel like dog years to you but it's really only six days to an agent — there are two days in a weekend, right? Two times three is six. So, the next time you're gearing up for a major anxiety attack because he or she hasn't called, go see a movie or run a 5K. If they like you, they'll call.

A KING OF THE HILL GOES ONE-ON-ONE WITH FRAN

LARRY HILL | SCREENWRITER | *THE BAR*
FIRST JOB IN THE BIZ | THIS ONE — WRITER

FH: Why/how did you decide to get into the entertainment business?
LH: Short version: I'm a masochistic fool. Long version: I read a book called *Do What You Are* which uses personality types to identify jobs that best suit each type. One of the jobs, to my surprise, was screenwriter. I was writing and producing videos for my day consulting firm job, and enjoyed that, so it intrigued me. Then, one night while traveling, I was bored and went to a bookstore. I stumbled upon the book of the screenplay for *Jacob's Ladder*; read it and was totally hooked.

FH: What was the one perception you had about being in the business that you found out was inaccurate?
LH: That it's easy to write 120 pages of anything good.

FH: What do you wish someone had told you prior to your diving in?
LH: That it would take a lot longer than a year to achieve any success.

FH: Who are/were some of the people you admire (d) in the biz and why?
LH: Mel Brooks, for obvious reasons; David Lynch, for obscure reasons; Kubrick for *Dr. Strangelove*; Bergman, Hitchcock, Alan Ball, Bill Broyles, just because they write/make great movies.

FH: What's been the most difficult aspect of being in the biz?
LH: Finding the time and the energy to write, while holding down a more-than-full-time job that requires a lot of travel. I'm fixing that in January as I'm leaving my "day job" to write full time. I imagine the most difficult aspect going forward full time will be worrying about the next paycheck and whether I'll have to go BACK to a full-time day job.

FH: What do you think you'd be doing if you weren't in the biz?
LH: Being very successful, wealthy, bored, and miserable as a consultant, waiting to die.

FH: Ever slept with someone to get a job? How'd you feel the next morning?
LH: Not counting myself? Uh, no. Two reasons: One, I'm a guy. And B, I'm not an actor, I'm a writer, and who ever wants to sleep with writers?

FH: Share one hard knocks lesson you learned.
LH: When someone options your first screenplay, don't jump up and down for about five years.

FH: Share one pattern or mistake you see newbies make.
LH: I made it myself. I put way too much stock in a single work, and had no other work to show.

FH: If you had the chance to start your career over, what, if anything, would you do differently?
LH: I would have started it years ago, when three hours of sleep per night was plenty.

FH: How do you handle rejection?
LH: I'm getting better at it. Someone once told me "Everyone will say 'no' until someone says 'yes'." Somewhat obvious, but it helps me realize that mass rejections are not part of some conspiracy to get me to go back to my old day job.

FH: Best advice given to you.
LH: If what you're writing makes you uncomfortable in any way, then you're getting close.

FH: One or two pieces of advice for anyone entering the business.
LH: One: Don't wait until you can afford to do it. It's too much work to do part time. Two: When people critique you, listen to everyone, but listen to yourself last. Three: Find people in the business to hang around with, whom you'd hang around with even if they weren't in the business; don't base your relationships on what they can do for you. That's cynical, and it sucks, and it won't work.

TAKE THE BEVERAGE... UNLESS YOU'RE IN AA

Have you ever gone to people's homes when they were about to serve dinner and they asked you if you would join them? And you said "no." Ever notice their reaction? Usually it sinks. That is a deflative moment. You have rejected an offer to join their families. It's not about the meal, folks, it's about family. So here's a twist on that same principle. If you go to a meeting and the receptionist gleefully offers you a drink, take it. Even if you're not thirsty. Take the drink. It's courtesy. It's good manners and even if you don't typically exhibit good manners, stretch yourself this one time for your career's sake.

Avoid making an unusual request. Typically, when you arrive in someone's office, an assistant or receptionist will say, "Can I get you some coffee, water, something to drink?" When this happens, do not say, "What else do you have?" If they had Crystal Light, they'd probably say so. So, be a good dog and make a selection from the menu.

If you're wondering how this subtopic made the book, check out a conversation I heard in 2000 at ICM (International Creative Management), a Hollywood agency. The names have been changed to protect the clueless.

Receptionist: Hi Cyndi, Mark will be right out. Can I get you something to drink? I just made some coffee and we've got some Evian.
Guest: Uh, I don't drink coffee and Evian tastes sorta funny to me. I don't know what it is, it's just weird.
Receptionist smiles weakly.
Receptionist: Well...?
Guest: Got any Perrier?
Receptionist: I don't think we....
Guest: What about cranberry juice?
Receptionist: I can check, but I don't....
Guest: If you've got cranberry that would be great.
Receptionist gets a pained look on her face and walks away. Meanwhile, Cyndi continues to choke me with her fragrance while reading *Elle*, never noticing that she's now become an inconvenience, not only to the receptionist, but also the firm, because you can bet the receptionist is going to tell Mark about the guest's special requests.
Minutes later, the receptionist returns. Empty handed.
Receptionist: Sorry, no Perrier.
Guest: Okay, well I guess I will take that Evian even though....
Receptionist walks off in a huff. Cyndi, as oblivious as ever, continues reading. Receptionist returns with bottled water, which she hands Cyndi, with a pasted smile.
Guest: Thanks, Lydia.
Receptionist: Lisa.
Receptionist walks away, really pissed now. You see what I mean? This is being difficult. Don't be difficult. Don't turn the receptionist into Dolores Claiborne.

THEY LIKE ME, THEY REALLY LIKE ME

You're witty and charming. In fact, four out of five dentists surveyed agree that you have a winning smile. But guess what? Everyone's still not gonna love you and guess what else? That's okay. Improve your craft and get them to like your work first, you second. Some people are so intent on getting everyone involved to like them. All the while, their art stinks, so they never get anywhere. And they wonder why. Gee, I'm a nice person. I bring cookies to the set. I send flowers to producers who reject my scripts. Why don't they like me? Because your work succcccccccks! Look, most people are going to be nice to you, it's in some people's blood, but at the end of the night, it's a business. You can be as nice as Mother Teresa but if your work is mediocre, your career will sink faster than a stone in a fish tank.

JENNA FROM THE BLOCK GOES ONE-ON-ONE WITH FRAN

JENNA GLATZER | EDITOR-IN-CHIEF | *ABSOLUTEWRITE.COM*
FIRST JOB IN THE BIZ | WRITER FOR SCREENWRITING MAGAZINES

FH: Why/how did you decide to get into the entertainment business?
JG: I was a professional actress, and then I was struck by a crippling panic disorder that left me housebound for more than three years. I had to find a way to make a living working from home, so screenwriting sounded like a great way to remain "in the biz" and possibly make a boatload of money.

FH: What was the one perception you had about being in the business that you found out was inaccurate?
JG: I believed I was better than most of the other wannabe screenwriters out there. I believed all I had to do was write my first spec and Steven Spielberg would be knocking at my door, begging to buy it. Then I started reading other spec scripts and finding out that there were LOTS of other talented writers in the game. I learned I had to get better to compete with them.

FH: What do you wish someone had told you prior to your diving in?
JG: Oh, people did tell me how difficult it would be, but I didn't believe them. I had to find out for myself!

FH: Who are/were some of the people you admire (d) in the biz and why?
JG: I admire M. Night Shyamalan for being one of the only screenwriters who can make me gasp out loud in a movie theatre — that's a master storyteller! I admire John Fusco for the way he lives life. I admire Blake Snyder for the way he made up his own screenwriting "rules" along the way, and for his openness to help aspiring screenwriters.

FH: What's been the most difficult aspect of being in the biz?
JG: Keeping hope alive. It's very difficult to keep coming "this close" and having a deal fall through. At those times, I remind myself of scripts like *Forrest Gump* that took, what, 10 years to get made? And then became blockbuster hits. I still plan to be an "overnight success," even if it takes me 30 years to get there.

FH: What do you think you'd be doing if you weren't in the biz?
JG: I'm a freelance writer and editor, in addition to being a screenwriter.

FH: Ever slept with someone to get a job? How'd you feel the next morning?
JG: Heck no. Though it was offered to me. A producer who was supposedly very interested in producing one of my scripts told me I "gave good phone" and wanted to know if I would come to his house. I felt like he was coming onto me, so I mentioned that I would bring my boyfriend with me. He rescinded his offer, telling me it was important that we meet alone. I told him I wasn't comfortable with that. The deal fell through.

FH: Share one hard knocks lesson you learned.
JG: There was a time when I had three or four option contracts come in all at once. I was "between agents" at the time, and decided it was time for me to get a "REAL" agent — one at a major, mover-and-shaker agency. I put my contracts and spec scripts in a briefcase and took a trip into NYC. I walked into William Morris, Paradigm, Writers & Artists, and a couple of other agencies, where I announced to the receptionist that I was there to speak with an agent, any agent. I was sure that, given the fact that I had all of these option contracts with me, **someone** would speak with me! Wrong. I was told that I needed to send a query letter like everyone else. "But I don't have time for that," I said. "I have these option contracts NOW, and I need an agent to negotiate them for me. Look, I'm handing you money on a silver platter. The agent doesn't need to do any footwork — I've already made these deals on my own." Tough noogies. Some of these arguments got heated, and security officers looked at me menacingly, making it clear that if I didn't walk out and send a query like a good little girl, I'd be thrown out.

FH: Share one pattern or mistake you see newbies make (e.g. not understanding how the biz works or not taking mailroom jobs if it gets them in the door).
JG: Sending out bad scripts. Not taking time to learn their craft before torturing Hollywood execs with their 150-page, spiral bound, no-character-arc opuses. Hey, I did it, too. But I learned.

FH: If you had the chance to start your career over, what, if anything, would you do differently?
JG: I wouldn't have signed with every agent who showed an interest in me. I would have started at the top and waited to garner the interest of a solid, WGA signatory agent.

FH: How do you handle rejection?
JG: Fine. I'm still cocky enough to know that I haven't wasted anyone's time with my scripts. I realize that there are many factors that go into a producer's decision — such as budget, roles for actors, genre, locations, etc., and that a good script may be turned down for reasons that have nothing to do with the quality of the writing.

FH: One or two pieces of advice for wannabes.
JG: Use the Internet! People are really making deals online. Take every possible chance at exposure. Almost all of my script options have come from producers I "met" through e-mail queries. Don't be shy — network with other writers. Trade leads, share contacts. Be a generous writer and karma will do its thing.

IS THERE LIFE AFTER REJECTION?

Look, it's a movie. It's a commercial. It's a song. It's a part, yeah, it's the lead, but it's still just a part. It's not going to kill you if you don't get the deal, the role, the movie. If you keep at it, there'll be more parts, more auditions, more deals. I should know. Last February my agent called with unusual news.

A producer at a major cable network wanted to bring me in to audition for an anchor/host position on a baseball show. "They really liked your tape," my agent said. I took the phone away from my ear and frowned. If they'd seen my tape, surely they knew that basketball, not baseball, was my thang. But they had seen my tape and they still wanted to bring me in for the audition.

So, I did what any self-respecting professional would do in that circumstance. I taped three baseball games and had a good friend (who knows everything about baseball) come over and administer a crash course. She took me through each play, rewinding the tape when I'd call a no-hitter a zero-hitter. "It's a no-hitter, Fran," she'd say, laughing. Or I'd asked her, "Isn't that Mark Maguire?" Only to be told that he'd retired two years earlier.

A week after my Baseball For Dummies class, I flew to the East Coast for my audition and met with the network producers, who said, "We know your thing's basketball but you're here for a reason — we think you have something special. We don't care about the baseball thing." Wow. Those words were music to my ears. But that melody would be the last good thing I heard that day.

Next up? Me in the anchor's chair getting ready for baseball highlights. Yikes! Now, for the record, I know what a baseball looks like and I know what a home run is, but that's about it. My baseball knowledge doesn't go much deeper or wider. And boy, did it show! The whole time I was stumbling over the plays, I kept telling myself that it was cool. "I'm not a baseball person. They knew that when they brought me in here!"

This was, of course, no consolation to me. Someone who's used to stepping up to the line and sinking the shot. Fortunately, the audition, er agony, soon ended and I was on a plane, on my way back home with a big "R" on my forehead. What a disaster! And as I sat in the airport eating a bite of my forbidden Popeye's fried chicken, I reflected on the remains of my broadcasting career. Then it was time to move past the rejection and on to the next opportunity.

The baseball audition had taught me one thing: sometimes people see things in us that we don't see in ourselves. But when they give us chances to shine, we need to forget about our shortcomings and just step up to the plate and knock that sucker out of the gym, er, ballpark.

THE LONG AND WINDING EXPLANATION

The longer you're in the business, the more feedback you'll get. You'll probably get more than you want. And definitely more than you asked for. Develop a stomach for input because once you decide to go into showbiz, everybody feels it's a duty and a right to give you an opinion often without your asking for it. Some people are resistant to feedback and handle receiving it by explaining or making excuses every time someone offers an opinion. Save it. You don't have to defend your work. You don't have to explain why you chose to sing something a certain way, write something a certain way, or shoot something a certain way. It's one thing to be in a meeting and an executive or instructor asks what was behind your creative choice. That's different. That's an invitation for discussion. But if someone says to you, "I didn't like that she died at the end," you don't have to explain why you killed this character, but it might be useful to gain some insight as to why this person responded that way to the death of the character. If someone says "I thought it would sound better if you went up on that last note of the song," that's an opinion. If you object to or defend yourself every time anyone has a different opinion, you'll find yourself spending an inordinate amount of time in conversations that do little to improve your art.

Here are some suggestions for handling feedback.
- Listen to it all.
- Embrace it all.
- Make note of feedback that rubs you the wrong way or intrigues you. What annoys us often presents us with a big growth opportunity.
- You may want to explore why you responded the way you did. Sometimes it will make sense to change, sometimes it won't.
- Don't be afraid to try it a different way. Sometimes the best outcomes are the results of listening to feedback and putting the suggestions to work. Don't be so set in your ways that you can't at least entertain the idea that your work can be improved by someone else's recommendations.

EVERYBODY USES EVERYBODY

If you haven't seen the sequel to *Saturday Night Fever*, the 1983 film, *Staying Alive* lately, rent it. In the movie, Tony Manero, played by John Travolta, is trying to land a role, any role, but what he really wants is the lead in a Broadway musical called *Satan's Alley*. He tries out for the musical and gets the part. And although he's already in a loving, supportive relationship with Jackie (played by the very capable Cynthia Rhodes), he can't help but go coo-coo for Cocoa Puffs when he sees the irresistible Laura, the lead dancer in the show played by Finola Hughes.

After some fairly believable rounds of hard-to-get, Laura gives in and gives Tony some play. And a few scenes later, they hit the sheets, which he denies when confronted by Jackie. He and Jackie ultimately break up. Shortly after he begins what he thinks is a relationship with Laura, she invites him to a party but, apparently, wants everyone there to know that she's "with no one."

Tony, in all of his Brooklyn bravado, is upset by Laura's dismissal and decides to call her on the carpet. Then, in remarkable rejective fashion, he asks her, "What we did? It don't mean nothing?" To which she says, "It was nice."

After a few rounds of verbal calisthenics, Laura tells Tony not to go nuts just because they had sex. Finally, when she's had enough of Tony's junior high school antics, she pulls away from him and announces, "Everybody uses everybody." And with that, she sashays away, leaving Tony looking like a little boy who's lost his mommy in the grocery store.

In that moment, Tony's introduced to some of the harsh, but true, realities of the entertainment biz. Actors sleeping with directors. Directors sleeping with dancers. It's a sad world, after all.

Now, maybe you think Laura's right. Everybody uses everybody. I don't. And when you're a starving wannabe, your desire to be seen or discovered is often so intense that you walk around with a sign on your head that reads, "I want something from you" to every industry person you meet. You meet a director, the sign changes. *I want to be in your movie.* You meet a producer, the sign reads, *I want you to read my script.* You get the picture. It's a fluorescent pink sign with black letters. There's no hiding it. But it's a turnoff. A huge one.

Nobody wants anybody to think the only reason you're talking is that you want a deal at the end of the night. If that's your approach to making it in Hollywood, keep the job at IHOP; you're better suited to balancing a short stack and a plate of hash browns. That's right. People would have you believe that you've gotta step on and over every man or woman in Hollywood to be successful. You don't. How do I know? Because in a span of about 12 weeks, I sold a book, had a reality show optioned, and almost had a script bought and made into a movie. And I didn't lie, cheat, or abuse one person. Well, there was that one person, but he deserved it.

BLADDER MANAGEMENT

For the record, you need to manage your liquids on meeting days. Yes, I know I said it's a good idea to take the beverage, but don't drink it all unless you know beyond a shadow of a doubt, that you'll have a second to run to the restroom before anyone comes out to get you. You cannot know this, so don't risk it. Who wants to come out to the foyer, call your name, only to hear from some other wannabe, "I think she went to the little wannabe's room." Nobody. So, take a tip. Sip. There are times when it's okay to rush to the restroom. The following two cases, for the record, are not those times.

- When the executive walks out to invite you into his office.
- During the meeting, right at the height of an executive saying, "So, does the hero get the girl?" Don't say, "I gotta go to the little scribe's room." Bad form.

Here's the deal with restroom interruptions. They disrupt the flow. It's not brain surgery, it's common sense. If an executive or agent is ready to see you and you're not ready — for whatever reason — it messes with the flow. Flow is very important. Smooth conversations make for better meetings and more importantly, future meetings. If you're constantly bouncing up to go the restroom or answer your phone, you break up the continuity of the meeting. Avoid it.

THE GOOD DOCTOR GOES ONE-ON-ONE WITH FRAN

SHEILA GALLIEN | SHEILA GALLIEN SCREENPLAY CONSULTING
FIRST JOB IN THE BIZ | CASTING ASSISTANT TO A CASTING ASSISTANT.
BUT MY FIRST REAL JOB WAS ASSISTANT TO A LITERARY AGENT AT CREATIVE
ARTISTS AGENCY.

FH: Why/how did you decide to get into the entertainment business?
SG: After my third bout with college, I finally graduated with a degree in theater arts, mostly because that was the field in which I had the most units. Plus, theater had seduced me, with its collaborative nature, away from the solitary world of fiction writing. After graduation, I wanted to do something creative, but wasn't sure what. My first love was writing, but it seemed so out of reach. I wasn't good enough at dance to be a professional dancer (and I was too old — 28). But I loved performing. So I thought I'd try acting (ha ha, the easy path) and I moved to L.A. to kind of check out the business, get a job, and study acting. My mother is a talent agent, so I wasn't completely naive about the business, and she had some people lined up for me to meet to learn more. People had warned me that a theater arts degree wouldn't help

me get a job, but I never believe people, so I started hunting for work, meeting everyone I could and sending out my resume. In the meantime, I started studying acting, and my mother informed me that I would need to get a boob job if I wanted to get any work. It didn't take long for me to figure out that the acting thing wasn't for me. I had a modicum of talent, and I liked it, but I was up against people who were full of fire for acting, were gorgeous, and would do anything to get a job, including a boob job.

FH: What was the one perception you had about being in the business that you found out was inaccurate?
SG: That successful people need as much sleep as I do.

FH: What do you wish someone had told you prior to your diving in?
SG: It's not just who you know, it's how you treat them. The smartest people treat everyone well, and everyone the same. Because today's assistant is tomorrow's studio head.

FH: Who are/were some of the people you admire (d) in the biz and why?
SG: Everyone I admire in the business I admire for the same qualities: they have passion, integrity, the ability to acknowledge the personal nature of the business without being controlled by it, and respect. Topping this list for me is William Broyles, Jr., and Fox 2000's Elizabeth Gabler. But there are many more.

FH: What's been the most difficult aspect of being in the biz?
SG: I think it's hard to remember that it's a business. Like Cameron Crowe's great line, "It's not show friends, it's show business!" You have to remember, at all times, that millions and millions of dollars are on the line. Whatever happens, it's nothing personal. And even if it is, it's nothing personal. To excel both creatively and at the business — that's extremely difficult, and unusual.

FH: What do you think you'd be doing if you weren't in the biz?
SG: Is it still too late for me to be an astronaut?

FH: Ever slept with someone to get a job? How'd you feel the next morning?
SG: Should I be offended that no one has ever offered?

FH: Share one hard knocks lesson you learned.
SG: When I first started at CAA, a client called whose script I had just read. I'd really liked it, and told him so, then just had to throw in how much it reminded me of another movie, in the same genre, that had done really well. There was a long silence, and that was our last conversation. Learning what not to say is at least as important in this business as learning what to say.

FH: Share one pattern or mistake you see newbies make.
SG: Thinking that they are the first ones to come up with the idea of being "refreshingly candid." Communication in this, and maybe any, business is quite subtle. The louder you are about it, the more of an amateur you appear to be.

FH: If you had the chance to start your career over, what, if anything, would you do differently?
SG: How could I beat the way my career started?

FH: How do you handle rejection?
SG: With my own writing, I grieve. I might eat ice cream. I used to drink tequila. Then I get back to it. When I have to be a part of dishing out rejection, I try to give writers as much time and room as I can to recover, then encourage them to get up and get back to it. Time to recover your dignity, that's all you need.

FH: Best advice given to you.
SG: Listen. That way you know what you know, and what the other person knows, as well.

FH: One or two pieces of advice for wannabes.
SG: Remember your soul.

IS THERE A DOCTOR IN THE HOUSE?

Unless you're on call to deliver a set of twins, it's probably a good idea to turn off the cell phone or two-way pager when you go to meetings and auditions. Execs don't play by the same rules you and I do. They can have pagers and cell phones going off all they want, but having your phone go off in a meeting that you had to scratch and claw to get, is not a good thing. Having your devices set to vibrate won't work either because if your phone's like mine, the voice mail indicator will go off sounding like the Emergency Broadcasting System signal. Remember to power them off so that nothing on your end disrupts your meeting.

THE ELEVATOR BITCH

When you go to auditions or meetings, you never know who you're gonna be riding on an elevator with, so, be nice. You don't have to discuss the day's headlines. People who launch into full conversations on elevators scare me a little, but it's okay to say, "good morning" or "afternoon." You don't really have time to carry on a conversation unless you're going to the 105th floor. Just know that being a grump to the wrong person, might botch the deal for you.

Last summer, while I was in L.A. attending a masters screenwriting class, my attorney helped me get meetings with a couple of producers and mini-studios to pitch some ideas for TV shows. One morning, rather early, I walked onto the elevator with a guy. We both smiled and said hello. "You played in the WNBA?" he asked. I was wearing a Lee denim jacket with a WNBA patch on it. "Yep. Houston." He smiled. The bell sounded and he got out of the elevator. When I arrived at my floor, I waited in the reception area for a few moments before they took me to the office where my pitch was to take place.

When I walked into the room, guess who was sitting in front of me? Yep. The guy on the elevator. The top dawg. Fortunately, we'd already had a pleasant exchange, so there was no need for me to try to undo any negative vibes I'd sent on the elevator. But imagine how my meeting might have gone had I been unfriendly on the ride upstairs. I don't even want to think about it. But I hope this little story serves as sufficient warning to all grim elevator reapers. Add a tablespoon of Metamucil to your coffee on the morning of your meeting if you have to, but don't be a grump.

> **"I saw losing my virginity as a career move."**
>
> — *Madonna*
> *recording artist/actress*

A TRAILER BLAZER GOES ONE-ON-ONE WITH FRAN

LESLIE SLOAN | EDITOR/TRAILER/TELEVISION ADVERTISING FOR MOTION PICTURES | WINSTON DAVIS & ASSOCIATES
FIRST JOB IN THE BIZ | WHEEL OF FORTUNE-RECEPTIONIST

FH: Why/how did you decide to get into the entertainment business?
LS: I knew it was the only business I wanted to work in but I didn't know what exactly that meant and what I could actually do. I was living in Chicago at the time and was about to move into a new apartment. Right before I moved in I got a call from the landlord saying the apartment had burned down. That was my sign to go!

FH: What was the one perception you had about being in the business that you found out was inaccurate?
LS: Coming from a little bit of a sheltered existence, I didn't have a true sense of the real world. I thought that everyone in Hollywood had huge ambitions, huge drive and that it was a very competitive environment... and I thought that's ALL it was. When you're living outside of the system sometimes you think only the "connected" have a shot at making it so, it was refreshing to get here and discover that there were so many smart, driven, and creative people in the business.

FH: What do you wish someone had told you prior to your diving in?
LS: I don't think anything could have been said. I'd imagine it would all make me worry.

FH: Who are/were some of the people you admire (d) in the biz and why?
LS: My current boss, Dean Blagg, who was driven, hard working, talented from a very young age and never let his (young) age get in the way of being very successful. My former bosses, Cathy and Pat Finn, who showed me love and respect always.

FH: What's been the most difficult aspect of being in the biz?
LS: Not knowing exactly what it was I was going to do that I actually enjoyed doing.

FH: What would you be doing if you weren't in the biz?
LS: Teaching or running an old folks' home.

FH: Have you ever slept with someone to get ahead?
LS: No.

FH: Share one hard knocks lesson you learned.
LS: The star of the show is the star of the show.

FH: Share one pattern or mistake you see newbies make.
LS: Not being satisfied with where they are.

FH: If you had the chance to start your career over, what, if anything, would you do differently?
LS: I would have jumped on the Avid when I had a chance about six years earlier. (But that's ok, I had other things to do)... Saved more money.

FH: How do you handle rejection?
LS: Try not to make it mean anything about you as a person. Keep it outside of yourself.

FH: Best advice given to you.
LS: Go for what you think you might want to do. If you are not crystal clear, that is ok, DO SOMETHING!

FH: One or two pieces of advice for wannabes.
LS: Don't wannabe. Do what you wannabe doing. And start where you think you want to end up, be direct in your route. Take the job that is the most direct route to where you want to be.

WOULD YOU LIKE SOME FRIES WITH THAT BUSINESS CARD?

I like realtors. Some of my closest ex-friends are realtors, but my God, they love to hand out their business cards, don't they? I mean, I've never seen realtors without business cards, have you? No, you haven't, because they are never without them. Their cards are like extra body parts just hanging around, waiting to be used. Sometimes wannabes are the same way. Quick to tell ya what they do and how they do it better than the next person. Realtors are good examples of what to do and what not to do. First, what TO do. Always have cards with you. It cuts out all of the unnecessary conversations revolving around, "Do you have a pen?" or "Got any paper?"

Some realtors are also terrific examples of what NOT to do — giving people cards who don't ask for them. Now, I think it's a great idea to have your cards on you. In fact, I can't think of one place I'd go where I wouldn't carry cards, but what I don't recommend is shoving 'em down people's throats before you even get out the last syllable of your first name. That's a little annoying. It's okay to carry your demos or scripts in your car, but flashing a CD or script at a luncheon is tacky. Unless you are asked to bring your stuff to a social event or lunch, don't. If your conversation turns to your work and the person asks for a copy, simply send it through the mail or have it messengered to the office. The only reason you should ever give someone materials over lunch or on the street is if someone says something like, "If you have a copy on you, I can take it back to the office with me right now."

Why? What's the big deal with handing someone materials at lunch or the doctor's office? Nothing, if only one person does it every once in a while, but imagine going from meeting to meeting and at every meeting having someone give you a script or a reel or a resume. Besides, there's less of a chance of materials being lost or damaged if they're delivered to an office where they can be placed in the company system upon arrival.

A PLUNGER GOES ONE-ON-ONE WITH FRAN

JOHNETTE DUFF | SCREENWRITER | *THE DEVIL WENT DOWN*
I MET JOHNETTE DUFF ONE WEEK AT A REEL WOMEN MEETING AND WITHIN A FEW WEEKS SHE WAS TAKING THE PLUNGE AND MOVING TO LOS ANGELES TO "GIVE IT A SHOT."

FIRST JOB IN THE BIZ | I DROPPED OUT OF LAW SCHOOL TO GO TO FILM SCHOOL IN THE '90s AND WORKED ON A COUPLE OF FILMS

FH: Why/how did you decide to get into the entertainment business?
JD: I've wanted to be a writer since the age of 10. Took me a while to figure out that the screenplay was the best medium for me.

FH: What was the one perception you had about being in the business that you found out was inaccurate?
JD: I expected people in L.A. to be snotty, but I have made so many friends and met so many kindred spirits (unlike my year-long sojourn in Austin, where I found the tech takeover had made Texas hospitality a thing of the past). Also, in film school, my biggest surprise was how dismissive the producers and directors are of the "talent" (i.e. the actors).

FH: What do you wish someone had told you prior to your diving in?
JD: That people were so friendly out here.

FH: Who are/were some of the people you admire (d) in the biz and why?
JD: I love writers.

FH: What's been the most difficult aspect of being in the biz?
JD: Talent plus determination plus networking skills and finally getting that lucky break!

FH: What do you think you'd be doing if you weren't in the biz?
JD: Probably go back to practicing law, although I sincerely hope this never happens.

FH: Ever slept with someone to get a job? How'd you feel the next morning?
JD: Nope.

FH: Share one hard knocks lesson you learned.
JD: Although I have won/placed in screenwriting contests, and have a loyal group of screenwriting friends who are convinced I know what I'm doing, the whole process is still so slanted toward rejection — takes so many "nos" to get to one "yes."

FH: Share one pattern or mistake you see newbies make.
JD: Not learning their craft. Not putting in the time.

FH: If you had the chance to start your career over, what, if anything, would you do differently?
JD: Go to film school before law school.

FH: How do you handle rejection?
JD: I expect it, so I am pleasantly surprised when it doesn't happen. Letting it get to you is the end — you have to jump over it and go on to the next thing.

FH: Best advice given to you.
JD: It's a battle of attrition — keep throwing it against the wall and, eventually, it will stick!

FH: One or two pieces of advice for anyone entering the business.
JD: Don't quit. If this is your dream, don't let anyone dissuade you. But, then again, make sure you are self-aware enough to listen to the other voices — if you are told over and over again that you don't have the talent or preparation, get the training and preparation. Not giving up is the only way to get there.

UNCHAINED MENTORING

I love it when people who are not in the business try to tell you how to be in the business. And I'm equally amazed at how much stock wannabes put in the advice of other people who have no clue about the entertainment world. Here's a tip. Get a mentor. Mentors are great for helping you move your career forward, but make sure your mentor is someone who's done the grind. Make sure he or she actually knows what it's like to walk in your shoes. Otherwise, they're not mentors, they're advisors. In other words, as a writer, one of my most effective mentors is going to be another writer, preferably with more experience. Someone who knows what this journey's about. My musician friend may be able to show me some of the ropes within the business in general (which is valuable), but she won't do me much good when I'm stumped on how to improve the second act of my screenplay.

So, where do you find a mentor in show business if you live in Buford, South Carolina? First, call your chamber of commerce and inquire about any Buford-Hollywood connections. There's a group called the Texas Exes in Hollywood that is, basically, a group of individuals who attended my alma mater, The University of Texas at Austin, and are now making a living in Hollywood. It's a terrific networking and support organization. Perhaps there's a similar group where you're from. Don't assume that because your town's the peach fuzz capital of the world that there aren't some Tinseltown hook ups there.

You can also check out some sites, such as the Writers Guild (*www.wga.org*) or The Writer's Channel (*www.writerschannel.net*), which boast different kinds of mentoring programs worth checking out.

SAY IT LOUD, I'M ___ AND I'M PROUD

Being ethnic is a good thing. I don't care what Trent Lott says. Sure, being white's always gonna be chic in Hollywood, but the good news for the rest of us is that there's never been a better time to be a non-white in the business. Society's changing. Movies are finally, slowly starting to reflect the face of the greater community. Commercials are becoming more racially and culturally diverse. The music industry's had a profound impact on the TV and film business, showing that it's not only cool to be urban or cultural, but it's good business to include multicultural themes and talent in properties. Yet, even though it's becoming more en vogue to look ethnic, some people are still afraid that their careers will suffer if they don't fit the mainstream definition of talent and beauty.

I used to work with a Latin woman who purposely "passed" as a white girl, even though she was Puerto Rican. I'll call her Mo. And Mo thought that even though she didn't look overly Latina that she wouldn't get as many parts if people knew she was brown and not white. It seemed like a lot of work to hide your identity, but she felt it worked for her. That is, until she discovered that being brown was suddenly in fashion. Almost overnight she began to let her Latina come out. She started using her natural accent and accentuating her culture in how she looked and dressed, but by then people had already decided that she was "too white" to be brown. Consequently, she missed out on tons of parts that she would have been great for, had she only stayed true to herself and let the chips fall. Who knows? Had she kept it real, we might be talking about Slo-Mo instead of J-Lo, although I seriously doubt that anything can stop *The Six*.

AGENTS: LOVE 'EM OR LEAVE 'EM?

It's a rule. Everyone has to have at least one agent from hell story in his career. Maybe yours will be on the front end, maybe on the back end, but whenever it happens, rest assured, it *will* happen. It's pretty inevitable.

I was fortunate enough to have one of my most unpleasant experiences early in my career and another semi-hellion within the last few years that, fortunately, never developed into full representation, because I decided to walk away before we got in too deep with one another.

Wouldn't it be great to find that first real agent love, get to know him or her, settle down, and live happily ever after? Wouldn't that be so white picket fence-like? I think Sir Isaac Newton should have created a law related to this phenomenon. He might have called it the "Law of Agentosity," but probably something much more clever.

Anyway, about the agent from you-know-where. We'll call him Sam. He was a referral through someone I didn't know and had never met. Let me explain.

I was in the bookstore browsing the business section and I came across one that really piqued my interest. The author's picture was on the front and he seemed like a nice person — at least from his photo — so I looked for his East Coast agency's phone number in directory assistance and called him the next morning.

His assistant put me through and we immediately began a seemingly effortless conversation. I told him that I had read his entire book while standing in the business aisle at the bookstore and that I liked what he had to say about integrity in business and how to maintain solid relationships with people at all levels. This was true, by the way. I wasn't pulling the old "butter up" maneuver. I only do that in case of emergencies and as best I could tell, no margarine would be needed in this initial conversation.

I told him that I wanted to write a book and I was wondering if he had any literary agency recommendations. To no surprise, he did. Of course, he did. Everybody in New York knows a lit agent, just like everyone in Los Angeles knows a producer or at least someone who's slept with a producer.

Anyway, he gave me the name of one individual, Sam, (we'll talk about why one is the loneliest number later) and told me to give him a call. He said that he was "really nice." Oh, for the record, be weary of people who describe other people as "really nice."

It took me about 10 minutes to gather the notes and outline for the book I wanted to write and then I called Sam. Now, notice what just happened here. In less than 12 hours, I'd found a person who didn't know me from the hot dog vendor at Fenway Park; he gave me the phone number of his agent who, in a few magical telephone moments, would also be my agent. That's the way the biz works. You find one person who's connected to the one person you need to talk to and 75% of your work is done. Why? Because 99.9% of us will talk to someone recommended by a friend or client. That's the first hurdle. The next hurdle requires you to be brilliant in that first phone conversation or meeting.

I was ready. I practiced my pitch and then I touch toned the number as confidently as I could. The phone rang and yes, my heart was pounding. I felt like Dena, the MCI telemarketer whom I hang up on every week — here I was calling to give this potential agent something he might want, but probably already had. Worse, I thought, he'll think I'm like the other 41 wannabe writers who've called him today, but had weak and unsellable book ideas and nothing intelligent to say. Above all, I wanted to avoid fiber optic hell. That place where people who don't give good phone languish for the first year of their careers.

All of the pre-game drama aside, it was time to put up. I was slightly nervous but excited at the same time. Sweaty palms and twitchy facial organs are all part of being a wannabe. Luckily for you, there is a remedy. It's called practice and you'll get lots of it by the time you finish this book.

When Sam answered the phone, I introduced myself and in the same sentence explained how I'd gotten his phone number. He didn't hang up, which was a good thing and my first minor success. I told him about the book I wanted to write. He said he liked the idea and wanted to see a proposal. I asked if he had any good resources for proposal writing. He gave me the name of a book that he claimed would walk me through the process. I rushed out to buy the book and Sam was right. For the most part, the proposal writing process was like filling in a template using my own words and style. Within a day or so I had a complete proposal ready to send to him for review.

The day he received the proposal he called. "I love it!" he said. He wanted more of my press materials but said that, basically, the proposal was perfect. We immediately began talking about working together. Sam said he had a simple agency agreement that he would fax to me for my review and that he believed we could do really well with this proposal, which was about succeeding in business.

I was in heaven, a place I wouldn't stay for long, but at least I was there for the time being. I never spoke to another agent after I began the journey with Sam, something I never recommend to anyone. It's always a good idea to talk to two to three agents, just to get different perspectives and to have some comparison material.

But I was new to the publishing game and when you're new, you make some interesting (read: stupid) decisions, unless you have someone in your life who knows the ropes or unless you own a book like this. In either case, I was about to get an education.

Sam called and said that the proposal "went out," a phrase you'll hear in screenwriting, acting, modeling, and other circles. When something or someone "goes out," it simply means people are reviewing whatever was submitted. In this case, the book proposal went out to a slew of publishers about five days after I signed with this agent. What happened next is enough to make any wannabe drool. You're drooling already, aren't you?

I had just gotten back to my house from a massage when the phone rang. I snatched it up.
"You ready for this?" he said.
"I think so," I responded. "It depends."
"Your book's about to go into auction," he said.
"That's great," I exclaimed, not knowing exactly what "auction" meant, but by the sound of his voice, it was really good, so I started smiling, too. "That's a good thing, right?" I asked.
He laughed. "That's the best-case scenario."

Now, I was pumped. A best-case scenario on my first time out of the gate? I was in the *penthouse* of heaven now!

Sam shared that editors from five of the country's largest publishers loved my writing, thought I had a unique voice and really liked the book idea. The next step would be a bidding war for rights to publish the book, a process that would take place via fax in a few days. I was ecstatic.

Friday came and the bidding began. Auctions can occur for books, screenplays, movie rights, just about anything. But when publishers bid on a book, it typically means that the publisher decides on an amount it's willing to spend on an advance for your book. And when several people are willing to make offers for anything you've done or written, it's always cause for celebration.

All day long I sat on a porcupine, waiting to hear the good news. About midday, Sam called and said that three of the five publishers had dropped out of the race but that for the last hour, two of them had continued to outbid each other. I liked the sound of that. Surely the end result would mean that at minimum, I'd be dining at my favorite five-star restaurant and this time, I could leave a tip.

Around 2:00 in the afternoon, he called and said that the larger publisher had acquired the book, that they were excited to have the chance to work with me and that the editor who had bought the book wanted to speak with me the next day. By early evening, the dust had settled and I was on my way to my favorite eatery, a successful writing career, and a happy marriage with my agent... or so I thought.

My first book sold within two weeks of writing the proposal. It enjoyed a healthy auction and upon receiving the first installment on my respectable five-figure book advance, I paid a hefty sum for a set of custom made golf clubs that now reside comfortably in my garage. But it was worth it and boy, you can't ask for a better on-ramp into the HOV lane of Hollywood than selling a book in 14 days or less.

So, you ask, where's the agent from hell part? Well, it started after the sale of my next non-fiction book. When you write a non-fiction book, you usually have six to 12 months to complete the manuscript. That's a long time in my world, so I was already thinking about where I could take my career. I've always enjoyed storytelling and I wanted to explore writing fiction.

So, of course, I shared my vision with Sam, who, surprisingly, didn't appear to be too enthusiastic about my two-sport aspirations.

"I think you should stick with non-fiction for now," he said, not really offering much insight into his way of thinking. And since I was the kind of child that always asked her mother "why?" I pursued the conversation.

"Well, Sam, am I hearing that you are not interested in repping me as a fiction writer?" I asked. "Will you at least take a look at it?"

"I think you should focus on your non-fiction," he answered. "I'd like to work on your non-fiction projects."

"That's fair. But since I've got a year to complete the next non-fiction project you just sold, I'm working on a novel, too."

There wasn't a whole lot of conversation on the line that day and to be honest, I wasn't sure why. I'd made every effort to stimulate dialogue, but never really got Sam to participate or to tell me why he was not open to the idea of my writing a novel.

My next step was to find someone to look at my novel. Through a friend, I found an agent who was willing to give it a weekend read. When I shared with Sam, what I thought was good news regarding my fiction, his reply was and I quote, "Well, if this agent likes your fiction so much, maybe he can have all of your work." End quote.

Ouch! That was not the response I anticipated hearing from this "really nice" agent. And I must admit, I was floored and hurt. I reminded Sam that I had made several attempts to have meaningful conversations with him about my novel. I'd even asked him to read it, but he never seemed to have time to get around to it. Yet, now that someone else was interested in it, he wanted to serve up attitude? That didn't seem fair and I told him so. It became clear in that final five-minute conversation with Sam, that I'd learned my lesson and that it was time for me to move on, so I did.

I'll always be grateful to Sam. You can't fault someone who gets excited about your work and truly fights for you with editors, and Sam got four gold sticky stars for those efforts. But when it came down to my vision for my career and more importantly, building a strong personal relationship, laced with respect and effective communication, Sam and I were like salt and pepper.

What I learned through my Sam years is that all that glitters ain't gold and that no matter how high profile or successful an agent is, no one has the right to treat another person as irrelevant, period. I learned that it's always a good idea to get a second opinion and that what makes for a good agent for one person, might mean a nightmare for you and vice versa. Do your homework and always, always listen to that small, still voice inside your heart, not your head. Take your time when choosing an agent. Don't just get an agent because you're desperate. Talk to more than one agent and decide who's the best match for you, given (1) your personality, (2) your career goals, and (3) their track records.

Now, let's turn our attention to clients from hell. You didn't think I'd let us off that easily, did you? That wouldn't be fair. And not nearly as much fun, either.

DO YOU KNOW THE WAY TO CLIENT PURGATORY?

Don't hide, little hellions. I see you clients from hell back there in the last row. Most of you know who you are. You're the clients who call your agent every day bitching about the job you didn't get. You threaten to leave your agent if she doesn't get you X number of jobs in the next six months. Is this starting to sound like you? If you're sitting there wondering if you're the client from hell, may I recommend that you rent the movie *Tootsie*, starring Dustin Hoffman. If you see any likeness between Michael Dorsey, the character Hoffman plays, and yourself, you are at least related to the client from hell.

There are tons of reasons people become clients from hell. First, they were little hellions as kids. Never learned to play well with others. Bossed their parents around. You get the picture. Second, most hellion clients are so narcissistic that they don't realize how much they're hurting themselves and their careers. If you're difficult to work with, nobody's going to be motivated to help you. Oh, sure, your agents may get you gigs here and there, just to shut you up, but they won't plow through brick walls for you as they do for respectful clients who always say "thank you" and "please." Your friends may concede to your tirades but, ultimately, even they will get tired of your antics.

And guess what else? Pretty soon, you won't be able to get anybody to work with or for you because the price is too high. If you're a client, writer, singer, or artist from hell, I'd be willing to bet that most of the people around you don't really *like* you, they tolerate you. Maybe because you're a talented person. Maybe because you have money or connections. Maybe because they think they deserve your treatment. But sooner than later, your behavior's going to catch up with you and when it does, I hope you've invested well, because it's going to be a long climb back from oblivion.

A MULTI-TASKER GOES ONE-ON-ONE WITH FRAN

BETSY AMY-VOGT | PRODUCTION ASSISTANT | *AT STAR*
FIRST JOB IN THE BIZ | P.A. AT A DIRECT RESPONSE AD AGENCY IN IOWA

FH: Why/how did you decide to get into the entertainment business?
BAV: I never really made a conscious decision. I wanted to be in theater, but I got a scholarship to study TV/video production, so, I decided that was close enough to theater, and since it was free, I took it! Then I got a job as an intern at an ad agency and a year later I married my boss's son, who was also in the business and so that was that... 10 years later I'm still working.

FH: What was the one perception you had about being in the business that you found out was inaccurate?
BAV: If you work hard you'll get ahead. Bullshit! You need to work hard AND know the right people AND be in the right place at the right time.

FH: What do you wish someone had told you prior to your diving in?
BAV: You're only as good as your last job. There's no resting on your laurels when you're freelance, you have to work to impress as much on your 100th job as on your first.

FH: Who are/were some of the people you admire (d) in the biz and why?
BAV: Anyone who sticks it out and keeps going, despite the odds. There are a million talented people out there who deserve recognition, but only a few ever get it.

FH: What's been the most difficult aspect of being in the biz?
BAV: Being freelance is difficult, never knowing when your next job or check is coming. A lot of people can't deal with it, but if you can learn to live without a regular paycheck, the rewards are enormous.

FH: What do you think you'd be doing if you weren't in the biz?
BAV: Managing a bank!

FH: Ever slept with someone to get a job? How'd you feel the next morning?
BAV: Do people REALLY do this? No one ever offered me! (Except my husband... and he doesn't count!)

FH: Share one hard knocks lesson you learned.
BAV: PAY ATTENTION to everything, ALL the time, ESPECIALLY the unspoken messages. Passive aggressive behavior is common in insecure people — and there are a lot of us in this business! I once misread a client who was really annoyed with me, but was "being polite" and not showing it openly. Come to find out he was bitching to the director and producer about me behind my back, and I never worked with that company again.

FH: Share one pattern or mistake you see newbies make.
BAV: There's a lot of down time on a shoot, but you can never relax. I see many new P.A.s who think that, because they're waiting around, they can goof off and stop paying attention. But then they're needed and they drop the ball. You have to learn to be on constant standby, completely alert for the time you're needed, but still able to chat and hang out with the other crew.

FH: If you had the chance to start your career over, what, if anything, would you do differently?
BAV: When we first moved to Austin I was worried about money and too scared to go freelance. I took the first job that was offered to me and spent three miserable years working in a non-creative position in advertising. If I could do it over I would be braver and run the risk of going freelance. Even when times are dry for production work, there are always other ways to earn a living rather than getting stuck in the daily office grind.

FH: How do you handle rejection?
BAV: Rejection? No one ever rejects me because I'm so wonderful at my job — they ALL call me back, and I can't handle all the work knocking on my door. Um... rejection. Hmmm. I deny that it happens and make excuses to myself as to why someone isn't calling me any more.

FH: Best advice given to you.
BAV: Again... "You're only as good as your last job."

FH: One or two pieces of advice for wannabes.
BAV: Make friends in the business. And I don't mean network or be sycophantic — spend time to search out genuine, real friends whom you truly enjoy spending time with. If you can't find anyone you get along with, then you don't have the right personality for this business. When you work really long days in miserable conditions, you have to have a certain personality to keep cheerful and keep having a good time. For me, 90% of it is that when I'm working I feel like I'm hanging out with my friends. On every shoot, I see people I worked with before and I get a chance to catch up with them, and I meet new friends I know I'll work with again. The other 10% is just the determination not to give in and to prove I can do it!

FH: Open forum, freelance – add whatever else you want to add.
BAV: That's it. I have to go be social and do things with my family now! I'll see if I can get my husband to fill this out as well... but it might be tough to drag him away from the mince pies!

THE RIGHT PERSON

The mistake lots of wannabes make is trying to impress "the right person." Let me dispel one myth right now. There are no "right people," everybody is "the right person." For some people that's going to take more time to sink in because we've all been conditioned to think that there are certain asses to be kissed when, in reality, ass kissing is optional in Hollywood. Respect and courtesy, however, go a long way in and out of Tinseltown. If you can learn anything it's to be as nice to the person who picks up the phone as the person who has the office with the view.

"… a vagina and a point of view —
that's a deadly combination."

— *Sharon Stone, actress*

FRAN'S GOLDEN RULE #4: CHANGE YOUR PICTURES

What are your pictures? What images do you hold for this journey? Do you see yourself as a success only if you...

> Become rich and famous?
> Become the highest paid actor or actress in Hollywood?
> Direct your first feature by age 30?
> Become a multi-platinum recording artist?
> Get nominated for an Academy Award?
> Sell your script for seven figures?

If those are the pictures you hold for what success is, then there's a chance that you will not reach those marks. Then what? See, the problem with most of us is that we've been suckered into defining success by what "they" say success is. Big mistake. You may never sell seven million albums and knock off Eminem's record. Your film may never out box office *The Lord Of The Rings*, but guess what? You can still be hugely successful in this business. The key is to redefine what you call success. Success for me right now is to sell one of my screenplays. When that happens, I'm going to be one happy soul sistah.

Would it be fun to follow in Nia Vardalos' *My Big Fat Greek Wedding* success? Absolutely! I'd be happy with a fraction of that film's profits. That would be off the hinges, but if it doesn't happen, I'll be fine. I'm more interested in having people love the story that I put on the page. For me, that would be the ultimate success. (Yeah, right).

OPEN MOUTH, INSERT BOOT

Loose Balls was the name of a basketball script I wrote several years ago. Within it was a gay man who flirted with a heterosexual man throughout the script. Several people had read the script and on one occasion, one agent made a comment about this straight guy being hit on by this "queen." I was flabbergasted, but I didn't say anything to the agent for two reasons. One, I was shell shocked by his comment and two, I didn't want to ruin what had been a great meeting, up to that point. Instead, I left that meeting very disappointed in myself for not speaking up, but vowing to be prepared the next time, if there ever were a next time. There was.

An affable, gregarious producer heard about my script from one of my screenwriting classmates and asked to read it over the weekend. He liked it but had several bits of feedback that he thought would make the script stronger. First on his list? "C'mon," he said. "You've got this suave guy being hit on by this fag. He wouldn't be that polite." I was stunned (again) and although my mouth was open, no words were coming out of it. I was terribly offended.

And the whole time I sat there, I knew that I could not be silent again. But I also knew that if I decided to say anything about his comment that I could potentially sever our relationship — and possibly lose lots of money. But the only thing I could think of was how terrible I felt the last time I didn't say anything. So I waited until he finished and then I said, "I appreciate your feedback, I think it's going to really strengthen the script, but I gotta tell ya, the "fag" thing sorta took me by surprise." He laughed. "I'm sorry. I have a foul mouth. I didn't mean to offend you." Phew! I had done it and I felt much better about our relationship and myself when it was over. It wasn't easy, but I promise you, it was well worth the risk and the payoff to my own sense of integrity.

What about you? What will you do when the awkward moments surface in your meetings? Will you suck it up and stand for what you believe in and have faith that you'll still get the deal, if it's to be? Or will you sit in silence and try not to rock the boat?

A HIGH FLYER GOES ONE-ON-ONE WITH FRAN

LITA-NADINE QUETNICK | ENTREPRENEUR/WRITER
EMPLOYER/COMPANY NAME | THE SILVERAIR GROUP, INC.
(NOT EMPLOYED YET!)
FIRST JOB IN THE BIZ | PRODUCTION ASSISTANT, ON *NEW YORK, NEW YORK*
(THREE DAYS FILL-IN FOR FRIEND) AND ASSISTANT TO ERIC MORRIS, ACTING
COACH (WROTE *NO ACTING PLEASE* AND TAUGHT ARNOLD SCHWARZENEGGER
& JACK NICHOLSON)

FH: Why/how did you decide to get into the entertainment business?
LNQ: Went to USC Film School for grad work... in my dreams and blood.

FH: What was the one perception you had about being in the business that you found out was inaccurate?
LNQ: Not much, they painted a pretty accurate picture of the business.

FH: Who are/were some of the people you admire (d) in the biz and why?
LNQ: I admired Tamara Asseyv and Alexander Rose, producers who asked for more of my work and I never kept in touch with them.

FH: What's been the most difficult aspect of being in the biz?
LNQ: Not being in it full time.

FH: What do you think you'd be doing if you weren't in the biz?
LNQ: Since I am starting my airline, that comes first. Getting in and staying in the business is second, for now.

FH: Ever slept with someone to get a job? How'd you feel the next morning?
LNQ: I interviewed Milos Forman and he put the moves on me and I left. In retrospect, I don't think anything would have happened if I had slept with him.

FH: Share one hard knocks lesson you learned.
LNQ: I had a chance to work for a top writing and creative agency, only I did not want to take the bus so, I turned the job down... foolish me... I would have been somewhere by now in the industry!

FH: Share one pattern or mistake you see newbies make.
LNQ: I am still blessed with wonderful contacts and so the most important thing is to stay in touch and follow through. You don't have to bug people, you just have to let them know that you are still there and then, when you are ready, they will be responsive.

FH: If you had the chance to start your career over, what, if anything, would you do differently?
LNQ: I would have taken the job at the creative agency, I would have been willing to start at the bottom and I would have kept going. Now the only place I can start is through writing.

FH: How do you handle rejection?
LNQ: Rejection is part of life, in EVERY industry and in everything. Internal strength and confidence comes from inside so you just have to keep going and know that sooner or later the law of averages is in your favor. Don't give up if you believe in something. Do listen to people and if, at least three people are telling you the same thing, then maybe you better make adjustments!

FH: Best advice given to you.
LNQ: If you believe in your dream, don't quit!

FH: One or two pieces of advice for wannabes.
LNQ: If you are going to do anything in life, be passionate about what that it is because there is no free lunch. Everything takes hard work and determination to succeed so, if you do not love what you do, then you will look back and have regrets.

FH: Open forum, freelance — add whatever else you want to add.
LNQ: If you are going to write, write from direct experience. Know something about your subject so that you can add some emotion from your experience. I think this is often why some things are really flat. Alternatively, if you have lived something — abuse, overcoming great odds — then this will come through in your writing and bring catharsis and real emotion to your reader and your audience.

OOOPS! YOU DROPPED SOMETHING

Spend enough time working in the entertainment industry and you're bound to see or hear names thrown all over the place. *Oh yes, Quentin was here last week. Cameron's people are reading the script. I hear Halle's got last say on casting.*

Now, to be clear, it's not name dropping if you really work with these people. It's only name dropping when you're using the name because you don't have a name yourself. We've been taught that it's crass to drop names, so why do people still do it? Because it's not crass to drop names, it's good business. It's all about how you drop the name. Nobody's impressed that you know Jerry Bruckheimer. I'm impressed that you have his cell phone number and that he answers the call. You can't drop names just because they read your scripts. Wannabes have it all mixed up. They think that if you say you know somebody that famous, people will perk up. They won't. The only people who perk up when you drop a name, are other wannabes.

Now, let's get clear on one thing. This business is 99% about who you know and 1% about how you know them. For example, if I were going to telephone a production company based on the recommendation of a star I really and truly know, then yes, of course, the opening line in my phone call would go something like this. "Thanks for returning my call. Whoopi Goldberg read my script, "Peaches and Cream," and thought your company might be interested in reading it." Bam! You didn't drop a name like Goldberg, you immediately bridged a gap between you (an unknown) and the executive (an established player). Your conduit was a celebrity. Nothing wrong with that. It's good business. Keep doing it.

On the other hand, let's take Willy Wannabe from Washington. He desperately wants Penny Marshall's company Parkway Productions to take a peek at his comedy set in the world of bobsledding. Only thing is that he doesn't have an "in" with Penny or her development department. Willy remembers that he met someone in his writer's group whose cousin got fired from Parkway a few years back for forgetting to tell Penny that her brother, Garry, called. His conversation goes like this.

"Hi, this is Willy Wannabe. Earl Lewis gave me your, uh, number. He used to work here, I think it was in 1995, no, wait, 1996. Yeah, that's it. 1996. Anyway, he said I should call because you were looking for something in the extreme sports arena. My script is about bobsledding, which isn't really extreme but it's pretty close."

Ehnnnk! Willy's lucky he didn't get an instant dial tone. First of all, never think that mentioning the name of a fired employee is going to get you bonus points. Second, you're better off sending a blind query letter than going in with a pitch as lame as that one. Third, do your homework; if they're looking for extreme sports scripts, don't call them to talk about anything except extreme sports movies. It's annoying and it's unprofessional.

The flip side of that is in the acting field. What if the part calls for a 25-year old and you're 30? Go for it. Even if you're 35, go for it. If you look 25, then by all means audition for a 25-year-old role. Don't let this industry define what's beautiful in your eyes. Just be prepared to deal with any consequences that might result. Trickery, as long as it's legal, is a part of the business.

MOWs: MORONS OF THE WEEK
"It's gotta be in the water because I have never seen a more moronic group of human beings than people trying to break into the business. And I would know, I graduated Cum Laude from the School of Morons... but I'm also a millionaire now, so there's hope."

That was the answer one exec gave me when I asked, "What do you see most often with people trying to break into the business?" I didn't really know what he meant about moronic behavior until I was trying to staff a pilot TV show two years ago. I needed a videographer for an event so I called one of the universities in the city where I live. I explained the project and sold the idea as a non-paid gig, but more of an opportunity to get some valuable experience and the possibility of a permanent role on a show that was already guaranteed a slot on a national cable network. Here are some of the responses I got:

> "I can't take on anything without pay."
> "I don't work for free."
> "I'm not willing to work for credit only."

I couldn't believe it. These were students with no professional credits to speak of and about $12.56 in their bank accounts, yet they turned down the opportunity to be considered for a show with built-in national distribution. I was baffled. This is what I mean about morons. Make no mistake about it, this was moronic behavior. First of all, you don't turn down the chance to work on a national show. Second of all, you don't turn down the chance to work on a national show.

MORE TALES FROM PLANET MORON

Last year I was looking for an intern to work on a video presentation I was doing for a pitch to a national television network. I went to the graduate department of my alma mater, The University of Texas, where I was told that I probably wouldn't be able to get any unpaid interns, because the students were looking for things that paid.

One by one, I heard people say things like, "Oh, I'm not interested in it if it doesn't pay." Or "Oh, I'm too busy to work on something where there's no compensation." By the end of my 10-minute stay, I was doubled over in laughter. I could not believe what I was hearing. Were these people listening to me? For about a day's work, they were going to have the chance to work on a show that had the potential to air in 80 million homes. And they were passing up this opportunity because they weren't going to get paid? For one day of work! I was shocked.

But apparently, I'm not the only person who thinks this is insane behavior. Some of the people I interviewed for this book said the same thing: I've never seen a more arrogant group of unestablished people in my life. One president of a company remarked, "When I hear film students or some other kind of wannabes saying that they'll only take this or they'll only take that, I know right then and there that I'm dealing with morons. People who don't understand how to play the game."

FAREWELL TO BLOCKS

You know what today is? Today is the day that you stop believing that you can't control blocks or what I like to call "creative cramps." Will you have days that are more creative than others? Absolutely. Do you have to throw in the towel when you do? Absolutely not. For whatever reason you're not feeling particularly inspired, honor it. Maybe you're tired. Maybe you've got major decisions bearing down on you. Maybe you're hungry. Whatever the reason is, it's okay. Nobody's great everyday. And anybody who says otherwise is a big fat liar. But instead of pouting about it, find an outlet for it. Instead of focusing on the fact that you can't seem to find a flow for your novel or screenplay, consider writing about the fact that you can't seem to find a flow for your novel or screenplay. Keep writing. If you can't seem to nail a scene while practicing at home, work on a scene about an actor who can't seem to nail a scene. If the lyrics to your love ballad won't come to you, try writing a song about a songwriter who can't find the words to his love song. You get the picture; turn your supposed block into a stepping stone to a better craft. What'll happen is that "not" focusing on your block or slump will open you up to other creative possibilities and, mark my words, sooner than later, you'll be back into the flow. And when you become rich, out of touch and famous, I will be calling you about my percentage!

HOW TO BE A GOOD LAY

Some of you need to get out of Pornville for a second — I'm talking about a different kind of lay right now. In Hollywood, "laying pipe" means planting seeds or laying the foundation for a relationship. I met a woman, by happenstance, through a friend of mine. Turns out this woman has all kinds of connections. Connections that would take me months to make, if I lived in Los Angeles. But because we vibed, she literally pulled out her palm pilot and started going down the list of people I should know. Company presidents, producers, writers, you name it. She was laying pipe. My job is to follow up on the connections she's helping me to make, which then makes me a good lay.

> "The only "ism" Hollywood believes in is plagiarism."
>
> — Dorothy Parker, writer

THE LITTLE NON-WHITE ENGINE WHO CAN'T....

Do I think there's racism, sexism, and classism in Hollywood? Without a doubt. Some of the people who are reading this book are racist, sexist, and classist but I'm certainly not going to let something as ignorant as racism, sexism, or classism get in the way of my dreams. And neither should you.

Since I started crashing Hollywood three years ago, most of my business dealings have been with people who do not, in any way, look like me. Sure, I've sent scripts to black filmmakers, directors, and producers. I've actually gotten a few responses from them, but the vast majority of the work I've been doing has been with white Hollywood, which is kind of an oxymoron, but that's okay. Every sale I've made has been bought by a buyer who wasn't of noticeable African descent. And guess what? I don't care. If that's the way the ball bounces, then I got next. And if you're the kind of person who's intimidated by white or powerful people, stay home. This game will overwhelm you. Because Tinseltown's nothing if not white and powerful.

A HAMM GOES ONE-ON-ONE WITH FRAN

BRIAN HAMM | NOVELIST | *ROLLER COASTERS & BRASS POLES*, LAS VEGAS
FIRST JOB IN THE BIZ | THE BOOK I'M WRITING RIGHT NOW.

FH: Why/how did you decide to try to get into the entertainment business?
BH: I had a story that I wanted to tell.

FH: What was the one perception you had about being in the business that you found out was inaccurate?
BH: I had no idea that agents were as busy as they are and publishers were as completely closed off as they are.

FH: What do you wish someone had told you prior to your diving in?
BH: Imagine yourself as a drug addict. At some point, you'll experience withdrawals... you'll sweat, cramp up, and shake violently, and you'll be out of money. You'll have to feed your addiction. If you get a job (non-industry), you can't shoot up as much or at all. If you beg for more from a pusher (industry), he'll abuse you and treat you like a leech, a non-human, in the end, like waste. Good luck!

FH: Who are/were some of the people you admire (d) in the biz and why?
BH: Gabriel Garcia Marquez. I had always been fond of his fiction, but when I read his nonfiction work *News of a Kidnapping*, I was even more in awe of his extraordinary talent. Man had never captured an image of the interconnectivity of modern mankind with such eloquently under-stated passages.

FH: What's been the most difficult aspect of being in the biz?
BH: It's been hard to weed out the educators and get to the successful achievers.

FH: What do you think you'd be doing if you weren't in the biz?
BH: A very friendly Black Jack dealer.

FH: Ever slept with someone to get a job? How'd you feel the next morning?
BH: I might have slept with someone who could have helped my career, but I never bothered to ask. Now, it'll be a prerequisite.

FH: Share one hard knocks lesson you learned.
BH: Editors are like psychologists: they can look at the same problem and come up with a completely different diagnosis. And let me tell you, when there's an editor involved, much like a psychologist, there's always a problem. I gave the same five-page sample to five different editors and got completely different styles, advice, and lists of problems. I believe in editors but, I think you need to be patient until you find one who believes in your style and vision and who's also willing to help you clarify it.

FH: Share one pattern or mistake you see newbies make.
BH: Not rewriting enough. No matter how great the plot, if the prose isn't polished, people will never see it, because they won't read that far.

FH: If you had the chance to start your career over, what, if anything, would you do differently?
BH: I would have given myself more time to develop. I let outside pressures to reveal something, to show *anything* of my work, take mental time away from my writing. I'm a workaholic, but the story doesn't care. It'll be done, when it's done.

FH: How do you handle rejection?
BH: I was ugly as a kid, so I'm used to rejection. The query letter process rankles me, though. There's something masochistic about paying postage for some stranger to write back that she's not interested. It's like taking a woman on a blind date, then paying for dinner and not getting laid. Ouch!

FH: Best advice given to you.
BH: The encouragement I received was far more beneficial than any advice I had been given. If you really need a technical answer, see question nine.

FH: One or two pieces of advice for anyone entering the business.
BH: Rewrite and persevere.

TIME OUT WITH PRESIDENT CARTER

NESTOR GREGORY CARTER
GREG | PRESIDENT – CEO | NEXUS ENTERTAINMENT
FIRST JOB IN THE BIZ | *THE FANTASTICKS* – EL GALLO (LEAD ROLE)
TAMU | AGGIE PLAYERS' PRODUCTION 1989

FH: Why/how did you decide to get into the entertainment business?
NGC: I was looking for an elective in my senior year in college, so I took an acting class after my brother suggested I would do well. I auditioned for my first play and got the lead. At that point, I decided I wanted to be in showbiz. Later, I decided to focus my energy on being a feature film writer/director/producer.

FH: What was the one perception you had about being in the business that you found out was inaccurate?
NGC: That you had to have a dog-eat-dog mentality to be successful.

FH: What do you wish someone had told you prior to your diving in?
NGC: All things being equal, always follow your gut instincts.

FH: Who are/were some of the people you admire (d) in the biz and why?
NGC: Spike Lee (prior to *She's Gotta Have It*, it was impossible for me to visualize what a black filmmaker was), Charles Gordone (Pulitzer Prize-winning playwright who taught me how to set high standards and not to settle for less, when it comes to first attempts), George Lucas (after seeing *Star Wars*, I knew anything was possible and that there's something special about telling stories with film).

FH: What's been the most difficult aspect of being in the biz?
NGC: Balancing friendship and professionalism, i.e., knowing that some friends who started out with you may not end up finishing with you because their goals and expectations are not the same as yours.

FH: What do you think you'd be doing if you weren't in the biz?
NGC: An engineer or inventor.

FH: Ever slept with someone to get a job? How'd you feel the next morning?
NGC: No.

FH: Share one hard knocks lesson you learned.
NGC: Even though people have the best intentions when they give me advice, I have to trust my own instincts, i.e., a friend of mine suggested it would be beneficial to hire this specific person who was a great talker. Since I trusted my friend's opinion, I hired the person against my gut feelings and he ended up being dishonest. He represented himself as the president of my company and tried to secure his own personal deals off of my company's name.

FH: Share one pattern or mistake you see newbies make.
NGC: People get so wrapped up in their projects and their positions, that they don't have the ability to step outside themselves and see the bigger picture.

FH: If you had the chance to start your career over, what, if anything, would you do differently?
NGC: I would have started at an earlier age.

FH: How do you handle rejection?
NGC: I try to view setbacks as learning experiences.

FH: Best advice given to you.
NGC: Everyone gets at least 15 minutes of fame, but being prepared for those 15 minutes when they come is what separates the doers from the dreamers.

FH: One or two pieces of advice for wannabes.
NGC: Seek to understand before seeking to be understood.

GUERRILLA MARKETING TIPS

I've probably said it a million times, and at least a few times in this book: ultimately the fate of your career falls squarely on your shoulders. Even after you've landed an agent, you still have to continue marketing yourself, always selling your talent. The term "guerrilla" has been around for ages. Guerrilla means "revolutionary" but I like to attach the words "all out" and "unrelenting," as well. As it relates to marketing, it means you are blanketing the world with your product: you.

Here are some effective guerrilla tactics to get you started. Strategies that are guaranteed to result in immediate and noticeable rewards. Yes, guaranteed.

#1: Make sure your Web site or Web page sizzles.
An effective Web site does one thing: calls people to action. If you're a model and you want people to book you, then your site should result in more shoots. If you're a recording artist, then your site should sell CDs or allow visitors to listen to your songs online. If you're a speaker, your site should result in bookings. If you're an actor, your site should result in more roles or, at least, more auditions. It doesn't need to be a 30-page site with crawling footnotes to be effective. It just needs to tell your story in a compelling and concise fashion.

#2: Consider producing a promotional item that you can hand out at events.
For this book I had bookmarks printed that not only promote it but also the *Crashing Hollywood* TV show, my writing workshops, and other projects. Maybe you'd want to put upcoming performance dates or available CDs on yours. Be creative.

#3: Organize a contest.
I'll tour select cities with this book doing signings and discovering upcoming talent, capturing it all on digital video — for what? You guessed it. To launch my television show about breaking into the biz. Instant guerrilla-ing!

#4: Provide appetizers for FREE.
Yep, give your stuff away. If you're a singer, burn one or two of your cuts onto CDs and either give them away or sell them for something like $1 a piece. If you're an author or singer, tease your readers by allowing them to go to your Web site and download a free chapter of your book or one of your songs. If you're a filmmaker, invite a select group of people to preview your project for free and then to an invitation-only reception afterwards.

Wait a minute? Doesn't conventional wisdom say that we should never give away anything we want to sell later? Yes, it does, but that's an old school way of thinking. Providing an appetizer of your product or talent says one thing to me: you are so sure of the quality of your work that you're willing to let me try it for free, because you know that once I've sampled a few dishes, I'll definitely buy the whole meal. Just be sure that when you give your sample away you provide a way for people to make an easy purchase of the product either via telephone, fax, mail, or Internet with check or credit card. There's a link to an online service called PayPal that allows you to send and receive payments online. You can sign up by going to this link.

Go to this link to register for free:
https://www.paypal.com/affil/pal=HH2TSCZ3ZCURQ.
They'll even give you $5 just for signing up!

#5: Get booked on local radio and television shows.

Appearing on these shows is easier than most people think it is. All you need to do is call the producer for the show you want to appear on a few weeks in advance, deliver your 30- or 60-second pitch, and send over your sample (a CD, DVD, audiocassette, video, book) for review. Radio is one of the most effective ways to get the word out about you and your work. Just be sure to do ample research so that you appear on the shows that cater to the audience most likely to respond to your work. If you're targeting a young, 18- to 34-year-old audience, you don't want to be on the all-news station. In contrast, television has the ability to reach mass numbers, so if you can get booked on a few television shows — such as your local network morning shows — you're going to really boost your marketing potential.

#6: Offer to perform for FREE.

There goes that word again, but don't be deceived by the word "free." Free doesn't mean that you get nothing in return. Clearly, if your band plays at a benefit concert, the benefits could be tremendous. If you do a reading at a local bookstore, you could sell books, get a deal or meet someone who could change your career. Whenever I hear someone say, "I never do anything for free," I know that person doesn't understand the power of guerrilla marketing and worse, is probably missing out on the opportunity to make millions of dollars. Some of my most profitable engagements have been when I've agreed to deliver a free speech with the understanding that I could sell my products before and after the event.

THE ANATOMY OF A THANK YOU NOTE

Part of your follow up will be a pithy, genuine note of thanks. This is one of the most forgotten aces in the game. I'm amazed at the number of people who don't say thank you. Don't be one of those people. In fact, this is one office supply you should never be without. You can actually buy them in bulk at places like Michaels or at some online retailers. Who gets thank you cards? Everyone you meet with, regardless of the outcome. Now, you're not going to send a thank you note to the guy or woman who sexually harasses you but everyone else should get one. Even those who "pass" on you.

Even if writing's not your thing, everyone can craft an effective note of gratitude. The most essential element in any thank you note is sincerity. Keep it real. Believe it or not, people can sense insincerity a mile away. The next important ingredient is brevity. Keep it short. The longer it is, the more fake it comes off. Finally, keep it light, if appropriate.

Here's a sample thank you note that I wrote recently.

Jamie Schamie, Title
Company
Address
City, State ZIP

Dear Jamie:

It was great to finally meet you in Los Angeles last week. I know how busy you've been with the Buena Vista deal, so I appreciate your squeezing me into your schedule.

I've got to polish my script, *Popsicle*, this week but I'll get that proposal to you by the end of the month. Hope to see ya in Austin at the South By Southwest Festival in March. Thanks again for the meeting and I'll talk to you soon.

Best,
FH

What about e-mail thank yous? They're great, almost immediate, and inexpensive. But while the Internet gives us the ability to communicate with people in a matter of seconds, it should never be abused.

> "Success in Hollywood is 10% talent,
> 90% follow through."
>
> — *Fran Harris*

AN INTERVIEW IN THE DEN

KEVIN BEGGS | PRESIDENT OF PRODUCTION | LIONS GATE TELEVISION

FH: How long have you been in your role at Lions Gate?
KB: Currently, as president of original production, about a year and a half. At the company about four years. Coming on next September, it'll be five years.

FH: Is there still freshness to the job you're doing?
KB: The good thing about being in TV and being an independent is that no deal is ever the same. Every one is different. Each has its own unique set of players and circumstances. We've never used the same deal memo twice. There's no cookie cutter business. As long as I'm meeting new people, working with new people, extending my working relationship with people I like and am working with already, it's great. It's a privilege to be in this business. Relative to most people, we get paid an inordinate amount of money. Relative to most people, that is. In the scheme of the world, for doing something that you love, it's terrific. I would likely do it for nothing.

FH: Which isn't the same as if you're gonna give the money back.
KB: No, but I'd still want to be in this business, even if there were no promise or guarantee of pay, if I didn't have to have another job to support myself and my family. And I have to think that most people in this business are saying, "How lucky are we? This is amazing." We get paid to be creative, we work with interesting people and meet interesting people. This year alone I've met some great people, General Norman Schwarzkopf, Senator John McCain, those are interesting political figures

whom I probably would never have met otherwise, but because I have a TV show to pitch to them, I'm in the room. That's great, how many people get to do that in their lifetimes? Nothing boring about it.

FH: What a life.
KB: It is. My wife is on my case a lot because I keep really long hours and my response is "I have to work these hours. I want to take care of the family." And she says, "You can't even take that position, because you like it! So don't come to me with your sob story about your long hours, because you like it. It's fun. Come suffer with me and the baby." And you know? She's not wrong, because my work is so much fun. I love it so much that I'd do it unregulated by my wife for 24 hours a day and not even think that it was unbalanced. She'd say I was sick though. "What's wrong with you? You're e-mailing at 2:30 in the morning." I always say, "yeah, but I just thought of this thing." So, it's intoxicating, but you do have to take those steps back and remember you're talking about a TV show. Then again, it is a business. Advertisers pay you to put a good product on and if you can entertain people, move them, then that's meaningful.

FH: Sounds good to me. I'm sold.
KB: It's not earth shattering, but it's a fun business to be in.

FH: What do you see from aspiring people in the business?
KB: Well, I think you can see the people who are committed to it and those who are dabbling. I have to go back to my first job as the cost control assistant. I had a college friend who had political aspirations. He needed a job and I told him he could be a driver at the production company where I was working.

FH: As the cost control assistant.
KB: Right, saving the company money. That was my job. Anyway, he lasted about three or four days. Then he came to me and said, "This is insane. They're driving my car to death. What are you doing? You could be working at Taco Bell and making more money. Why are you doing this?" He didn't view it the same way I did. I saw it as my way in. If you get through the six weeks of boot camp, you'll be a Marine. He saw it as exploitation. We were both political science majors so he was saying "rise up." There are a lot of people who have the attitude of, "hmm, that's interesting. I'd like to make a documentary. That would be cool." And these are people for whom being in the business would just be a

fun experience, but they're not in it for the long haul. Within one meeting I can probably pick someone who's in it. And the truth is you want to help people who are serious about the business. You want to steer them on their way. Give them the breaks that you received. You have to think that every person who walks into your office, walks into your life, could have been you. So, treat them nicely because you could be working for them one day, and just because it's the right thing to do. I know where I was and people helped me, gave me opportunities.

FH: But a lot of people don't have a clue about what to expect. They think this is what they want.
KB: One experience in the business will tell them everything they need to know. I really believe that if you are not 100% sure that this is what you want to do, then don't do it. The people who stick with it, for however long that is, end up on top. Is that too different from anything else in life? Probably not, but in this business a lot of what you're selling is your creative ability and it's not quite as bad as being an actor where you're selling you. People feel that if they don't get the part then they didn't like *me*, which is hard for most people to take. But take one step back from that and know that it's not about how I look or perform but do they or do they not think I'm creative enough to take on this job. Which can be an ego boost or...

FH: Deflator.
KB: Right. But if you're confident and you keep working, you'll get there.

FH: Remember anybody who blew you off?
KB: I remember all of them but I don't harbor any grudges because I've been short with people too and it's not a definition of who they are. And most of the time, it's not personal at all.

FH: What is it, so I can report back to the wannabe tribe? Busy-ness?
KB: It's just sorting out what I've got to get done. It's making priorities for that day, that moment. It's ever changing. And if you've got a phone sheet and you've got 28 calls, you have to pick the five most important calls and you may never finish that list that day. It's never easy. So, if I don't get a call back myself for a couple of days I don't stew and fret because there are a bunch of people waiting for my call. That's why e-mail has been a good tool, because you can contact people at night.

FH: When your wife's sleeping?
KB: Right. I get on the computer and I tell them that I wasn't in for their calls and I'll try to get back with them via e-mail.

FH: And you e-mail people while you're on the phone with other people? Tell the truth.
KB: It's true. Every now and then someone will say, "You're not listening to me." I say, "Oh sure, it's a Civil War movie, a period piece." Then they say, "No, actually it was an action movie with Stallone."

FH: Did anybody give you any grand advice when you were trudging through those early years?
KB: It was probably not distilled down to one piece of advice but more through their actions. My first big job in the business was on *Baywatch*. One of the big things I learned from Doug Schwartz (one of four executive producers on the series) was to be fair and treat everyone equally. To deal with actors and actresses the same. He learned the importance of that because through his uncle, a producer, he got a job on the set of *Gilligan's Island* and he would run lines with the actors. Unbeknownst to him they wanted him to count the lines, until he got in trouble with his uncle.

FH: Count the lines as in "tell me who's got more lines?"
KB: Yep and there would always be mayhem on the set when one actor had more lines than another one. I learned a lot from him about not being adversarial in business negotiations. There are basically two schools of negotiation: The bull in the China shop approach, where you charge in and, when you retreat, you've gotten everything you wanted. The other team is bullied into submission. But that wasn't Doug's approach. I've watched him do deals for ridiculously low amounts of money but, doing so in a completely non-adversarial manner. In sports parlance, make sure it's a win-win for everybody. He wasn't a yeller, a screamer.

FH: Negotiations are really about, "How can we make this work?"
KB: Right, they should be and I actually learned a good lesson from my current boss, Jon Feltheimer (CEO of Lions Gate Entertainment). One time we were discussing a deal and I was erring more on the bull in the China shop approach and he said, "Wait a minute, you don't want to do that. How would it feel to be on the receiving end of that deal?" His point, which was a great one, is that stuff always comes back around in some way or another. He also emphasizes saying everything up front.

If you're not interested in the project, tell them immediately. If you see a potential problem, say so. If you know there's no budget for five producers and the five producers are in front of you, don't be diplomatic, tell them you can't afford five producers. Don't let things dangle, tie things up.

FH: And how has that worked? You've got people coming into your office with high expectations, good vibes, you like 'em but you know you can't do their movies.
KB: As hard as it is to say "no" to a good project or someone you like, you have to. The direct approach has really worked well. It's not easy to do but, 99.9% of the time, it's the best thing to do and when you sit on the other side of it, you know that you'd actually appreciate it more if people were up front with you.

FH: Are there people at Lions Gate whom you're formally or informally mentoring?
KB: Yes, because I was lucky enough to be mentored myself, I try to assume the same role in someone else's life. I've got an amazing head of development, Joanna Klein, whom you've met, who started as my assistant, but who's now vice president, doing all the things I do and is completely capable of taking over. I'm proud of that. I am proud of her. And my method is one that I learned by being on the *Baywatch* show. They shared everything with the assistants. They were very inclusive, so everyday was a teaching situation. I'd like to think I am the same way. Give everyone as much information as possible because someone may have a solution or an idea that you hadn't thought of or weren't expecting.

FH: Yeah and it also helps people to know what NOT to say.
KB: Exactly. Who wants to put someone in a position to say something that can be harmful to anyone involved. Nobody wants an assistant to be in a meeting and say, "Yeah, heard your client got fired." Bad.

FH: What goes into your process of deciding to be in business with people? I've heard people say, "I like the project, can't do it right now, but we'll find something to do together because I like you." Ever walk away from a deal because you didn't like the person sitting across the room from you?
KB: Yep. It's a lot easier to do business with people you like, no question. If you don't like people in the pitch meeting, it may be hard to say "no" to them if their projects are good, but it'll be 10 times harder down the line to be in production with them. If you don't like them,

then to try to work with them everyday would be tough. And you'd have to be a pretty offensive person for me not to like you, but there have been some.

FH: What's gone into a decision not to work with someone?
KB: There are only a few things that would prevent me from working with people. If they were dishonest. If I found out that they'd cheated someone in the past or lacked integrity and my barometer of that is fairly loose.

FH: Have to be scratching the bottom of the moral code barrel? Is the business really that small?
KB: Yeah, it is. It really is. There are probably 50 or so people who control the television business, if that. A lot of people participate in the business but only a few who really control it.

FH: Okay, last words for someone trying to break into the biz.
KB: No matter what it is, be tenacious about finding an opportunity. If it pays 10 cents and you can somehow still live, take that first job. Because a job will beget another job. I've heard people moan and say, "Well, I don't want to take this job as an assistant, I have a degree, I went to film school." But it doesn't matter because, unless you're in the game, in some job, you won't make the contacts to get you to the job you want. So even the worst job can lead to something great, but you have to get in the game. It can be as menial as driving scripts around town. There should be no job — at least not your first one — that is beneath you. You won't be picking up that producer's laundry forever and you can't lose sight of that. And unless you are willing to do whatever it takes, legally and ethically, to be in this business, don't do it. Go teach elementary school. Like I did.

YOU'LL NEVER EAT CROW IN THIS TOWN AGAIN

It's one thing to turn people off, quite another to burn a bridge. You can turn someone off by making an odd statement but that statement's not likely to end all business dealings. Now, granted, you won't become best friends with everyone you meet in Hollywood, but the goal is to leave the door open for future interaction. Remember, relationships are as fragile as glass and they must be treated with care. I'm not saying that you have to always be on alert with what you say, I'm suggesting that you go the extra mile to be courteous and professional.

Here are a few sure fire ways to burn bridges.

Make off color remarks. This includes comments that are sexist, racist, classist, homophobic, or otherwise insensitive in nature.

Bad mouth anybody. Even if the exec says, "I hated that movie," you never say things like, "Yeah, I hated it too. I can't believe Scott Rudin made that piece of crap." If the exec thinks Britney Spears has no talent, that's her business. You keep your opinions to yourself. Rest assured that what goes around always comes back around much faster than it went out.

Gossip or spread rumors. I don't care what kind of inside track you think you have on a particular person or event, never, ever take it upon yourself to speak badly about anyone. Even if the exec invites your opinion, try keeping your comments on the straight and narrow. Use those trusty window-opening communication phrases you learned earlier.

Get a funky attitude when you're rejected. I could sum up this section by showing you outtakes of Fox's *American Idol* auditions. I don't care if you think *Idol's* Simon Cowell is the biggest jerk this side of the Rio Grande River, you don't have to stoop to his level. Actually I appreciate his honesty, though his choice of words often leaves a lot to be desired. In any case, when you are auditioning for a role, interviewing for a job, pitching a television show, or submitting a screenplay, you are at the mercy of the recipients' opinions of you and your work. You don't have to buy into their assessments, but you never want to lash out at them. This very well could be professional suicide. It's silly and it's not worth it.

There's a way to leave a bad situation without having it blow up in your face or come back to haunt you later on. Remember, you cannot control someone else's behavior, only your own. So, no matter how rude, nasty or inappropriate someone else is, you don't have to respond in a similar fashion.

I'll give you an example of something that happened to me many years ago when I was selling health and beauty care products for Procter & Gamble. I was pitching a decision maker on a new skin care product when, in the middle of my presentation, he started to make some sexually inappropriate comments. I was shocked and yes, unnerved by his behavior. I took a deep breath and said, "I don't really see what that has to do with Oil of Olay or this proposal and I'd appreciate it if you wouldn't make those comments." He laughed nervously and told me not to be so serious. Then he apologized. I suspect that very few women had the nerve to let this guy know that his advances were not welcomed, because he acted like I'd somehow insulted him. I continued to call on his store for another three or four months but I never had another encounter like that with him. Hollywood, I hear, is home to people like this, but I think they're probably in the minority. At least I've yet to have a similar interaction with anyone like my grocery store manager.

KNOW THY COMPETITION

You know the people in front of the line at the auditions? They aren't your competition. What about the select few who have been invited to read for the director? Nope. And what about the thousands of people who moved to Los Angeles this past year in hopes of that big break — aren't they your competition? Sorry.

I got news for you. You don't have any competition. What a relief! It's true. I know I've already asked you to shift a few of your paradigms but now I'm gonna challenge you to change your perspective about competition. Rather than seeing it as you versus everybody who wants the part or the deal or the money, focus on what you do best.

As a basketball player on one of the finest college teams in the history of the game, I was surrounded by athletes who had been the best in their respective states, on their respective teams. Collectively, when we all decided to attend UT, we became the cream of the crop, which meant that our practices were often better than some of our games. This level of talent also meant that sometimes I was going head to head, neck and neck with someone who was my best friend. But because we'd set our sights on a national title, we needed to make one minor adjustment if we were going to reach our ultimate goal. We had to stop seeing each other as competition. Even though only five people could be on the court at one time, we still had to realize that the only way we were going to be able to keep our eyes on the prize was to see each other as fellow warriors, people we went to battle with every day.

Some nights I would be the star, on other nights my teammates would shine. With this minor shift in perspective, we were able to amass an incredible 34-0 record en route to the NCAA's first undefeated national basketball championship. All because we didn't view each other as the "comp." This attitude has helped me in this business because I share what I know freely with other writers, producers, filmmakers, and actors. I do not operate from a deficit model. In other words, I don't believe that if I give to you, I lose or fall behind in the race. Remember, you can only do what you do best. And it doesn't matter how stellar your performance, if you are not what "they" are looking for, you won't get the job. It's that simple.

At auditions, don't start comparing yourself to the people you see. It's not a game of comparison. It's about what the people sitting in that room think they're looking for. Maybe you think you're perfect for the part. It doesn't matter. If they don't think you're the right person, you're not. End of story. Roll the credits. It is completely counterproductive to torture yourself by sizing up your supposed comp. You don't have any comp. So, rather than hating the person who's up for the same job, focus your energies on delivering the best performance you're capable of.

I had a great lesson in this area a few years ago. In 1999, I heard that they were beginning auditions for the movie *Love & Basketball*. My TV agent at the time was with ICM, the company that also repped the director and writer of that movie, Gina Prince-Bythewood. I was sure there was a part for me in the movie, seeing that I was a former WNBA champion and all, so I asked my agent to get me an audition. She made a few phone calls and they agreed to see me. When I spoke to the casting agent she said, "We don't want you to make a special trip out here just to audition." That's industry-speak for "we're probably not going to cast you, but if you're goofy enough to fly 3,000 miles to audition, that's your business."

I told her I wanted to do it anyway. I read, didn't get the part and was out almost $800 bucks after the flight and car were paid for. Would I do it again? I don't know. It was fun and had I gotten a part, this story would probably be in a much happier section of this book. But here's the reason I'm telling you this story anyway. While I was waiting on them to call me in to read, several established actresses showed up, including Tisha Campbell-Martin (*My Wife & Kids*). When I saw her I had to quickly remind myself that everyone in the audition line had an equal shot at landing the role.

Remember, it's not about the star power necessarily; it's about what they're looking for. Don't knock yourself out of the running because you don't feel you belong. You do. And if you truly know that, it will show in your meetings and auditions.

COME AND LISTEN TO A STORY 'BOUT A MAN NAMED JED

Remember how much the Clampetts stood out in Beverly Hills? They had more money than The Donald (Trump) but no one took them seriously. No one had any real respect for them. Now, it's a shame that people couldn't get past the package to see the inherent beauty and innocence in the product, but that's how it is. You don't need to change who you are to make it in Hollywood, but if you stand out for the wrong reasons, you may be doing yourself a disservice. In an effort to distinguish yourself from the rest of the pack, try elevating your talent rather than focusing on something external.

IS THAT WHAT YOU'RE WEARING?

Everybody makes such a big deal about what to wear in Hollywood when it's the least important thing about you. Hold on. I'm not saying you should look like a hobo because nobody will care about anything except your script or your acting or singing talent. People will focus on your clothes if you force them to focus on your clothes by wearing something that's distracting. But it's useless to spend hours trying to find the perfect garb for a meeting that will last about 30 minutes, if you're lucky. Remember, these are busy executives. They are often going from meeting to luncheon to meeting. They don't have time to focus on the color of your pants or your choice of blouse. They want to know if you have talent, period. So, pick something simple and don't draw attention to what you're wearing.

In one of my first real Hollywood meetings I wore a pair of khaki Capri pants, a sweater, and a pair of leather clogs. I needed to be comfortable so that I would be "me." That outfit is me. If I had worn a Brooks Brothers black suit, I would have probably acted as serious as a pallbearer and I didn't want that.

After my meeting, a few of my girlfriends asked, "What did you wear?" "Did you wear this, did you wear that?" I said, "Nope, I wore a pair of Capri pants and a sweater... and some clogs." They all looked at me like, "You've gotta be kidding me." But I wasn't. I met with the president of a mini studio in a casual outfit. And guess what? I got the deal. My friends, it ain't about the clothes.

But if fashion truly is not one of your strong suits, here's my suggestion. Get some black, white, denim, and/or khaki stuff. Mix and match. These four colors or styles go well together in any combination. Why black? Because you can dress black up or down, which means that if suits are not your thing, you're still in business if you need to go to a dress-up affair. If you're the type who would be out of place in anything but jeans, wear jeans. Yes, you heard it here. Wear what will enhance your meeting, not detract from it.

Now, here's the caveat. I'm encouraging you to be yourself, but not a slob. Don't wear the jeans with the ripped pocket and the dried up cheese whiz on the leg that you just pulled from your hamper on the way out the door. That's not professional, even if it *is* your signature style. Don't do it. If you're the kind of woman who likes to show off her bosom buddies, invest in a blouse that's a little more conservative. You don't have to dress like a nun, but you definitely don't want to convey the idea that you're a slut or that you expect to win favor by being sexy. Even if you do.

A RENAISSANCE WOMAN GOES ONE-ON-ONE WITH FRAN

GIGI GASTON | WRITER/DIRECTOR

FH: Why/how did you decide to get into the entertainment business?
GG: I couldn't help it... I had so much to say. I wanted people to go to one of my movies and feel healed, or be given hope when they had none, like Capra did.

FH: What was the one perception you had about being in the business that you found out was inaccurate?
GG: That you could make movies that were different, not formula and commercial... idealistic movies. I wanted to write about the human spirit with people who were not considered normal. Major studios only want what is formalized and what will sell to the public, which has a very short attention span now. I am just learning all this stuff that goes into it all.

FH: What do you wish someone had told you prior to your diving in?
GG: Be commercial first, don't try to stray off into unexplored territory

and be political. I wasn't. I believed that art would triumph over com-mercialism... it won't in a business, well not all the time. Sometimes a great film slips through.

FH: Who are/were some of the people you admire (d) in the biz and why?
GG: Writers, directors, and actors who take risks. I just recently saw *Apocalypse Now*. What Coppola had to do to make that film was daunt-ing... it took two years, didn't it? What a film, what a sacrifice. There are so many studio films made in the last years that are all action and more expensive and have so little meaning. Music has paralleled this. The world of music is all about the youngest, the newest. Look at John Huston. Where would he be today? Didn't he direct his first film at 40? Today he would have been buried at 40. What is wrong with being 40? I pray there is a newcomer who directs his or her first film at 40. I don't like that writers now have to lie about their age and only the young get chances... it is stupid.

FH: What's been the most difficult aspect of being in the biz?
GG: Starting so late and my perception of what I thought Hollywood would want.

FH: What do you think you'd be doing if you weren't in the biz?
GG: Writing.

FH: Ever slept with someone to get a job?
GG: No, never and I don't recommend it and I don't know many women writers who have. I think that is more for actresses.

FH: Share one hard knocks lesson you learned.
GG: Don't argue with studio executives. Try to do it their way. Their jobs are on the line.

FH: If you had the chance to start your career over, what, if anything, would you do differently?
GG: Yes, I'd look at it as a business first and write commercial formu-la movies and then, after I had a hit, I'd try to do something uncom-mercial and artistic and entertaining. Something with risk, something that says something different. Like I hear *The Hours* does. I can't wait to see that film.

FH: How do you handle rejection?
GG: Fine... I keep going. I don't consider it rejection.

FH: Best advice given to you.
GG: Garry Marshall once said to me, "You have all the talent, you just have to learn to swim with the sharks better!"

FH: One or two pieces of advice for anyone entering the business.
GG: There is no greater business.

TO LIVE AND DRIVE IN L.A.

I hate being late to anything and I hate it when other people are late. And more importantly, executives hate it when people are late. They can be late. You can't.

And I'm even more livid when I learn that there are people out there who are perpetually late and that they brag about it by saying things such as "I'm never on time" or "Give me an extra 15 minutes because I'm always late." What is that? You know what's funny? Even people who are perpetually late aren't late to things that matter to them. But I also know that no matter how conscientious you are, there are going to be times when it's nearly impossible to be on time. Like when you're driving in L.A. That's why I've developed a way to decrease your chances of being tardy anywhere, anytime. Here goes.

- First, buy a Thomas Guide. No real wannabe living within or without the Los Angeles area should be without this book. It's a map that enlarges areas so you can actually see where you're going.

- Second, open the Thomas Guide and plot your trip at least one day before your meeting. We all learn differently. I like maps, but they tend to make me a little nervous when I try to look at them while I'm driving. So, that's why I recommend going to your meeting the day before. Sit down with your Thomas Guide and plot the trip from your point of origin. If you have multiple meetings in succession, plot them all. Here's the magic in doing this little exercise. The day of your meeting you can count on a combination of at least three things that can potentially make you late: (1) nerves, (2) adrenaline, and (3) traffic.

Nerves & Adrenaline. You're meeting Paula Wagner, Tom Cruise's producing partner, because she goes to the same salon as a friend of a friend of a friend. They're thinking about casting a total unknown opposite him in his upcoming blockbuster *"Majority" Report*. It's your one shot (you think) and you want to blow her hair back, right? It's Friday, the end of the week and since Monday, you've bombed two auditions, gotten evicted and to make matters worse, they left some foam in your tall, non-fat, no-foam latte. You get the picture, things are not going your way right now.   But it's about to change.   You're about to become a five-year overnight success and by gosh, you're not gonna blow it.

So, you get in your car and head north on the 405. Uh oh. You left the directions on the laser printer. Now you're really in a pickle. Do you call Wagner's office and fess up to not having directions, even though they just gave them to you two hours earlier? Or do you pull out your Thomas Guide and try to maneuver rush hour traffic while turning the pages of the book? It's one helluva dilemma. What happens? Your heart starts pounding out of your chest. Little beads of sweat form in a marching band line across your top lip. Your palms are so wet, they keep slipping off of the steering wheel and guess what time it is? 2:55.

Your meeting starts in 20 minutes and you haven't even gone two miles. Now, your stomach gets sick and the "omigod" soundtrack starts to play in your head. I'm never gonna make it. If I call them, they'll think I'm an idiot. If I don't call, I'll be even later. I'm never gonna get this part. My one chance and I blew it. I'm so stupid, why did I even move here? I should've stayed in Iowa. And so forth and so on. Now, is there any way to avoid this scene? Yes, two things: First, always leave at least 45 minutes earlier than you need to. If it's supposed to take only 30 minutes to get to your meeting, plan on it taking at least 45. Always take something to read or work on. Don't look bored in the waiting room. If you arrive too early, they feel like they need to entertain you, so don't be too early. About 10 minutes before your scheduled meeting time is cool.

Traffic. I don't care what anybody tells you, never, ever underestimate Los Angeles traffic. Never, ever believe that there are windows of time when there's no traffic. You have to always expect traffic, period. So what, you plan 30 minutes for your trip to your meeting and it only takes 10, at least you can get there and relax.

THE FLY AT YOUR FAMILY REUNION

We've all been there. You're about to bite into a juicy piece of barbecue but there's this nagging fly that won't stop trying to get you to kill it. You shoo it, you even talk to it. "Get outta here! Go on, get outta here!" But what does it do? It just buzzes away, circles the picnic table and comes back tempting, almost forcing you, to turn into The Fly Killer. Your cousin's laughing, giving you the fly logic sermon, "If you just leave it alone, it'll go away." But you don't listen, do ya? You start running around the table trying to catch it, all the while talking to it. "Come here. I'm gonna getcha, just wait." You've forgotten about the 'cue, and now your single, most solitary mission in life is to kill that damn fly, right?

Well, guess what? That's how some of us make other people in the business feel. Like killing us. One of the most difficult things to gauge when you're breaking into the business is how "visible" you need to be with decision makers. You don't want people to forget you but you also don't want them to get tired of hearing from you. The goal is to be pleasantly present through a variety of communication mediums. The best ways to stay in touch are e-mail, phone, and hard copy correspondence. The combination of all three is the best.

Another word about e-mail communication. The Internet has changed the way we do business and maintain personal relationships but, unfortunately, it's also opened the door for some people to abuse this form of communication. Here are a couple of things you can do to avoid being hunted like the fly at your picnic.

Rule #1: Ask the people you're meeting with if they like to correspond via e-mail.

Rule #2: Do not inundate anyone with e-mails, jokes, chain letters, or other junk mail. It's bad manners, it's unsolicited and it's a quick way to get your e-mail privileges revoked. Remember, you want people to be glad to hear from you. You don't want them to frown or sigh when they see your e-mail address in their mailboxes.

BLING! BLING!

That's the sound I hear when I'm receiving an instant message in AOL. Are you in love with IM-ing people? If so, I suggest you back off a bit. Instant Messaging someone is like showing up for dinner without being invited. And never, ever send an instant message to an executive.

A few years ago I met a woman at an event who somehow got one of my AOL e-mail addresses from a distribution list. She decided that she would send me an e-mail telling me how great it was to meet. I sent her a reply thanking her for the note and thought that would be the last time I'd hear from her.

Soon afterwards though, I started to get these serial instant messages from her. I'm an early riser and a night owl, which meant that I'd get these IMs from sun up to sun down. It was irritating, to say the least. The funny thing is that I never answered her IMs. Not once. Instead I sent her an e-mail explaining that I work on my computer and that when I receive an IM, sometimes, it's like walking into my office while I'm in the middle of an important meeting. She promptly shot back an e-mail telling me that she'd never e-mail me again and that her time was precious, too, but at least she had time to IM her friends. Huh? Now, I was her friend? I'd seen this woman once in my life! She was clearly offended, but not half as offended as I was by the daily onslaught of asinine instant messages.

On another occasion, a friend of mine started to IM me every day, just as I'd begin my administrative tasks of checking e-mail, answering mail from the day before, etc. Most people don't realize that most of the time that I'm online, I'm not really online. Meaning that my browser is almost always minimized because I'm working on a project. Or, sometimes, I'm connected to the Internet, but I could be in a meeting.

My friend sent me a somewhat scathing, somewhat humorous e-mail asking me why I ignored his instant messages. I had to tell him that the times he chose to e-mail me was primo work time and that I couldn't take time away from my work day to chat online. I also used the analogy about having a string of visitors show up at your doorstep unannounced. He apologized and said that he'd never really thought about it that way because he was just trying to say hello. I told him to try sending me a simple e-mail. That I always answer e-mail.

The moral of both of these stories is to use the Instant Messaging feature sparingly and don't expect someone to welcome your unannounced visit whenever you do it. In fact, in general, keep your e-mail communication with contacts very brief, and spread them out. A good rule is to e-mail a professional contact every few months, unless there's an obvious need for more frequent contact, such as a deal.

AN INTERVIEW WITH THE VEEPS OF VEEPS

ANA CLAVELL | VICE PRESIDENT OF PRODUCTION | TAURUS ENTERTAINMENT

FH: You are one of the few true independent production companies still standing. How have you maintained your independence in the midst of mergers, buyouts, and collapses?
AC: Oh, my God, we have a library. When you have a library you have a constant influx of money, which then allows you to expand and explore other areas, but it's not easy because, being independent, we don't have anyone we can go, run, and cry to for more money to complete anything. We have a set amount of money and that's it. Once it's gone, it's gone. Sometimes we get projects where the budget exceeds what we can finance on our own. We usually shepherd them to a studio because we learned the hard way that there's a limit to how much money one should be handling in a production before it starts to get scary and out of control. It's not that we cannot do it because we can, we've handled very big budgets, but why incur the headache? When you're handling large amounts of money, it gets pretty dicey.

FH: Where's the checks and balances system to say that we're not gonna get into that kinda game?
AC: Exactly, it's not worth it. You need your money on the screen, because if you're building a business, you need to put all your quality where you're going get the most money back. We've even done films for nothing, or next to nothing, that are playing and they're simply made, with every penny that a producer brings on board going on the screen. And on catering, of course. Listen, you cannot have pizza every night.

FH: Oh, for sure, ya gotta get your grub on!
AC: Right. We're independents, but health and safety come first. We eat well. They may be complaining by week two, but any show will complain. That's another law. The crew will complain no matter what you give them. It could be lobster and it'll be, "this is overcooked."

FH: So, if this is a business about who you know, who did you know to get to be the vice president of Taurus Entertainment?
AC: This is funny. True story. I was finishing this event and I stayed in town for Christmas. It was 1994. So the director of photography for that project said Christmas time is a tough time for a lot of working

folks who are in AA (Alcoholics Anonymous), they get really depressed, really lonely. Why don't we hire people and shoot three short films? And I said "Hey, let's do it." And you have no idea how many people really cannot be at home during the holidays, because they're recovering from addictions. We got the whole crew for free. It was hysterical. All these recovering people — the actors, crew, everyone. So, I was at FourMedia, formerly Digital Image, formerly LiveWire, and now Ascent Media. I was with my rep and, at the same time, Jim Dudelson, (Taurus president) came in and was fighting with the rep. Jim and I took sides against the rep and we clicked. He saw what I was doing. He was finishing a series for Showtime and he needed someone to come on board for a film that was… let's put it this way, they forgot to shoot the ending. And it was lying in cans somewhere in the building. They needed someone to come in and supervise that, so they could finish it and deliver it. And they were going to embark on a new series. That's how it started. I was just freelancing with my company doing what turned out to be a 90-minute long music video. It totally works because it's so outrageously bad. It's so bad. It plays all the time, people seem to like it.

FH: They like it?
AC: I know. Another law of Hollywood. You have to step away from your art and look at it as product. Even if it's something that's near and dear to your heart. Because if you don't, you're going to get heartbroken real quick.

FH: Yes, people, not me, of course (*wink wink*), tend to be very attached to their stuff, their scripts, and their ideas.
AC: Right and the problem with that is as soon as you get comfortable, they say, "Yeah, I like your character but why don't we make him a girl. Oh, and let's make her Chinese. And she knows Karate."

FH: [*Laughs*]. And you sit there and you say, "it could work!"
AC: Right, you nod and say, "Yeah, uh huh, that's nice." So that takes a little bit of learning. Jim and I did a film for Showtime and then a sci-fi film. Fifth law of Hollywood…

FH: Wait? Where are laws 1 through 4? Never mind, go ahead.
AC: Fifth law. Never get excited until it's showing on TV or until you're standing on the set. That's when you know it's happening. Because, before then, anything can happen, anything can fall through. It's so incredible.

FH: It's insanity.
AC: It is. We're trying to figure out the laws around it. And everything is out the window. Because as soon as you settle on something, something happens to the deal. For instance, it never rains here. Never rains here... except when you need to do an exterior in sunlight.

FH: So, you're too nice. You have to be an outsider!
AC: We've always been considered an outsider, to a degree, but at the same time we're very much insiders. We have something that the rest of the independents didn't have. First of all, we've been around the longest. Most people who started around the same time as we did either folded or were bought out. Second, we have clout. When we call a company, we talk directly to the VPs or presidents. We don't talk to development people or junior execs. We talk to decision makers. We have access to do that type of thing. When it comes to money, all of us Indies suffer, because there's no corporation behind us. Very rarely are there investors. The first law of Indie — they ask "What are my returns going to be." You always say "Zero."

FH: So, the juicy stuff. What's it like to be a woman in this business?
AC: Oh my God, it's hell. It's a guy's town. So I guess, first of all, being an Indie woman is interesting in and of itself. I've worked on the R-rated stuff. But really, how long can you stand being around the centerfold women who are drop dead gorgeous, while here you are short, stubby? It lasts like seven minutes because then you realize, these women can't even sleep on their bellies. That's when you start recognizing the castes in Hollywood. A fellow female executive told me, "you're the lucky one: you don't need to use your body to earn a living. They depend on it. That's the choice they've made and they think they cannot get out of it. So, you are the lucky one that you don't need to do that." So we think, anyway. I've been very lucky because I landed with a couple of the biggest screamers, yellers, moaners, and whiners in town, but they are also some of the most straightforward, honest, and just good guys you'll find. Some of my female friends have not been that lucky. The worst part is that I usually get more respect from guys than from women. You're finding it out, too? Guys actually, if you're good, they don't care. If you're good, you're in trouble with another female.

FH: Right, because a guy's game is fairly transparent. They hit on you. You reject them. They hit on you again. You tell them "no." They hit on you again and you marry them! [*Laughs*]. No but, you know what I mean. With guys you pretty much know where they're coming from. Not saying that I agree, but it's pretty much right in your face.

AC: Unless they're really slimy and there are some slime balls out there. I'll give you a whole list later. I remember going to this office — it was still decorated in 1972 fuzzy shag carpeting. He forces me to go the bathroom, he says "We don't want to have to stop for gas, because you know you girls always have to go to the restroom on long trips."

FH: Were you going to Napa for God's sake?

AC: Santa Monica! [*Laughs*]. Anyway, I go to the restroom, I go in the stall, and I'm standing there in front of a big mirror. I'm thinking "oh my God, it's a two-way mirror." Beware. There are many like that in town. So I wash my hands and smile at the mirror. It starts out being disgusting and then it's outright stupid. But women are not like that — they will encourage you in ways. You need to be weary of, and measure out, how women relate to you. When you think you're helping them, they will turn around and say that you were setting them up. It breaks your heart. No matter how many times you help them, it still breaks your heart.

FH: So what kind of advice for aspiring folks.

AC: I give everyone equal chances. I've learned that women and men must be given equal chances but every time people have come through that door saying what you just said, invariably they don't last. They don't. Because either you've got — it's not talent at this point — it's the balls, or not. It's not that you have to behave like a guy but you need to understand that it is a boy's town and you need to understand how they think. And as an independent, the biggest thing you need, and it's clear that you've got it, is discipline. You've got to be very disciplined. As a woman, you've got it twice as hard. If you're a woman who doesn't mind getting dirty and breaking a fingernail, you'll make it. But with guys, here's what you get. At certain levels, some guys resent a woman telling them what to do. They don't know how to behave. So, as a woman, if you get to the point in your career where you wield a certain power, you have to command fast crowds and have to measure out how much power you exert, and how you exert it. Some people who feel vulnerable will respond badly to females in authority positions. I don't do anything to perpetuate the myth. If you're going to call me names, call me names that really stick. The biggest tag you'll have is "bitch." The guy in your position...

FH: ... No, he's strong. He's tough.
AC: Right or they say it must be that time of the month. I say, fine, then beware. No, but really, it's getting to the point where you can deal with the handful of people who hate your work, because you discover that there are also people who love it, too. You just have to be so many people for yourself. That's why people get so lost in this town. Always remember who you are.

FH: People get so disillusioned out here. The small town girl from Dayton, Ohio comes to Hollywood and...
AC: ...discovers new religions or drugs. The rampant use of drugs and stimulation, artificial stimulation.

FH: Not to be confused with insemination....
AC: Right. Stimulation because there's this big hole. It happens very quickly. You don't even notice it's happening and it's already on you. It takes over you.

FH: So how did you... or did you avoid that spiraling?
AC: I discovered that I hated the Hollywood party scene. I cannot talk to people who are saying "yeah, right," looking around the whole time.

FH: Not paying attention.
AC: "Yeah, uh huh, what are you working on? That's great. Magnificent." The whole time they're looking off. They pretend to be interested. It makes me want to say, "I'm a mortician's assistant, you would look good in red." One of the EMI execs is a woman and she always says she's in a Fed program so nobody knows what she does. I don't blame her because you cannot open your mouth about what you do anywhere, because everyone is a producer/writer/director. Their cousins are related to so-and-so, three times removed. Or, he works at Universal and it hurts, because you want to help everyone, you want to give someone the opportunity you had, you want to pass it on. But you know what? Nine out of 10 of those you think about helping are going to claim that you're trying to sink them. You've gotta watch out.

FH: That's just maddening. Who wants to keep all of the agendas straight? Subtext and back story, it's crazy to just have a conversation.
AC: I have nothing in common with most of the people out here. They're so caught up already in themselves. You have to protect yourself from the craziness here. I'd just rather be baking than to go to a

party. I like the one-on-one. This business has made me hate it so much. Now when I go to Cannes, I just work. Take my clients to dinner. We avoid the parties. It's a waste of time. As an independent, you'll work seven days, 24 hours a day. No holidays. Do you want to waste your spare time with people who are not really worth your time? It's so empty.

FH: Sounds very lonely. The pretension. The lies. Where's that come from?
AC: You feel lonely because in this town, sometimes, you feel that nobody's to be trusted. You get very tired of blowing smoke up peoples'... butts. You get to the point where you prefer your own solitude. You figure you're safer that way. You concentrate on your real friends. It's harder as a woman, the older you get. Very few people ever find happiness and a spouse here because it's an industry town. Then you start making rules for yourself. Never date actors. Never date musicians. Never that.

FH: Susan Sarandon said something that really resonated with me. It was on, I think, *Inside the Actor's Studio* with James Lipton. She said, "I don't trust anyone who hasn't had at least one meltdown." This is a town where that seems inevitable.
AC: People will be dying of hunger outside of the Beverly Hilton, but they see a star and their days are made. Wake up! And then you do have to incur expenses to keep going. As an Indie you're not fabulously rich. Have a second talent in hand for the downtime. So, if you're a writer, you can do something else. Because when the down time happens, there's no work and you need income. When we're not in production, I program HTML. I learn something new every year.

FH: Nobody's said that to me yet.
AC: Come to Hollywood armed with a principal talent and another skill, so that, at the drop of a hat, you can get hired as a bartender, or whatever it is. Waitressing? No. You don't make enough money. The hours are horrible and you need something that's related to what your main talent is. That's another thing that will kill. We'll call that the 12th law. Be true to yourself.

FH: Right. In Tinseltown.
AC: Lie to everybody else, but be true to yourself. You're going to be your own worst enemy. A lot of people set goals and when they don't work out they turn their anger, fury, and frustration out on themselves. Not worth it. That's when you need to have a secondary skill. You need

to rethink plan b, c... Initially, handy hands keep your mind free to do your work. Depression hits very hard here and that's why they're so many crazies. And you don't want that to happen to you. Sometimes I see people on the street and I think, "Oh my God, that could be me. Talking to the tree." Oh yeah. You have to try. You're not going to give up.

FH: Best/worst thing you've ever done in the biz.
AC: I was being interviewed on one of the sexy shows that we were doing for Showtime and one of the production assistants on the set turned to me and said, "So, how do you feel about denigrating women the way that you do?" And I should have punched her, but I didn't. The key is to learn something from every experience you have. There are no mistakes. Every opportunity to show your art and get better at it, is okay. That's when you need to separate your art from your product. It comes to the point. Unless it's close to your heart. If they want to change your script to a Chinese martial arts expert...

FH: With an Afro.
AC: With an Afro, right! You can handle that, right? You say, "Love it, keep it, print it." You're not destroyed by someone else altering your "product." It's product. Not you, not your art. You're safe inside. You don't feel corrupted or polluted.

FH: That's good. I like that. Can I steal that? Oh no! I'm already fitting in!
AC: See, it's seductive! My friend's mother used to say it is you who makes your own bed at night and you have to sleep in it. That's important.

FH: Best advice for wannabes.
AC: Stay home. Get good at your talent and strengthen your second skill. Don't come out here unless you're willing to work. Come out here. Try it. If you believe it, try it. We can wax lyrical about the pros and cons of making it in Hollywood but anyone who has this dream should at least try it. But now, here's the deal. You have a better chance at winning big in Vegas than you do at winning a part here. It's totally true. The Quentin Tarantinos and Drew Careys of the world happen once in a lifetime. Come here knowing that. Come here expecting it to take some time.

FH: This was great, thank you. You're wacky.
AC: I know and I'm not even venting, I was just talking.

> **FH:** Then in my next book, *Venting In Hollywood*, you will be my first interview. And please, next time, no holding back. You gotta work on that, you're too inhibited!

THE FIRST TIME YOU GET PAID FOR IT

You scored! You got your first deal, what's the first thing you should do? Celebrate. Squeal like you've won the Lotto. Then, get a lawyer, if you don't already have one. Don't let anybody tell you that you don't need professional representation. In most medium and large agencies, there's a department called business affairs. This is the legal department. If you sign with a manager or agency without a business affairs department, start asking around for recommendations. Don't sign anything that a liar, I mean, *licensed* lawyer, hasn't reviewed. Don't commit to anything verbally. Don't sign a napkin or handkerchief until you're clear on the terms of the deal.

Now, when you hear the words, "We love it" or "We want to sign you," it's hard not to start turning cartwheels or moon walking on the spot, but you have to keep a clear head now, more than ever. It's okay to be excited and even to appear excited. In fact, scream if you want, but don't sign a damn thing because many a bad deal has been consummated in the heat of emotion. That's also how a lot of unwanted children are born, by the way.

Take a step back, share your excitement but tell the person that you want to think about it for a few days. We always need to think about it. If the person hearing this says, "What's there to think about? I'm offering you the deal of a lifetime?" that's when it's truly time to beware. Anybody who scoffs at a little reflection is not someone you want to be in business with. Even if everything about the deal sounds like it's on the up and up, still take the time to talk it over with one sober person. Mark my words, if you don't do your due diligence at the front end of the deal, you'll be doing a lot of crying on the back end.

I'M GOING BACK TO INDIE-ANNA

One of the most effective ways to elevate your skills and move you closer to your dream of Hollywood fame is through independent film and television projects. Let me repeat that. Independent projects are your HOV lane to Tinseltown. Do not diss Indie productions. You need credits. You need practice. You need exposure. Independent projects afford you all three plus, potentially, the opportunity to meet Hollywood producers.

By independent, I'm not just talking about films such as *Boys Don't Cry* or *Do The Right Thing*. I'm also talking about the film the local producer's shooting with his Canon XL-1 over the Thanksgiving holidays. By independent, I'm talking about the pilot TV show that's shooting on Lake Erie all day Sunday. By independent, I'm talking about the community stage play that's being cast for Cinco De Mayo. By independent, I'm talking about hooking up with the filmmaker who needs music for his first feature. You get the point — if there's work, paid or unpaid, and you have the time to do it, do it. Remember, you're building your resume. Always make sure you are compensated for your work, if not in actual dollars, at least in meals, fringe benefits, and/or a copy of the production. Never stop building your reel and credits.

KARMA, KARMA, KARMA KARMA, KARMA KHAMELEON
It's the basic law of reciprocity — you get what you put out — and it needs to be pasted on your rear view mirror so that you are always aware of how to bring good things into your life. Think twice before you screw someone. Think twice before you talk badly about someone. Think twice before you back door somebody. Think twice before you allow your jealousy of someone else to make you do something you'll regret. When in doubt, do the right thing. Ultimately, you will be rewarded and you'll save yourself a lot of grief and heartache down the line. Yes, *you* will.

FAKE IT, 'TIL YOU MAKE IT
The first time I heard someone tell others to fake it until they made it, I had to laugh. It sounded so ridiculous to tell someone to pretend to be someone she's not. That's why people think Hollywood's the City of Plastic. Listen, you don't need to do this. I don't recommend pretending to be anything or anyone. You are enough. Avril Lavigne's an 18-year old platinum-selling rocker because she came to the table looking like herself and let her talent speak for itself.

You can make it in showbiz without an American Express card. You can even make it in the Wood without a Beamer, but it's gonna be hard to make it in Tinseltown without a hook. You thought I was going to say talent, didn't ya? Nope. There are lots of insanely rich celebrities who are short on talent. Sometimes all you need is a hook, an angle, something that distinguishes you from the next singer or actor or director. So, if you want to spend time creating anything in your laboratory, make sure it's real. We don't need another fake.

CELEBRITY 101

Pull out your paper and pen, this is important. There's a right and a wrong way to treat people. Remember that law of reciprocity I discussed earlier? No? Then go back a page and read it again. One sure way to build your fan base and increase your status as a celebrity is through kindness and generosity of spirit.

Why do I prescribe kindness and generosity? Because I don't care how friendly you are, you will never be able to sign every autograph. It doesn't matter how many hands you shake, you will not be able to reach (touch) everyone who wants to touch the hem of your garment. It's not humanly possible. So, your charge is to send warmth and kindness even when you can't meet everyone's demands of you. And because you won't be able to be everything to everyone, there will be people who will become upset, even angry. This is normal and to be expected. No matter how far you go to please people, you will never be able to please everyone, so don't beat yourself up over it, just do the best you can.

CONFERENCES, FESTIVALS, AND SUNDANCE, OH MY!

Don't just go to a conference to say you went to a conference. Go to an industry event with a purpose: to meet experts or peers, to learn something, develop a new skill, or get a deal. Going to an event just to see or be seen is a waste of time and money that will do little to accelerate your career.

I recommend planning your events and attaching clear objectives for attending them. With goals that are definitive and measurable, you'll be able to track your success much better. In other words, don't just say you're going to the Hollywood Pitch Fest to make contacts with established producers, say you're going to meet X number of executives, get X number of requests for your scripts and X number of pitches. If you're setting targets for the year, don't just say "I want to be in a movie this year," try something like this, "I will get X number of film auditions and X number of roles this year." It's a lot easier to develop a system of success when you're serious about where you want to go with your career and you set crystal clear goals for getting there.

AMATEURS 'R' US

There are some things that just scream AMATEUR. Here's one from my vault.

I needed to copy my basketball-themed screenplay and drop it off at a Beverly Hills literary agent's office. So, I popped into a print center on Wilshire Boulevard and stumbled upon these orange, leather-basketball looking 8" X 11" covers. How perfect. They were so cute! I had to have them. How clever was I going to be by submitting a basketball-themed script with an orange basketball-like cover?

Probably too clever for my own good. I didn't want to send my script in the patent white card stock cover, I wanted to be different. I wanted to stand out. Boy, if I had a nickel for every time I heard a wannabe say that! Unfortunately, the standard screenplay cover is white and no matter how boring I found white to be, it was the standard and that's how my screenplay needed to be uniformed. So, what did I do? I bought the orange leathery paper anyway and now I use it as my personal script cover. This, of course, happened after a year of sending my script out with solar orange, fiery red, and orbit blue covers. I can still hear the readers laughing at me. And you, too!

There's plenty of room for individuality in Hollywood, but if there's a particular standard for submitting something in your particular industry, just do it.

A FUTURE OSCAR-WINNING SCREENWRITER GOES ONE-ON-ONE WITH FRAN

NATASHA WILLIAMS | P.A.W. PRODUCTIONS

FH: Why/how did you decide to get into the entertainment business?
NW: Ever since I was 10, I remember watching the Academy Awards and fantasizing about winning one. However, being shy and unpopular, I never envisioned myself as an actress, so I didn't think it was possible. It wasn't until my late teens that I realized I could win an Oscar for my writing, but since there weren't any film schools in my small, Louisiana town and I didn't have any money to go to one out of state, I had no idea how it was going to happen. As fate would have it, in my early twenties, I met a German film and TV producer and screenwriter who helped me gain the confidence to pursue a screenwriting career, nonetheless.

FH: What was the one perception you had about being in the business that you found out was inaccurate?
NW: The most profound inaccurate perception I had that actually jumpstarted my career once I discovered it was that you don't have to live in Hollywood or have attended film school to write and sell a feature film.

FH: What do you wish someone had told you prior to your becoming whatever you are?
NW: That it takes a long time and a lot of patience to succeed in this business. My perception was that I could write a great script, sell it and it's made into a movie. In reality I've found that the first step, making the sale, is the most nerve wrecking part of the entire process and even if you are fortunate enough to make a sale, it may take years to see the script made into a movie, if ever.

FH: Who are/were some of the people you admire in the biz and why?
NW: I admire each of the 13 African-American screenwriters featured in Erich Leon Harris' book *African-American Screenwriters Now – Conversations with Hollywood's Black Pack*. Every time I feel hopeless or fathom the thought of giving up, I read one of their inspirational stories and I feel a new burst of hope, energy, determination, and assurance that I will succeed, because they have succeeded before me.

FH: What's been the most difficult aspect of being in the biz?
NW: At first getting my work read was a tremendous challenge. Now that producers are requesting my scripts, giving them something that "meets their developmental needs" has been the second challenge. The third challenge has been to stay positive and motivated. One of my mentors in the biz told me to just write the movies my heart desires and, eventually, good writing sells.

FH: What do you think you'd be doing if you weren't in the biz?
NW: Actually, since I have convinced myself that I will write and sell movies, I don't think about doing anything else. I will always write and if I write novels in the interim, that I'll do. But if my screenwriting career went absolutely nowhere after 10 years, I would probably seek employment in some other aspects of the film industry, even if it's working in a studio's accounting department, since that's what I do when I'm not working on a script.

FH: Ever slept with someone or would you consider sexual favors to get a job?
NW: No, I've never slept with anyone nor would I consider giving sexual favors just to get a job, for two reasons. One, I wouldn't feel good about myself if I did that and two, I don't trust what people say, I trust what they do. My point is for them to give me the job first and when they make money from my work, I won't have to sleep with them, because they'll find out that I'm really talented and making money is a lot better than sex, at least where the movies are concerned.

All in all, that's the ideal, but I have been propositioned. Actually, a German producer I met, who became my first mentor in the biz, invited me to L.A., all expenses paid, for a meeting. He was in L.A. to scout locations for a film with his film partner and wanted to introduce me to some of his colleagues. I was very excited about it, but not totally naïve. I bluntly told the Einstein look alike that I would love to go to L.A. for the weekend but I had no interest in having any intimate relations with him. That promptly ended our mentor-mentee relationship. I was kind of hurt when he had his assistant block all my calls and e-mails, but I knew I had made the right decision.

Although he turned out to be a sleaze in the end, he really helped me to build my confidence and to believe that I could be a screenwriter if I stick with it. One day, when I'm on stage winning my Oscar for best screenplay,

I hope he's still alive to witness that I did it without degrading myself. Or, if he has to witness it from hell, that'll be fine, too.

FH: Share one hard knocks lesson you've learned.
NW: There are a lot of "balls" in Hollywood and not the kind we throw at each other. Besides discovering that people will use you to get what they want without any real intention of helping you get what you want, I learned that some people in Hollywood, or even the wannabes, are selfish sharks motivated by money and will chew up anyone to get it.

My first hard knocks lesson came when my story plot was stolen right in my face. I had taken a screenwriting course where the objective was to write a script throughout the course and have our classmates critique it. Each week we had to read 15 pages of script out loud. Four weeks into the program, one of my classmates decided to scrap his story because it wasn't going anywhere. His new script had the same plot and story line so closely related to my script, that it *was* my script! Furious, I confronted him in the classroom and he pointed out that since my scientist was a man and his was a woman, and the settings were in two different cities, that it wasn't the same story. I wanted to jump over my desk and wring his neck so that his beady little eyes would pop out and I could stomp on them, but instead I said, "I don't care if your story is set in the middle of the Amazon, you stole my plot!" The teacher refused to comment because ideas are not copyrightable. So that made the remaining four weeks of class awkward and frustrating. I stopped reading because I didn't want to give him any additional information to add to "our" script. Great ideas are like gold and I guard mine like a hungry lioness in front of a big piece of meat.

FH: If you had the chance to start your career over, what, if anything, would you do differently?
NW: If I had the chance to start my career over, the only thing I would do differently is to start it sooner than I did. I feel that if I had had the courage to go to film school instead of a regular university and studied film/scriptwriting instead of accounting and writing for fun, I would be a lot further along. However, I believe everything happens in its own time and because of my accounting degree, I am able to pay my bills while I wait for script deals to be made. No starving artist here.

FH: How do you handle rejection?
NW: I learned not to take it personally. They are not rejecting me; they are just not interested in that particular script. When I began to take this outlook on being rejected, rejection started not to bother me. Of course, I get disappointed when someone passes, but I usually try to interest him or her in another project or just move on to the next person. I stopped trying to figure it out. "The right script will get in the right person's hand at the right time." That's what I tell myself and keep chugging along.

FH: Best advice given to you.
NW: I'm fortunate to have two great mentors in the business. Both love my writing style and believe in me. The best advice that they've given me over the years is:
- You are a great writer.
- Guard whom you share your ideas with. Ideas are golden. (I learned this first hand).
- Network, don't be afraid to be yourself and tell everyone you meet what you do because you never know who knows whom.
- You will be a success because I believe in you.
- Never give up, no matter what.

FH: One or two pieces of advice for fellow warriors.
NW: Everywhere you go, tell people what you do, find a mentor in the business and never ever give up.

FH: Open forum.
NW: In addition to the advice that has been given to me, my final comments for everyone are the principles I use to keep myself motivated and inspired.

- Believe in yourself and your work
- Always look for ways to stretch yourself
- Know in your heart that you'll succeed
- Quitting or giving up is never an option
- If one door closes, look for a window and when another one happens to open, no matter how small, stick your foot in it!

WHEN THEY SAY THIS... THEY MEAN THIS

I know you want it. You want it really badly. The director who saw you audition said she liked your work. The producer who heard you sing said, "You've got something special." The agent who read your script e-mailed you saying, "I didn't fall in love with the characters." All of this is industry speak, but what in the hell does it really mean? Four words: keep your day job.

Basically, if people really vibe with you, they almost always say so immediately. Occasionally, if a casting director likes you but someone else has final say, you may not get a strong response after your audition but rather something like, "I liked it." Or they'll ask you to read again or with another partner.

Most wannabes are so desperate to make it in the biz that they blow simple comments out of proportion. My advice is not to get excited until you're standing on the set of a movie or looking at your film on the screen. Anything short of these two things is likely to be all smoke and mirrors. I don't mean to sound cynical but we all have to see things for what they are, not for what we'd like them to be. We're always looking for that little ray of sunshine when you audition or get feedback on your work, right? Well, unless you're standing in front of *Idol*'s Simon Cowell, you're not going to get brutal honesty about your work. People are far too polite to be rude. So, I've put a few phrases together to help you sift through the Hollywood speak. Brace yourself.

When they say: "Thank you for coming in," they mean:
You didn't get it. They won't be calling you. They won't be following up. There'll be no callbacks for you. Next!

When they say: "It didn't work for me," they mean:
I didn't like what you showed me. Maybe I don't really think you have "it." Don't call us and we won't call you.

When they say: "I think you're amazingly talented, we're just not signing any new talent right now," they mean:
I *don't* think you're amazingly talented but I needed to say that in case one day you're rich and famous. I may think you have talent, but I couldn't get enough people in the company to agree with me. I couldn't get the most important person in the company to agree with me.

When they say: "Gee, this one wasn't right for us but please feel free to send us other __," they mean:
I didn't think your materials were exceptional, but may want to keep the door open in case you do finally produce or write something great.

When they say: "We'll keep your tape on file for future consideration," they mean:
Maybe they'll keep your tape, resume, reel, or headshot on file for future consideration but it's likely that they tossed your materials that day.

When they say: "We're not taking submissions right now," they mean:
They didn't like what you sent them. They will not be buying whatever you're selling. They won't be signing you or calling you back. True story. I got a rejection letter from a producer who said, "I liked the story but I'm just not taking submissions right now." I said okay and continued to build the attachments on my project. A day or so passed and a recording artist, who happens to be a very good actor, heard about my project and possibly wanted to be involved, so I called this producer again with an update. All of a sudden he was very interested in the project. Why? Because the more viable attachments you have to your project (even if your script's not good, sad to say), the more interest you'll get. Just make sure your attachments are verifiable, not figments of your imagination.

Remember, people in the entertainment business are in the business of making money. If you can help them do that, then they will ALWAYS take your call or meet with you. Don't ever believe that people are not taking new talent, new pitches or new clients, etc. They are. You've got to figure out how to make yourself more attractive, either by sharpening your talent or by bringing famous people on board with your project.

HOW BADLY DO YOU WANT IT?
The popular Gatorade advertisement asks a compelling question, "Is it in you?" Anybody can aspire to be famous and rich. That takes no work at all. But how many of us are willing to put in the time that it takes to achieve our desired level of fame and celebrity?

Know this. The extent to which you'll be successful in the entertainment world is in direct correlation to how hard you're willing to work to improve your craft. I am amazed at how easy we, yes, we, think this journey's going to be, at the start, but most of us learn quickly that making it in showbiz is no picnic. I learned that from the jump. It's the rehearsals and rewrites that end up making you what you are. So, give yourself a reality check by asking, "Am I really using my time and resources in a way that will yield the greatest rewards for me?" A lot of people think that working 23 hours a day means that they're working hard. Not necessarily. Some of my best work has come out of 90-minute intervals. Sometimes my best workout at the gym is a quick 45-minute combo weight and aerobic training session. It's not about the quantity, it's the quality. So, just because you've only slept four hours in the last week, doesn't make you a smart worker. It's possible that you could have accomplished the same results in half the time.

HOW TO SELL YOURSELF WITHOUT SELLING YOUR SOUL

"I want you to make me into whatever you want, I want to be your product." Those are the immortal words of a contestant who stood before a panel of talent show judges. I buried my head in my sweater. And it wasn't just this kid who said this. Scores of other wannabes shared the same sentiments as they waited on their turn to be judged. The next great talent won't be the person who lets "them" remold and remake her. The next great talent won't be the guy who lays himself at the altar of Hollywood so that it can reshape him into the next Vin Diesel. The next great talent will be the person who walks into a room and blows folks away with incredible talent and possibly, charisma, although that's usually a bonus, not a requirement for stardom.

Here Are Some Quick Tips for Selling Yourself.
Know yourself. Who are you? What are your core values?

Know what makes you or your product unique. This is what I call your Unique Selling Point(s). These are the things that you should highlight. If you're beautiful, be beautiful not sexually provocative. If you're smart, quick, make sure those qualities come out in a way that makes people take notice. I'm not talking about "trying" to wow people with your intellect — that'll just irritate the hell out of 'em — I'm talking about "being" quick and sharp naturally.

Know your boundaries. Have some idea of how far you'll go for the deal or success.

THE 10-MINUTE RULE

There's something magical that happens every 10 minutes in face-to-face meetings or in two-minute conversations over the phone and at parties. There are no long conversations in Hollywood, because attention spans tend to be nonexistent there. So, you've gotta learn to make your point quickly.

When you get a meeting with an executive, plan on it being about 10 minutes long. It may be longer, but you want to work in 10-minute intervals. If you can keep someone's attention for longer than 10 minutes, you're doing great. So, with that in mind, I'm going to give you some tools for rocking your 10-minutes.

First, have a short version to every long story you have. Practice it with friends and have them time you. Try to keep the story interesting and peaking at every 30-second interval. So, if you're pitching a movie, this keeps the pace fairly brisk and safeguards against boredom.

Second, just because you're on a time crunch doesn't mean you need to talk so fast that no one knows what you've said. Make your points, but you don't want to sound like you're on drugs (even if you are).

Third, be ready to move to the last part of your pitch earlier than you'd planned, because the person listening may say something like, "So, what do want from me?" Or "So, what happens to the main character in the end?" And if you get that question, you go immediately to the last 15-30 seconds of your pitch. Instead of saying, "He died," you might try something like, "He hunts down the guy who killed his mother and they have this big shootout on top of a 20-story building before he's shot." The end result is the same, but this dramatic explanation makes for a more exciting close to the story.

THE INTERVIEW THAT ALMOST WASN'T

LIZ OWEN | PRODUCER – PRESIDENT | GIRLIE GIRL PRODUCTIONS

Imagine sitting in Starbucks, waiting on someone whom you've never met. You watch the clock as you prepare for the inevitable questions, "Are you ____?" I'd gotten to this particular store about 20 minutes early to make some phone calls. But about 20 minutes into my wait, I decided that the area where I was sitting, a little enclave by the back door, was too obscure, so I decided to move to the table by the main entrance. Another five minutes passed and I decided to make a quick run to the restroom. Unbeknownst to me, when I went to the restroom, Liz Owen, my interviewee, walked around the store looking for me. Then she stepped outside to see if maybe I was out there.

While she's outside I emerge from the restroom looking for her, even though I have no idea what she looks like. So, I head back to my seat, glance at my clock and wait patiently. Surely she'll be there shortly. I head to the register. "Have you seen anyone looking for anyone?" I ask. They hadn't. So, I move out of the line and start checking out the pastry case. All the while, Liz is sitting in the place by the back door where I'd originally sat. Waiting on me, someone she's never met.

This goes on for about 15 minutes. My going to the restroom and looking around for someone who looks like she's waiting. Her walking around every time I left my seated area. Finally I sat down and she walked over. "Are you Fran?" We both laughed and the interview started.

FH: Who are you, now that we've found each other?
LO: I was just about to leave.

FH: I'm glad you didn't because I just wrote my next short film.
LO: My name is Liz and I sit at Starbucks and avoid people I'm supposed to be interviewing with.

FH: You're very good at it, by the way.
LO: Thank you. I'm with Girlie Girl Productions. I started this company officially in 1997 but didn't start doing it full time until mid 2000. In my previous incarnation I was an actress, I went to Northwestern as an undergrad in theater. Did my graduate work at New Actors Workshop

in NYC, and then moved back to Chicago. I was lucky, I went from show to show. Then woke up one morning and was bored. I knew I still wanted to be in the arts but didn't want to be on stage anymore. Knew I wanted to transition into film and TV but thought it would happen as an actor. I researched and assessed my strengths and weaknesses and found that producing was a good fit for me. I had an offer to come work for someone who was a producer. I really admired her. Only thing is that she'd just hired someone. She said "Give me six months to fire her and then I'll hire you." Welcome to Hollywood. Instead of doing that I decided to start my own company. Then I took a hiatus and co-founded FilmBureau 606, a not-for-profit for filmmakers in Chicago. I was executive director for three years. Hit a crossroads where I was deciding whether I was going to stay in the nonprofit world and help people get their films made or go back to focus on my own stuff. So, I focused on my own stuff and my husband and I picked up and moved out here.

FH: Did you move to L.A. or the Valley?
LO: L.A. First to hooker central over on Sunset, now in the Hollywood Hills.

FH: Who's Girlie Girl?
LO: Originally it was just me, but while I was doing my NPO, people started writing articles about us. Our goal was to get people to talk to one another, it was very scattered. I got a call from this woman in L.A. who was working for a major manager/producer at the time. She was his head of development and she was looking to make connections in other cities. We spoke to each other for about a year and a half via phone and then I came out here, met with her face to face, and decided to partner up. Then we started interviewing to find some interns to read for us. In between, I met a woman in Chicago who'd been working for a lit manager in Boston and was moving to Chicago. And I knew I was gearing up to move to L.A., but I didn't want to lose my Chicago connection, because there are great writers there. So I asked her how she felt about being my Chicago eyes and ears. She signed on as a development associate in Chicago. Then there was another woman in New York whom I met in Chicago and had a long-time working relationship with. She's our senior vice president of production. We interviewed 20 people to read for us, but a lot of the ones we talked to had more experience — they were looking at this as a stepping stone. We have an opportunity to give people that next step up.

FH: How difficult was it to create this nucleus of people whom you felt would be right for your GG family?
LO: In some ways I have the opposite problem. Coming from a theater background, it was really collaborative. Studying at Northwestern, they really pushed the mentality that, even though you're an actor, you still have to take design classes, crew classes, and lighting classes. So I've had the philosophy that I'd better know how to set up my own lights and know something about costumes before I have the right to stand in the spotlight and wear the costumes. So my feeling is anytime I meet people who are great I want to work with them. I think my best and worst quality is that I'm quick to work with people, because our commitment is sometimes different. Not in terms of commitment but more in terms of focus. My partner and I parted ways — we're good friends, but we have very different approaches to the business. She likes to find one project and work only on that project. That works for some people. That would not work for me. I want to have 20,000 things going at one time, because when one drops off the map another one is going. Our approaches were so different, and both are equally valid, but they did not coincide and rather than not be friends we went our separate ways. The people I am working with, we all share the same focus. Even with my former partner, though, we always respect the writer, we feel the writer is not expendable. I'm working on a feature that we've been on for about three years and we've stuck with the original writer because we felt like he was the right person to work on it. But, finally, he said, "I don't think I could do it, but my son's a writer." Sure enough, we took the project to his son and got a brilliant first draft four years later. Literally four years later. And it worked out. Now, the last writer's got two huge projects going. One at Warner Bros. Another at Universal. Now we've got another film and a TV deal with him, so who knew? Who knows what would have happened had we dropped him to bring in another writer.

[*Her phone rings*].

FH: Your cell phone is on in our meeting that almost didn't happen?
LO: [*On phone*]. We were just talking about you. [*It's the writer*].

FH: Where were we? Two years out here, you've got a lot of stuff swirling on. You seem to be moving along.
LO: We're kind of in a weird gray area. We're not straight studio stuff. We've got some TV stuff. I pitched some stuff a few years ago that I

thought was really good, timely but nobody bit. Then a couple of years pass, the world changes politically and all of a sudden my phone was ringing off the hook because all of a sudden it became a...

FH: Viable project.
LO: Viable and artistically appropriate. Now to me, it's always been artistically viable. It's written by an amazing writer, but from a business model, things just need to be happening at the right time. So, I don't close any door.

FH: So, what was that conversation like when you called to pitch and they throw that "what are your credits line" at you. How is that conversation for you?
LO: Short. Normally I don't always pick up the phone and call people directly. I will send a short query letter and fax it and because I'm not a writer, but a producer, they'll accept a faxed query from me. Just a quick synopsis about the story. A little about the writer — in this case, he's a Tony Award-winning British writer and he's attached to write the screenplay — saying "we think you'll see the value in this story, as we do." And everyone I queried called back. Every single one. I sent about 20 queries out. I don't go wide because if it doesn't go well the first time...

FH: You don't wanna blow yourself out of the water.
LO: Exactly. So I went very targeted and specific to a lot of places. Some thought it wasn't big enough. With one cable channel, for instance, it wasn't big enough for them, but it's funny, two years before, when I originally pitched it to them, while they were still empire building, it would have been perfect for them. Now, I'm working with another producer who's produced for cable and knows the playwright, so we're going out with it again. He has something I don't have. He's got a track record. So, my queries are simple, short and I follow up with a phone call.

FH: You sound like you're really loyal to people, but with all of this love, faith, trusting, and believing, are you getting any work done?
LO: It's funny that you say that because the first project I did, we didn't have a contract and I busted my butt to get it all together and then the writer wouldn't sign a contract. We're three days before shooting, my name's on every contract and I get a call from the director saying "the writer refuses to sign a contract, you're not producing this anymore, I am. You can still be a part of it, you can be a P.A. if you want, but we can't get this done if you're involved at this level."

FH: Doesn't sound like this was an easy escape deal on your end.
LO: I had thousands of dollars sitting in the bank that I'd raised for this project. So, I told the director that I couldn't, in good conscience, keep my investors' money tied up in a project that I wasn't involved in because I could no longer guarantee that their money would be well spent. So, I sent the investors their money back, rewrote all the contracts in two days, so that the director's name was on them and mine wasn't. I pulled out. I subsequently saw the film and it's a shame, because it could have been a good film and it wasn't what it could have been.

FH: Too bad.
LO: I learned so much by completely screwing it up. It was the best lesson because I learned that everything has to be on paper. If it isn't on paper, don't do it. For example, I just had a great kid's script that came our way and we were going do a short, non-exclusive shopping deal, but I wanted it on paper. The writers said, "Well, if it's nonexclusive, it doesn't need to be on paper." I said "Sorry, bye, let me know if you change your mind."

FH: Sometimes ya gotta walk away.
LO: Yep. I had a TV deal that fell apart because the paperwork couldn't be worked out. We'd put in hours of work having a lawyer draw up documents. We presented the paperwork and they said "We can't agree to any of this" and we said "Sorry, we can't do the deal." So, with all of this trust and faith, even if it's your best friend, write it down. The best-laid plans go awry. If it ain't on paper, it ain't getting done. With this TV deal, it was simply a matter of writing down our oral agreement and they didn't want to do it. And we'd already pitched it to one of the networks.

FH: This brings up a good question from the land of desperation. Some people are so eager and dire to get into the biz that they sell their souls. They get caught up in the excitement of deal making and then, a week later, they're sipping a frappucino wondering what happened. How do you come back to the middle, knowing that you want to do business with someone, but not being too pushy about that little contract thing? I've told people that they have to get it in writing and they've said, "But she might get mad." My response is if people have a problem with simple written agreements, you do not want to be in business with them because people who are for real do not frown at getting it written.

LO: Yep. One of my best friends is a phenomenal screenwriter and he had a screenplay, but his script wasn't getting any hits. So, we started talking about me taking it out. So, I had my lawyer draw up a one page memo that basically said if I get attached to produce it, I'll take my fee and you'll get your money. And if I don't get attached to produce it, because I don't have a track record, then I'll take a percentage of the sale and it's yours to run with. One of my *best* friends. It's on paper. I took it to three places, a couple of the studios and to a producer manager. And consistently down the line I got feedback and it was all the same. Everyone came back with the same thing. I'm thinking well, since this is the feedback, then maybe we should do a little work on this. I contacted him and his response?

FH: Upset.
LO: Very upset. He said "No; I want to get paid to do this work." We had a huge fight about it. Then I realized that I agreed with him, he was right and I was wrong. I signed on to pitch this thing as is and if they're interested enough, then he should get paid for the script and then they can tweak it as they see fit. So I called him and said "you were right, I was wrong." I then spent some additional time trying to sell it and after a year, I had the option to continue shopping it and I didn't renew it. We walked away friends because you have to be able to admit when you f----d up. I don't ever have a problem with that because you have to be honest with yourself.

FH: So, has he sold it?
LO: Not yet, but he just signed with a manager and he's got other scripts out there. He's going to sell something; he's a great writer. That's one scenario. On the deals that I've been striking with people, I'm fortunate that I've had to spend very little money. My contracts, I feel, are pretty fair, but now I've been doing these nonexclusive shopping deals, which, in some cases, have me paying five dollars for six months. But you can still take them to other people. Here's a list of places I know I can take these. You will be okay with this list of places. If it leads to other places, you will sign off on those and I'll take them there. If this property sells through another channel that you have, I'm entitled to nothing and you get what you want. And this method really works because I get what I want, which is to have everything on paper and it doesn't limit them from taking it to other people. It can't get more flexible than this. But some people aren't comfortable with it and by all means, don't sign anything that you aren't comfortable with. Spend $30 and have the Lawyers For The Arts look at the paperwork.

FH: How much networking do you do?
LO: Not enough. Part of it is because I'm married. I work a lot of hours, my husband works a lot of hours and it's real important that when I have down time, it's truly down time. It's never been me to get out there and go to parties every night. Even when I was single, that was just not my thing. I don't want to have a Hollywood marriage.

FH: There are marriages in Hollywood? That's right, there's Tom (Hanks) and Rita (Wilson). I have to admit, I will be devastated if they ever break up, because they're the only couple who look like they'd be together, even if they hadn't met on the set. They don't look as if they're "acting" like they love each other, when they're on TV. We sit at home — and this is horrible, I admit — but we're watching other Hollywood couples on the red carpet, my friends and I, and I'm thinking, "I give that duo about six weeks. St. Patty's Day for them. They'll be lucky to carve the turkey together this year!"
LO: My marriage is the single most important thing to me, so it's priority. If it's a choice between the big party and the husband, it depends. Did I see the husband yesterday? If so, I'll go to the party. If I didn't, chances are I'm going to watch a movie. Oops! I just revealed my big secret; I'm not evil and hungry. But I meet a ton of people through the Web. You're a case in point. I'm always getting e-mails from people who want to get together — I don't know how they find me. Maybe it's my company name.

FH: It's intriguing. It was compelling enough for me to seek you out. Seriously.
LO: Well, that's good. I have an open door policy. I like meeting people but also I think it's important to be open to meeting people at all levels. I know that will change because the more work you do, the more you have to scale back. But I'm hopeful that, by then, people will know enough about me to know that if I can't talk to them it's because I'm busy and not because I'm a bitch.

FH: Which you are, by the way.
LO: I know. I feel like the only thing I have to carry around with me in this world is my name and who I am as a person. I want my work ethic to reflect the kind of person I am. When I query people on the phone I'm aware of what I'd want people to say to me when they call me. What would I not want to hear? Would I be uncomfortable receiving this call? I also have things that just tick me off. Someone sends me a letter that starts off "Dear Sir."

FH: [*Laughs*].
LO: Hello? That makes me insane.

FH: What's wrong? Maybe it's Marcie from the Peanuts gang writing ya! [*Loud laughs*].
LO: [*Laughs*]. That's true, I guess. It makes me nuts! It's not the "Dear Sir" and I'm actually a woman that bothers me but what it tells me, is that you haven't done even the most basic homework. I have a whole Web site that tells you to whom you address your query.

FH: I know a man named Elizabeth, by the way.
LO: You do not! No, but I'm serious, if you send me a generic query, you're getting off on the wrong foot. Some writers are so sloppy. They misspell my name, the name of the company, it's sloppy. Read the instructions. Like right now we're only taking queries via e-mail. Make it hard for me to say "no" to you. I want to like your work.

FH: Most writers think producers and readers are dying to say "no."
LO: I know. It's not true. Who wouldn't want to love something they read or discover a great new writer? A quick story. I had these two guys who'd just graduated from NYU and they e-mailed me a query. I loved the letter. It was genuine, fresh, and funny. It was one of the best queries I've ever received and it hooked me. I said if their query letter is this funny and they're sending me a romantic comedy, it's probably going to be funny. And it was. It needs some development, but it was funny. So, I sent them an e-mail saying I loved the script but "I think you can get money for this script. Keep me posted and if you really exhaust your possibilities maybe we can do something together." Flash forward a few months later. I get an e-mail from them saying they hadn't really gotten any bites on the script. So I turned them on to a friend of mine who's a manager, who's going to read their script. Now, they're coming out here and we're going to meet and talk about possibly working together. Why? Because of their query letter.

FH: You mean they didn't send you a dozen flowers or some other gimmick?
LO: They don't typically work. I've had people say, "Well, my movie's a bubble gum love story, blah blah" and they send me a pack of bubble gum. C'mon, don't. I have enough shit on my desk as it is. I don't need your chewing gum.

FH: What else have writers done that made you wonder about the depth of their drug addiction?

LO: When someone sends me an e-mail query letter that has 17 synopses in it. This tells me that you're prolific but haven't sold anything. That you cannot focus on one thing. This does not say, "Oh, great writer, I have 17 things to choose from." Just don't. One, then see what my response is.

FH: Yeah, true, my experience is that if my query gets their attention but the particular script I query isn't what they're looking for, they'll ask me what else I've got.

LO: Absolutely. I've had situations like that. I don't believe you only have one shot, but you do have one shot to make a first impression and what is that going to be? And if your first impression is that you've written 20 things, you got my name wrong and you faxed me your query? That's all I need to know to make a note to ignore your next query.

FH: What's the most common crap you see with new writers?

LO: Hmm, well certainly if you're sending me a comedy, please make sure it's funny. It can't just be funny if I'm drunk and it's midnight. It's gotta be funny. Proofread. Your spellchecker's not going to catch everything. Get a pair of human eyes on your script. My feeling is if I'm going to spend an hour reading your work, make it easy for me to visualize the story. If I keep stumbling on your typos, I'm taken out of my imagination. You don't want that.

FH: Okay, best advice given to you.

LO: My family just saying "go for it." I mean, they let me major in theater twice for two degrees. I think the people who are trying to talk other people out of being in the business are the ones who are successful. If it's the thing you want, make it work. Five years ago I didn't know any-thing about this business, now I do.

FH: Big advice for anyone starting out?

LO: Stay true to who you are. Don't become what you think other people want you to become because, ultimately, your success will be very shallow success. If you've corrupted everything you believed in your whole life for a paycheck, you have nothing. You have cash, which is great but it's built on such a hollow foundation. It reminds me of a story Mike Nichols told us in grad school — he was one of my teach-ers. He told this story about those chocolate Easter bunnies. He said you can get the kind that disappoint you, because, when you bite into them, they're hollow. Or, you can get the solid chocolate bunnies, the really good bunnies. Then he met his wife and thought, "wow, she's a really solid bunny." So, I guess my big advice is to be a solid bunny.

FH: Hey, I'm already a chocolate bunny. I'm a solid chocolate bunny! Thanks, Liz.

ACT II CHECKLIST

√ What's the best way to get a meeting in your industry?

√ How many people stand between you and the Dream Filler who can change your career?

√ What does it mean to detach from outcomes?

√ What is intentional goal setting?

√ What is one of Fran's Top One-on-One Questions?

√ When is it okay to drop a name?

√ What's an MOW?

√ What's the best way to clear a creative "block?"

√ How often should you e-mail an executive if you're NOT in the middle of a deal with him or her?

√ List one or two things that stuck out in the interviews in Act II?

√ What's a pitch?

√ What should you do the night before a big meeting or audition?

ACT III

MASTERING THE GAME:

ADVANCED SKILLS FOR FUTURE POWER PLAYERS

HOW TO FOLLOW UP LIKE A PRO

The key to following up like you mean it, is precision. You have to keep a log of your activities, that's the only way you're going to be able to manage the madness. Check out the sample Success Log below. It's really helped me to keep it together. Knowing who got what, when, will help you to follow up like a pro. Don't just send your script to producers and count on them to remember you. Don't just send your tape to an agent and expect her to know you from the next reel she looked at. Don't send your headshot to a scout and think you're going to get a call like clockwork in a few weeks. You've got to be the leader of the pack. So, when you make your follow-up calls, it's "Hey Cathy, I wanted to follow up regarding my script, "Victory," which I sent to you on December 15."

SUCCESS LOG

PROPERTY/DATE	SUBMITTED TO:	EXEC/CONTACT	RESULT	FOLLOW UP NEEDED
SP/12/16/02 Loose Balls	Cathy Wilson Associates	Cathy Wilson	Liked script, wants to meet on 1/20	Confirm 1/17
Q/12/16/02	ABC agents,	Larry Tate	Requested Loose Balls	Send scripts
BP/9/02 Crashing Hollywood	Michael Wiese Prods	Ken Lee	Bought	Deliver manuscript 2/15

BP = Book Proposal   SP = Screenplay   TR = Treatment   Q = Query
TVT = TV Tape   AC = Audio Cassette

HE'LL CALL

It's so hard not to bug people when you're waiting to hear if they liked you or your work, but if you do, you'll live to regret it. I said it earlier but let me say it again. Money's at stake. Jobs hang in the balance. Face is constantly being saved. Things take time. If executives like you, they will call. It may not be soon enough to suit you, but they'll call. Your job is not to drive yourself (or those close to you) insane in the middle of a deal or while you're waiting to hear if ya got the part.

Here's a Quick Rule of Thumb.
Give decision makers at least a week (five business days) before following up, unless they've said, "Call me tomorrow." Now, business days are all of the days except Saturday and Sunday. Don't count those days. I'm telling you this because there are people who, when they meet with someone on Friday and hear "Call me in a week," begin to bug executives by Wednesday. That's not a week, that's three days since your meeting.

Your first follow up should be via e-mail, if possible. Why? Because if they haven't gotten to you yet, your e-mail will serve as a reminder that you'll be calling them soon. They'll be more likely to do something if you give them a soft reminder such as an e-mail. If they haven't gotten to your deal, they're probably not going to take your phone call anyway.

Be sure to include a line in your e-mail follow up that says, "I'll be following up with you in a few days." Now they know that the next contact will be your phone call.

Your next follow up should be a phone call somewhere between three to five days after your initial e-mail contact, unless you've been otherwise instructed. If the person responds to your e-mail with something like, "I'm behind, give me another week," then of course, you're not going to call three days after the e-mail, you're going to wait a week.

Finally, be sure you file or save all correspondence, so that you can track your contacts.

PICK A POCKET, ANY POCKET
This is a term used when agents like you but don't want to do any paperwork on you. In other words, you're on their list of clients, but not really. They're holding onto you in case you "pop." Then they'll sign you. In the interim, they are servicing you a little, but not that much, which is not to say that they're not doing anything. They probably are. They don't pocket someone they can't do something for.

If you're wondering if being pocketed is a good thing, ask yourself this question. "Can I do better at this stage in my career or find a better rep?" If the answer is yes, move on. If the answer is no, continue to work your buns off out there marketing yourself. There are advantages to being pocketed by a well-known agency. If you happen to meet someone who wants to hear your demo, for example, but needs to be contacted by an agent because of potential legal issues, you're set.

Some writers don't mind being pocketed because it's an easy way for them to have their scripts submitted in Hollywood. You have to decide if it's worth it for you. It does you no good to be able to say, "I'm repped by Creative Artists" if you haven't had one meeting, sold one script or gotten one option in the 10 years you've been with them. Always weigh the advantages of having an agent versus the disadvantages that come without representation. But never, ever stay with an agent who's not doing anything for you. You can do better by yourself.

Wannabes are so eager to get an agent that they'll sign their lives away just to say those elusive four words, "I have an agent." But if you have a bad agent, you may as well not have an agent at all. I once interviewed with a commercial agent who couldn't find my headshot at the beginning of our meeting. She rummaged through her bag for about five minutes and then pulled my headshot out. It was wrinkled beyond recognition. "Here we go," she said, as she straightened it out.

No, we don't, I thought. I read for her but didn't sign with her. Remember, you're interviewing them, too! As desperate as you may feel, you've got to hook up with someone whom you trust, first. Second, sign with someone who can actually get the job done. This particular agent didn't inspire a great deal of confidence in her ability to handle my career, so I didn't sign with her.

IRRECONCILABLE DIFFERENCES

When is it time to divorce your agent? When you don't get along and there's no good ending in sight. Look, it's a relationship. And nobody wants to be in bed with someone who bails at the first sight of danger. Nobody. Agents, the good ones, invest a lot of time and energy into building your brand and managing your career. Their reward comes in three ways (1) your relationship, (2) the 10% they get from your paycheck, and (3) your success.

There are going to be up and down times, it's inevitable. There will be times when you'll be upset that so and so got a part that you wanted, but couldn't even get a read for. That may not be your agent's fault.

It's important to keep your emotions directed at the proper recipients. Never lash out at your agent because things don't go the way you want them to. Unless of course, it's your agent's fault, then lash all you want. But no agent worth sofa lint wants to bust her hump for a client who's always looking to defect when a bigger name agent shows interest. That's not cool. Some people do it, but it won't get you any points in Hollywood.

When is it time to start looking for a new agent? Does this sound familiar? *"I've been calling my agent for a week, he hasn't called me back."*

If you were in a relationship with someone you'd been trying to reach for a week and he or she didn't return your calls, would you be upset? Most of us would. Now, I'm not saying that an agent/client relationship is on equal footing with a marriage, but it's in the neighborhood, that's for damn sure. A week is plenty of time to return a call. An agent who doesn't return your call after seven days does not place you in the highest priority. No exceptions. Yes, it may take the head of Sony two weeks to get to your demo. It may take a lit agent a month to answer your query. And it may take a scout 21 days to respond to your submission for representation. These are all people who are juggling a million things, people, and projects. Your agent, the lump of flesh that you've agreed to compensate handsomely when your ship comes in, is juggling a stable of talent, but not a million people.

"If I had known what it would be like
to have it all, I might have been willing
to settle for less."

— *Lily Tomlin*

FRAN'S GOLDEN RULE #5: BLOWING UP TAKES TIME

If you don't commit, you're gonna quit.
Sounds like something Johnnie Cochran would say, but it's true. Don't even think about giving up on your dream until you've committed at least 10 years to your art. As electric and dynamic as Hollywood is, it takes time to become a star. There's no such thing as an overnight success. So, if you go into it expecting to microwave yourself to stardom, you're simply setting yourself up for a lot of sleepless nights.

AN INTERVIEW WITH THE IRISH CATHOLIC KID WHO BROUGHT US SNF

KEVIN McCORMICK | EXECUTIVE VICE PRESIDENT
THEATRICAL PRODUCTION | WARNER BROS. PICTURES

FH: I couldn't wait to talk to you, only because I've heard such different stories about making it in the business since I've been here. What's your story and what makes it unique or unusual?
KM: I don't know how unusual it is, but it's kind of funny, I think. I had gone to an experimental Quaker school. I'd spent about a year and a half in Mexico — it was all work-studies. I'd go to the University of Mexico in the morning and then I'd work for a director in the afternoon. The next place I went was England. I was first at a university in Norfolk and then I went to London to work at the Institute of the Contemporary Arts. It was the end of the '60s and everything was experimental. My parents were bewildered in terms of what I was doing, exactly. I got a job basically as the talent booker on this year-long program called *The Body is a Medium of Expression*. I got to book the leading mimes of the world. I brought in all sorts of speakers and dance companies; it was really an incredible job, and I was already working part-time as a stringer reviewing theater. At a certain point my parents said "we don't understand what this is, you have to come home and go to a real school."

FH: A real one, huh?
KM: Right, so I ended up dropping out of school and returned to the States after about a year. I only had one American friend and this one friend of mine was the same age, early twenties. He was leaving to move back to California, which was going to leave his job in England open. It was a desperate situation because his replacement couldn't report for about three months. So, he asked me if I'd take over for him. He said "it isn't a long-term thing, it's basically a three-month job, but I'd like to get back to California to open this new office." So, I jumped at the chance, because it meant a three-month postponement for me to move back to the States, re-enroll in college and all of that. And in the end, the guy they'd originally hired decided that he was going to stay in whatever job he was already in, so it worked out and I stayed for 10 years.

FH: And your parents were cool with that?
KM: Well, eventually they understood that I had a real job and it was a really interesting stint because they had 10 shows running in the West End. There were lots of aspects that I liked about it. I began to travel back and forth from London to New York, but at the end of the day I became executive in charge of film production and development, mostly because it wasn't a very big company, but also because I just stuck it out. You just never know where the opportunity is going to come from and a decision you make to do something for a short term could end up leading to a long-term kind of gig. You may not know what course you're on, but sometimes not knowing leads you down the path to your ultimate goal.

FH: You seemed to have a love affair with everything about your life at the time. What enticed you to come back to the States?
KM: The company I was working for was public and ultimately someone made an offer to the owner to buy his company. So, they said to me, "If you stick it out, you may get stock ownership, and so forth. We'll determine all of that when the time comes." The company went private and basically I got to invent a job that never existed, because there was no one else to do it. One of the first projects I bought was *Saturday Night Fever*, which was my first movie. That was it. I got to move back to New York, open the new office there and ultimately found myself back in California.

FH: So after *Saturday Night Fever*?
KM: I came here to Los Angeles, went back to New York. Back out here in 1981 and started doing some stuff on my own.

FH: And eventually ended up at Fox?
KM: Five years before Warner Bros. I was part of a new division called Fox 2000. I'd never been an executive in a big company. It was wild and by the seat of your pants and evocative of that time. I was coming to it late in the game. I knew a lot about the magazine and publishing business, but most of my colleagues, including myself, had never worked for a studio. So it was really fun. We got to develop a lot of good materials. Some worked and some didn't.

FH: So, are you in a lateral from your position at Fox?
KM: I would say it's a different company. At Warner Bros., you're really playing in the big time. Fox 2000 was just one piece of the company,

whereas here, Warner is the company. We make more movies than anybody else. I think we do make movies well. There's a certain kind of history here at Warner Bros. and it's a company that really celebrates film.

FH: What do you like most about what you do?
KM: I love working with talented people, writers and directors. Tiny movies or big movies, just great properties. I'm working with people I've dreamed of working with all my life and I don't know that I'd have that same opportunity in some other places.

FH: Did anybody give you any feedback as you were transitioning from N.Y. to L.A.?
KM: Because *Saturday Night Fever* became such a big hit, I literally went to the head of the line, but I had to learn the business all over again. I did a variety of jobs, some which interested me, some not at all, but I had to make a living. I had to really learn my way into the system. So, I had a producing deal at Universal in the early '80s. Had a video company, which won the first video Grammy. Then I became Sally Field's partner. Ran an animation company.

FH: Is there anything you haven't done? A lot of stone turning.
KM: In a way I sort of did my career in reverse, but there's still a lot of learning, no matter where you start in this business.

FH: What do you see with new people just getting into the business?
KM: People can be highly educated and I think going to film school is great but what I feel is a deficit, and what I see in some of the people I interview, is that they are not as skilled in the movie business and the history of the movie business as they should be.

FH: Where do you acquire that kind of knowledge beyond the books?
KM: You go to movies all the time, you want to understand what a Billy Wilder movie is. You need to know that the history of the business didn't begin in the '70s or now. It began many, many years ago. It's incumbent on all of us to know this stuff if we're in this business. WB is the studio that did the Al Jolson movie, we did the first talking picture movie. We pride ourselves on being ahead technologically in the business.

> **FH:** So, know your industry.
> **KM:** Know it.
>
> **FH:** Best advice for someone wanting to break in?
> **KM:** See everything, read everything. Know that it's not just what something grosses, it's what a movie makes.
>
> **FH:** Best advice given to you.
> **KM:** Stay focused. If it's what you want, stay focused on it.

YOUR EXTREME TEAM

I'm starting to sound like a broken record, I know, but ultimately, my career rests primarily in my hands. Not my agent's, not my manager's — mine. Given that paradigm, I'm an active participant in my career. I'm always pimping and promoting myself. In the past, I have had relationships with people my agent couldn't get return phone calls from. In one instance, I was coming to Los Angeles and I'd set up a meeting at Fox because I knew the executive over the department. In the hustle and bustle of preparing for my trip, I forgot to tell my agent that I'd gotten this meeting with Fox. The day I arrived in Los Angeles, my agent called me and left this message. "Yeah, Fran, I called Fox to set an appointment for you and they told me I was too late — you already had an appointment. That's great. You might've wanted to let me know about that."

He was right. My actions were not intentional, I'd had such a full day that I'd neglected to keep one of the key players on my team in the loop. Not a pattern you want to develop. Always let your agent know what you're doing so he or she can support your efforts, or in some cases, provide feedback or knowledge about how to make something work.

THE SHAMELESS PROMOTER

Listen up. If you don't advertise, nobody will know that you're out there. This doesn't mean that you have to paste your business cards on your forehead, but it does mean that you're always ready to tell people what you're up to, what your latest role was, what script you're working on, when your demo will be complete. You get the point. Be ready to promote yourself. There's no such thing as a shameless promoter. The only shame is on the person who's too shy to spread his or her own gospel.

In 2001, I directed my first stage production, a play based on the work of acclaimed poet Nikki Giovanni. The week before we opened I had a talk with the five-woman cast, none of whom was shy about making sure that we sold the place out. We were playing a small coffeehouse that was so intimate the people on the front row knew what we all had for lunch. At capacity, we're talking about 50 people. When I turned the production meeting to the topic of marketing, these normally crazy and raucous women turned silent on me.

"I don't know about marketing, Fran, I'm an artist," one woman proclaimed.

"I feel uncomfortable asking people to come and watch me perform," another one said.

"It feels weird asking folks to show up, but if you'll give me some post-cards or flyers I'll try to muster up the courage to hand them out," a third one said.

This bellyaching went on for about 10 minutes. One lousy excuse after another until finally I laughed and said, "Okay, fine. If you're cool with playing to empty seats, fine with me. It'll be fun. In fact, it'll be just like rehearsals." They all laughed. "Look," I said. "It's not just about the art, it's about entertainment. When I played ball I gave my best, whether there were 10 or 10,000 people in the stands. But I'd be lying if I said the game wasn't more fun with butts in the seats." We opened to a packed house that Friday.

WHEN TONY ROBBINS TALKS....

It's 2:30 in the morning and I've shut down my computer, but my mind is still churning with ideas and things to put in this book. I grab the notepad next to my bed and go to town. I'm thinking about all of the TV shows that I'll sell. The scripts I'll write. My directorial film debut. Finally, I turn the television to one of my 3,200 worthless cable channels and I hear this guy who's so fired up about whatever he's talking about that I'm ready to get out of bed to go join something. I don't see him yet. Only the effervescent faces in his audience of thousands. The camera pans and guess who it is? The pimpdaddy of motivation, best-selling author, and multi-millionaire Tony Robbins. And I have no idea what he's talking about, but I'm not changing the channel. It's the end of the program and all I hear are his parting words, "Love what you do and don't think about the rejection."

It was just what I needed to hear because the next day, I was about to ask someone to become a founding sponsor for a fitness show that I want to produce and host. Twelve hours later I get the meeting with the sponsor who says, "It's funny you should stop by, we were just talking about how much we need a show like this."

Intentional living works every time.

WILL YOU RESPECT ME IN THE MORNING?

There's an overused axiom, "You have to give respect to get respect" and that's not true. It's possible to respect people without having them respect you or themselves. Your job is to show yourself as a person worthy of respect. The way to do that is to treat every person you encounter with respect and dignity. If someone is rude to you, resist the temptation to be rude back. It is possible. Treat people with the respect that they do not show you. You will be rewarded for doing the right thing.

I'll give you an example of something that happened to me in 2002. I was working on one of my independent sports projects in an editing bay in a television studio. A full-time employee of the station walked over and said, "I need this editing bay." I didn't fully understand what that had to do with me. "Well," I said, "I'm working here. I should be done in about…" He interrupted with, "Look, I don't know who you are and I don't care, I gotta get this package done and I need this bay." "Well, ya see, it doesn't work that way," I said. "If you'd like to use this bay, perhaps you could try something like this: 'I'm on a deadline and I was wondering if I could slip in here. All of the other bays are taken and I really gotta get this done.'" His face was redder than a Roma tomato. His response: "I need this bay." "Sorry," I said, "I should be done in an hour or so." He starts bringing his things over, as if I was going to be intimidated by this very junior high school bullying technique. I continued to edit my work with no intentions of budging. "I need this bay," he demanded. "You don't seem to understand. You may get to talk to other people like that and get your way, but that doesn't work with me. It's rude and I'm not moving. I will be happy to help you meet your deadline with a reasonable request from you." He grimaced and then forced a, "Would you please let me use this bay,

I really need to finish a package and get it on the air." "Of course," I said. I gathered my things and promptly moved aside. It was that simple. He got what he needed and I got what I needed in a civilized fashion.

Now, do we think he would have done the same thing to another guy? It's debatable, but I doubt it. And I didn't care if that little incident had resulted in me losing that contract; I was not going to be treated like a piece of navel lint. Now, when I see that reporter, we are cordial, sometimes friendly with one another. I have no grudge to harbor. I assume he doesn't either, but I don't care, either way. We teach people how to treat us. No truer words were ever spoken. Don't ask yourself why you're being treated a certain way. A better question is, "When did I give this person the idea that I was okay with being treated this way?" Then change it.

YOUR BRAND

We all have something that brands us. Those things that make you uniquely you. Avril Lavigne has a distinct style. She's not a prissy, over-glamorized star. She looks like the millions of teenagers and young adults who buy her music. Besides her obvious talent, what defines Avril Lavigne is her unmistakable style. Ultimately you'll be welcomed into the kingdom because of your talent, but in the meantime, don't get booted out because you look like you're in a time warp. Hollywood's a happening place. And while I don't recommend going out and spending thousands of dollars on a new wardrobe, I do recommend taking a long hard look at your brand. Do you have a signature look or style? Do you need a haircut? Are your glasses the size of Poindexter's? Are you still wearing the same pants you wore 20 years ago? You want people to remember you, not laugh at you.

I'M GOOD ENOUGH, I'M SMART ENOUGH AND DOGGONIT, PEOPLE WANNA DO BI'NESS WITH ME

That's my mantra. And it's gotta become yours. It's about the business. Look, you've got to feel good about who you are. I can't help it, the spiritual, self-help, rah-rah thing is bound to come out. It's who I am. It's not some cute little addendum to this book, I believe this crap!

If you think you're too young, too old, too fat, too skinny, too white, too black, too ethnic, too whatever, then guess what? You are. And that's what you will sell to people. You can't fake what you really feel inside for long. Make who you are work for you.

I go to screenwriting conferences, festivals and I kid you not, sometimes I am the only brown face in the place. I don't care. It works for me. I never have trouble getting anybody — the teacher, the speakers, or my classmates — to remember me. I just say, "I was the African-American woman who…" and immediately they know who I am. Who can beat that? So, instead of walking into the room with my Caucasian peeps and saying, "Oh no, I'm the only one." I say, "Wow! I'm the only one."

DON'T GET IT WRITTEN, GET IT WRITTEN DOWN

Many a feeling has been hurt by bad memory. I interviewed 10 people over a week's time on my last trip to Hollywood in 2002 and nearly all of them said one thing: get it in writing. Not only did they say it, they said it with conviction. "I don't care if you have to write it on a napkin and get everyone present to sign it, get it written down," one executive stressed. So, you heard it here. If you enter a verbal agreement with someone to do anything, it's worth the effort to commit it to paper. Even if it's your 75-year old Aunt Gracie… get it on paper.

GET LOCAL

It's a longstanding debate. Do I need to be in Los Angeles to succeed in the business? The answer is a resounding yes… and no. Hollywood is where the business is taking place, so would it help if you were here? Maybe. See, it's not enough to just physically be in Hollywood. You have to also be in the game once you get here.

Now, there are certain areas of the business that can be done from a hut in Tahiti. Screenwriting for example, is something that can be done anywhere. If you want to be a screen actor, however, you need to be in the screen actor's mecca, Los Angeles. If you want to produce or direct, you can do all of that from wherever you live. Once you blow up and become a much sought after producer or director, you'll probably spend more time on the West Coast.

There is one major advantage to being in L.A. — access. Access to industry events, resources, and the people who make movies. Access is king because it allows you to cover much more mileage than you would if you lived in say, Roanoke, Virginia. If you live in Los Angeles, your agent can set up meetings and auditions for you whenever they come up. If you're only in the city two or three times a year, it means that all of your meetings have to be scheduled around those visits. And what if someone needs to reschedule outside of your trip range? It can be difficult to establish or even jump-start a career that way.

There are a couple of ways to deal with living outside Los Angeles, though. These ideas are basically for anyone who's not an actor or actress. As I said earlier, if you really want to be a working actor, move to L.A. But if you're producing, directing, writing, or even singing, and you're not ready to move to L.A., what I'm about to suggest might be a good alternative for you.

Make a commitment to go there at specified times of the year. This means pulling out your calendar and strategically planning your trips. Maybe you'll want to make quarterly two-week visits. A lot can happen in two weeks. I also recommend getting a Los Angeles area address and a voice-mail box. Even if you don't live there, you can access your phone messages and probably get a friend to pick up your mail once or twice a week.

SAFE SEX

There's a lot of paranoia in the world. Most of it in the writing profession. We've all thought at one time that somebody was going to steal our brilliant ideas right out from under our noses. Those vagabonds in Hollywood are just waiting to get their grubby little hands on our scripts, slap their names on them and make a skillion dollars. Does this happen? I'm sure it does. But the reality is that there are tons of ideas floating around in the universe. Maybe you were the first one to think of it, maybe you weren't. But I've learned from painful experiences that it's rarely about who thought of it first and more about who "executed" it first.

In 2002, I saw seven of what I was convinced were "my" ideas made into or bought to be produced into television shows. I won't mention which ones they were, but let's say three of them are among the highest-rated programs on television right now. That's the nature of the business. Good ideas typically find themselves a home no matter who thought of them first.

But remember, beating someone to the punch on an idea is secondary to protecting your intellectual property — a script, song, play, etc. It's always a good idea to make your work official. One way to do this is to register it with the Library of Congress at *www.copyright.gov*. There you'll find out about copyright laws for different kinds of properties.

MY BIG FAT GREEK PAYDAY

As you go away to become megastars, never underestimate the power of a basic story through a film or even a song. Some themes will always stand the test of time. Look at the great singers, filmmakers, actors, actresses, and writers of all time. Their work transcends decades and manages to remain classic no matter what trends and fads momentarily take our attention.

A basic story is sometimes all you need to succeed. That's what I took from the phenomenal success of the hit movie *My Big Fat Greek Wedding*. Yes, it's seems rather alluring to be able to create a movie such as *Men In Black* or *Minority Report*, films that are made for 100 million smackaroos. But you wanna know what's sexy? Sexy is making a movie for $5 million and raking in more than $180 million... and counting. That, my friends, is sexy as hell. So when I hear filmmakers talking about these gargantuan movies with all of these futuristic features and gizmos, I say have we learned nothing? How about writing a movie that regular people can dig. You can bet that's what a lot of writers are doing these days.

THE SMARTEST THING YOU CAN DO TODAY IS...

Form a production company. There's so much talent right there, wherever you live. But don't just form a company with people you don't know. Get your producer, director, musician, actor, and writer friends together and form a company that can help elevate all of your careers. Commit to making two or three films a year that will showcase all of your talents! This is a fantastic way to get better at whatever it is you do. Once the films are in the can, market them. Enter them in contests and festivals. If your work is good, everybody gets exposure and everybody wins.

ACT III CHECKLIST

√ Name your career's Dream Team.

√ What's one of the fastest ways to turn off an exec?

√ What business tool should you always have with you? (Act II cheat question)

√ What's pocketing?

√ Name one guerrilla marketing technique that you'll use in the next three months.

√ What is the philosophy behind the 10-minute rule?

√ What did you learn from the Lion's Den Interview?

√ What's more important, having an agent or having a good agent?

√ What's the most unique aspect of your brand?

EPILOGUE

At the beginning of the book I told you that I had discovered that there were two kinds of people. But over the course of writing this book I found that there were three more kinds of people...

> Those who are doing their thing
> Those who are thinking about doing their thing, and
> Those who ain't doing a damn thing

Which one are you?

Now, regrettably I must say goodbye. Thank you for e-mailing me your personal stories over the last six months; I can't imagine having written this book without your insights, woeful and triumphant stories, and enthusiasm. Go forth and multiply, always remembering the immortal words of the great Jackie Gleason, "I have no use for humility. I am a person with an exceptional talent."

I'll see ya at the Oscars....

ABOUT FRAN HARRIS

Fran Harris is president of Tall Tree Productions, a film, television, and multimedia company that specializes in nonfiction, documentary, sports, reality, entertainment, and lifestyle programming. A national broadcaster who has worked for ESPN, Lifetime Television, and Fox Sports, Fran is also the executive producer, show runner and host of several television shows including *America's Fitness Show, Entertainment Texas* and soon, *Crashing Hollywood.*

Fran is a screenwriter, consultant, and inspirational speaker who addresses thousands of people through her seminars and keynote speeches annually. To inquire about scheduling speaking or workshop engagements please send an e-mail to *fran@franharris.com* or *frantv@aol.com.*

Got a success or war story?
Share them in the Crashing Hollywood community at
www.crashinghollywood.com

Other books by Fran Harris available at *www.franharris.com*

How I Made Nearly $50,000 on My First Book Before It Was Published

About My Sister's Business: The Black Woman's Road Map to Successful Entrepreneurship

In the Black: The African-American Parent's Guide to Raising Financially Responsible Children

Summer Madness: Inside the Wild, Wacky, Wonderful World of the WNBA The Dream Season

Tall Tree Productions
P.O. Box 5285 | Austin, TX 78763 | PH: 512.443.0716
www.franharris.com
www.talltreeproductions.com

THE WRITER'S JOURNEY
2nd Edition
Mythic Structure for Writers

Christopher Vogler

Over 100,000 units sold!

See why this book has become an international bestseller and a true classic. *The Writer's Journey* explores the powerful relationship between mythology and storytelling in a clear, concise style that's made it required reading for movie executives, screenwriters, playwrights, scholars, and fans of pop culture all over the world.

Both fiction and nonfiction writers will discover a set of useful myth-inspired storytelling paradigms (i.e., "The Hero's Journey") and step-by-step guidelines to plot and character development. Based on the work of Joseph Campbell, *The Writer's Journey* is a must for all writers interested in further developing their craft.

The updated and revised second edition provides new insights and observations from Vogler's ongoing work on mythology's influence on stories, movies, and man himself.

"This book is like having the smartest person in the story meeting come home with you and whisper what to do in your ear as you write a screenplay. Insight for insight, step for step, Chris Vogler takes us through the process of connecting theme to story and making a script come alive."
— Lynda Obst, Producer
Sleepless in Seattle, Contact, Someone Like You
Author, *Hello, He Lied*

Christopher Vogler, a top Hollywood story consultant and development executive, has worked on such high-grossing feature films as *The Lion King* and conducts writing workshops around the globe.

$24.95, 325 pages
Order #98RLS
ISBN: 0-941188-70-1

FILM DIRECTING: SHOT BY SHOT
Visualizing from Concept to Screen

Steven D. Katz

This classic with the famous blue cover is one of the most well-known books in the business, and is a favorite of working directors as an on-set quick-reference guide. Packed with visual techniques for filmmakers and screenwriters to expand their stylistic knowledge, this international best-seller contains in-depth information on composition, previsualization, camera techniques, and much more. Includes over 750 storyboards and illustrations, with never-before-published storyboards from Spielberg's *Empire of the Sun*, Welles' *Citizen Kane*, and Hitchcock's *The Birds*.

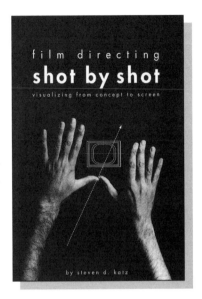

$27.95
Order # 7RLS
ISBN: 0-941188-10-8

Both Katz Books Only $47

Save 12% when you order both books
Order #KatzB

FILM DIRECTING: CINEMATIC MOTION
A Workshop for Staging Scenes

Steven D. Katz

This follow-up to the phenomenally popular *Shot by Shot* is a practical guide to common production problems encountered when staging and blocking film scenes. Includes discussions of scheduling, staging without dialogue, sequence shots, actor and camera choreography, and much more. Also includes interviews with well-known professionals such as director John Sayles and visual effects coordinator Van Ling (*The Abyss, Terminator 2*).

$24.95
Order # 6RLS
ISBN: 0-941188-14-0

ORDER FORM

MICHAEL WIESE PRODUCTIONS
11288 VENTURA BLVD., # 621
STUDIO CITY, CA 91604
E-MAIL: MWPSALES@MWP.COM
WEB SITE: WWW.MWP.COM

WRITE OR FAX FOR A FREE CATALOG

PLEASE SEND ME THE FOLLOWING BOOKS:

TITLE	ORDER NUMBER (#RLS _____)	AMOUNT
	SHIPPING	
	CALIFORNIA TAX (8.00%)	
	TOTAL ENCLOSED	

PLEASE MAKE CHECK OR MONEY ORDER PAYABLE TO:

MICHAEL WIESE PRODUCTIONS

(CHECK ONE) _____ MASTERCARD _____ VISA _____ AMEX

CREDIT CARD NUMBER _____

EXPIRATION DATE _____

CARDHOLDER'S NAME _____

CARDHOLDER'S SIGNATURE _____

SHIP TO:

NAME _____

ADDRESS _____

CITY _____ STATE _____ ZIP _____

COUNTRY _____ TELEPHONE _____